The 1990s
Teen Horror Cycle

ALSO BY ALEXANDRA WEST

*Films of the New French Extremity:
Visceral Horror and National Identity* (McFarland, 2016)

The 1990s Teen Horror Cycle
Final Girls and a New Hollywood Formula

ALEXANDRA WEST
Foreword by STACIE PONDER

McFarland & Company, Inc., Publishers
Jefferson, North Carolina

ISBN (print) 978-1-4766-7064-5
ISBN (ebook) 978-1-4766-3128-8

LIBRARY OF CONGRESS CATALOGUING DATA ARE AVAILABLE

BRITISH LIBRARY CATALOGUING DATA ARE AVAILABLE

© 2018 Alexandra West. All rights reserved

No part of this book may be reproduced or transmitted in any form or by any means, electronic or mechanical, including photocopying or recording, or by any information storage and retrieval system, without permission in writing from the publisher.

Front cover: Poster art from the 1998 film *Urban Legend* featuring (clockwise from top right) Alicia Witt, Joshua Jackson, Tara Reid, Michael Rosenbaum, Rebecca Gayheart and Jared Leto (Tri-Star Pictures/Photofest)

Printed in the United States of America

McFarland & Company, Inc., Publishers
Box 611, Jefferson, North Carolina 28640
www.mcfarlandpub.com

For all the Final Girls, on screen and off

Acknowledgments

The impetus for this book started about two decades ago when my parents bought me *Scream* on VHS for Christmas. Even though I was still a bit too young to see the film in theaters, I was drawn to it; it felt like the next step from all the Tim Burton films and other oddball, horror-leaning late 1980s and early 1990s offerings I was consuming at the time. It was love at first watch and that film led me on a path to writing what I do now. Watching *Scream* for the first time was like Dorothy going to Oz: suddenly everything was in Technicolor—bloody, gut-stained Technicolor.

I cannot remember how many times I watched that VHS but it was a lot. In watching *Scream* repeatedly, I finally worked up the courage to rent staggering amounts of horror films from my local video store, in part because I could not get enough of them and in part because I wanted to understand all the references in *Scream*. *Scream* was a gateway to horror for me, and as I passed through those gates I could already sense how deeply lucky I was to have parents that would not only be fine with their child spending all her allowance money on renting movies but who also took her to see most movies, which she would later write about, in theaters. I still remember family outings to see *The Craft* and *Scream 3* as well as my mom taking me to see *Halloween H20*, *The Rage: Carrie 2* and *I Still Know What You Did Last Summer* in theatres even though she's not a horror fan. I have vivid memories of my dad taking me to see *Buffy the Vampire Slayer* in a multiplex in Montreal and the way he laughed louder than anyone in the theatre when the dog got microwaved in *Urban Legend*. Without those outings and my parents' love, support and encouragement, this book would not exist. I am forever grateful that they continue to support my horrific leanings to this day.

I also feel deeply lucky for a number of friends and colleagues who, lending me their ears and advice, believed in this book and topic. I feel I owe a great debt to all of them but since they don't believe in that kind of thing, I hope my thanks here will suffice.

I am in awe of the women in my life who I know would be the Final

Girls of any movie they were in. Andrea Subissati is not only a partner in crime, but a great friend, writer and editor. Her unwavering support is felt throughout this book and her talents constantly push me to a better writer, thinker and person. Alison Lang's level of love and encouragement are matched only by her own abilities. She always had time to talk and offer advice or just listen to a Bush album with me. Joanne Sarazen and I had a similar experience with these movies and her insights into these films helped many of the ideas found within this book evolve. I hope I make her proud with the Alyssa Milano portion found within these pages. Jennifer Frees is one of the toughest women I know in real life so I'm glad I finally wrote about films she could watch. Alice Berg transcends being a friend and a sister. Even though she was half a world away throughout most of the writing of this book, she helped in more ways than I can ever possibly articulate. Stacie Ponder is one of my favorite writers. Her blog *Final Girl* set me on the path to writing this book, and the fact that she wrote the foreword means more than I can ever say. If you ever find yourself being hunted by an unkillable killer, find her. She'll help.

I'm grateful to have Giles Sander, who keeps me honest while also supporting my ambitions, as an older brother. Penny Kroll is an awesome bastion of encouragement. I also owe a great debt to Darren McLennan whose own love of the weird and macabre may outmatch mine. Getting to watch, talk about, and get weirded out by movies with him is one of my favorite things. And Magnus—one day when you're old enough we'll watch all of these movies again. Chris Hayes and Adam Driscoll watched a lot of the movies within this book with me while I was doing research and were instrumental in helping develop the analysis within these pages, if only to describe how truly bonkers some of these movies are. Paul Erlichman and Neil Rankin's support and friendship for 15-plus years is nothing to sniff at so I won't start here. I will always be grateful for Danny Lindsay, who jumped in and read a lot of very early, very rough drafts with great insight and excitement, helping push this book along. Paul Corupe is one of the great writers in our community and I'm lucky to call him a friend. His advice and support have helped keep me on track over the years. Kim Snider and Patrice Baillargeon have been constant supports throughout my entire career and their minimal book collection inspires me to write something good enough to belong on their bookshelf. And thank you to Zuzu for keeping me company while I wrote.

Table of Contents

Acknowledgments vii

Foreword by Stacie Ponder 1

Introduction 3

1. They Never Had It So Good: America in the 1990s 13
2. Imitate Us: America's Youth Culture 25
3. Co-Deads: *Buffy the Vampire Slayer* (1992) and *My Boyfriend's Back* (1993) 34
4. First Blood: *The Crush* (1993) and *Fear* (1996) 43
5. Generation Hex: *The Craft* (1996) 55
6. Bowling for Woodsboro: *Scream* (1996), *Scream 2* (1997) and *Scream 3* (2000) 63
7. Hit and Run: *I Know What You Did Last Summer* (1997) and *I Still Know What You Did Last Summer* (1998) 82
8. Circulate Widely: *Urban Legend* (1998) and *Urban Legends: Final Cut* (1998) 92
9. Cutting Class: *Disturbing Behavior* (1998), *The Faculty* (1998) and *Teaching Mrs. Tingle* (1999) 103
10. Re-Generation: *Halloween H20* (1998) and *The Rage: Carrie 2* (1999) 121
11. Lust for Life: *Wicked* (1998) and *Idle Hands* (1999) 131
12. The Millennium Approaches: *Cherry Falls* (2000), *Final Destination* (2000) and *Scary Movie* (2000) 140

13. It's All Coming Back to Me Now: *Urban Legends: Bloody Mary* (2005), *I'll Always Know What You Did Last Summer* (2006) and *Scream 4* (2011)   156

Conclusion   169
Chapter Notes   173
Bibliography   181
Index   183

Foreword
by Stacie Ponder

> "What's your favorite scary movie?"
> "Oh come on, you know I don't watch that shit."
> "Why not? Too scared?"
> "What's the point? They're all the same. Some stupid killer stalking some big-breasted girl who can't act who is always running up the stairs when she should be running out the front door. It's insulting."
> —*Scream* (1996)

Ask your average genre fan about the 90s Teen Horror Cycle and chances are he or she will call it as dull and flavorless as a week-old loaf of store-brand white bread. Nestled between the gore-drenched, hyper-violent slasher flicks of the 1980s and the gore-drenched, hyper-violent torture flicks of the 2000s, 90s teen horror often feels homogenized, corporate-driven, and tepid at best.

Lucky for us, then, that Alexandra West isn't your average genre fan.

With the sharp eye of a scholar and the knowledge stockpile of a true horror junkie, she's remarkably deft at picking out the patterns and seeing the bigger picture. So what if 90s teen horror feels homogenized and corporate-driven because more often than not, it was? What was it about the 1990s that pushed the genre in that direction? What do the trends say about the industry, and what do they say about us? More than any other film writer I know, Alex is able to show how horror's shiniest treasures and trashiest trash piles reflect and affect culture and society at large. The films give—and are given—context through examinations of history, sociology, politics, and feminism.

More than her critical thinking and her observation droppin', however, it is Alex's straight-up affection for horror that shines through. She's writing about these films because above all else, she loves them—*hard*. And she's not afraid to show it, to let you know what a movie or an actor means to her. It's thanks to this love that I met Alex where all of the best people meet: the Internet. It was a much more innocent time (2011) and the online horror community was robust, rife with blogs and sites and pundits aplenty. I ran a film club at my blog *Final Girl*, wherein I would choose a movie and folks could write about it on a specified date; Alex joined in a few times, we started chatting, and the next thing you know, there we were: bona fide cyberfriends sharing a passion for horror movies great and terrible, from classics like *Hellraiser* to clunkers like *Hellraiser: Hellworld*. We spend time ruminating on *Amityville* sequels, films featuring not Final Girls, but Final *Women*, and the trends and tropes we adore and abhor.

Since those early days, it's been a pleasure and a privilege to watch Alex find her feet and stand her ground, to embrace the fact that she has a voice and something to say and you should most definitely listen. She can no longer be constrained or contained by the blogs of her horror youth, and she's taking over nearly all media with books and magazine articles for your eyeballs while lecturing and podcasting (co-hosting the critically-acclaimed Faculty of Horror alongside Andrea Subissati) for your earholes. My impulse is to say that witnessing her rise to beyond-well-deserved prominence in the horror field makes me proud ... but that seems unnecessarily condescending. And it also makes me feel old.

I'll say, then, that I'm duly honored to be writing this and to get to spout off a bit about Alex and why she's supremely qualified to write this book. Really, there's no one more suited to the task of championing one of the most overlooked and underappreciated subgenres, to saying that while some of the films may not ever be fan favorites, they're still worth talking about. As society evolves, so, too, do horror movies. No matter which direction they may take, no matter how bloody or PG, how puerile or progressive, Alex will there, ready to dig deep, dissect it, and tell us what it's all about.

Stacie Ponder is a writer and artist based in New England. Her writing has appeared in Rue Morgue Magazine, Sirens of Cinema Magazine, *and* Butcher Knives & Body Counts: Essays on the Formula, Frights, and Fun of the Slasher Film, *but she is perhaps best-known for her long-running, award-winning horror blog* Final Girl.

Introduction

The 1990s Teen Horror Cycle has been dismissed by most major publications, film journals, spectators and critics as a Hollywoodized iteration of the now beloved slasher subgenre of 1970s and 1980s horror. This cycle of films has been called "pandering,"[1] "frustrating,"[2] "sheer tedium"[3] and even "a bit misandrist."[4] The main concern around this cycle of films is that they took what was once a powerful force in the independent film scene and commodified sacred elements into something sleek and refined and ready for mass consumption. To many horror fans, the 1990s Teen Horror Cycle took what was an underground movement and made it palatable for the masses while ignoring the elements that made these films of the 1970s and 1980s unique. Many have felt that this movement led to watered-down versions of beloved horror films from the previous decades in order to ingratiate themselves to a larger teen audience, marking them as products rather than films with any kind of artistic merit. However, in ignoring these films, film criticism and film fandom are ignoring a cultural moment that integrated multiple social and political forces within the film industry to create a cycle that made money rendering them an undeniable force in popular culture. These films hit at the right place, at the right time and, for a brief period, were an omnipresent force in the film industry. They were rapidly made with increasing budgets and box office expectations, making for a mixed bag in terms of quality, but what other film cycle has not suffered from those same expectations? While the main successes of these films occurred from 1996 to 2000 there are multiple films that came before and after which helped tell the story of their seemingly rapid ascension and quiet decline.

For many horror critics and fans, the notion of the 1990s as being anything but a bizarre anomaly that featured a few great horror films such as *Candyman* (Bernard Rose, 1992), *Silence of the Lambs* (Jonathan Demme, 1991) or *The Blair Witch Project* (Eduardo Sánchez and Daniel Myrick, 1999) is suspect. The 1990s Teen Horror Cycle, which, for this book, begins with *Buffy the Vampire Slayer* (Fran Rubel Kuzui, 1992) and ends with *Cherry Falls*

(Geoffrey Wright, 2000), was too glossy, trendy and sleek to be considered worthwhile horror, lacking the grittiness and earnestness of previous films. The 1990s Teen Horror Cycle, however, was a reaction to the oversaturation of the slasher subgenre in the 1980s with seemingly endless sequels to *Halloween* (John Carpenter, 1978), *Friday the 13th* (Sean S. Cunningham, 1980) and *A Nightmare on Elm Street* (Wes Craven, 1984), which were laughed off by critics but consumed by fans who still saw merits in them. While some of the films in these franchises offer genuinely great filmic moments and a few likeable characters, others have become better known for the gluttonous, elaborate on-screen deaths and semi-naked co-eds about to have sex. The beloved elements of practical effects and sexually available women offered an enticing entrance for many heterosexual male fans of the genre as the films stayed steadily in their gaze. Writer John Kenneth Muir describes the Teen Horror Cycle of the 1980s thusly:

> The flip side to these freedoms and excesses [the explicit gore and nudity depicted in 1980s horror films] however, came in the thematic subtexts to these films. It was not hard to divine that these slasher movies appeared designed and executed as conservative precautionary tales. Although the Moral Majority and conservatives railed violently against popular horror films in the 1980s, the very movies they loathed actually toed the party-line with dedication. To wit, a display of vice (drugs and sex) would invariably precede the slice-and-dice (a new kind of capital punishment!). The actual content of these films may have been quite naughty, skirting the very edge of socially accepted mores and taboos about violence and sexuality, but most of the films also carried the conservative (and contradictory) theme that if you sin, punishment shall be meted out.[5]

The 1990s teen horror films situated the terror in America's backyards, communities and families. The films were no longer in remote locations like abandoned summer camps where the killer could terrorize victims in their dreams through supernatural powers unfettered by societal intrusions. The antagonists in the 1990s were friends and family members who sought revenge for very specific incidents relating to the protagonists. The teen horror films of the 1990s situated the horror in the heroes, making the terror harder to escape or recon with. Horror had truly come home.

Carol Clover's seminal book *Men, Women and Chainsaws: Gender in the Modern Horror Film*, which not only helped codify the slasher film and give critics and fans terms such as the Final Girl, but also placed a gendered critique on the films, was published in 1992. Clover's work helped encode a potential feminist reading on horror films, which had often been derided as misogynistic. While the vast majority of these films, particularly from the 1970s and 1980s, have deeply problematic elements, they also offer some subversive reprieve:

The "play of pronoun function" that underlies and defines the cinefantastic is nowhere more richly manifested than in the slasher; if the genre has an aesthetic base, it is exactly that of a visual identity game. Consider, for example, the by now standard habit of letting us view the action in the first person long before revealing who or what the first person *is*. In the opening sequence of *Halloween I*, "we" are belatedly revealed to ourselves, after committing a murder in the cinematic first person, as a six-year-old boy. The surprise is often within gender, but it is also, in a striking number of cases, across gender. Again, *Friday the 13th*, in which "we" stalk and kill a number of teenagers over the course of an hour of screen time without even knowing who "we" are; we are invited, by conventional expectation and by glimpses of "our" own bodily parts—a heavily booted foot, a roughly gloved hand—to suppose that "we" are male, but "we" are revealed, at film's end, as a woman.[6]

Clover writes extensively about the pain inflicted on the male body versus the female body and gender transference that can take place between an audience and a character (most notably the Final Girl). The Final Girl is simply the character who survives the events of the film, though usually at some great cost to her mental health or selfhood. She has become an embodiment of the trauma and if she shows up again in any of the sequels, such as Alice in *Friday the 13th Part 2* (Steve Miner, 1981) or Kristen in *A Nightmare on Elm Street 4: The Dream Master* (Renny Harlin, 1988), she is quickly dispatched by the killer who finally has their revenge. In the 1980s in particular, horror worshiped at the altar of the villain with Freddy Krueger, Michael Myers and Jason Voorhees becoming more iconic, recognizable, and, to some, even more sympathetic than their victims. Freddy Krueger started as an invention from the mind of Wes Craven as an undead child murdered but soon evolved through the popularity of the *Nightmare on Elm Street* franchise to have his own television show, toaster, board game, misguided rap career and telephone hotline among other licensing opportunities. *Rolling Stone* reported on the Freddy phenomenon in 1988:

> One of the nicest touches in these films, after all, is that they take the side of the unloved—the children... Yet when these same brave youths invariably get wiped out in the sequels, the message seems to be that even their courage and intelligence and determination will not save them forever. Eventually, Freddy Krueger *always* wins, and perhaps the greatest obscenity of all—he is the one character in the series who continually survives.[7]

Throughout these franchise sequels it was the killers whose stories and mythologies evolved, not the survivors' or victims'. The victims and survivors were a means to an end in the 1980s slasher films; they were archetypes who fit into different slots and embodied different trends (see Debbie and her fitness obsession in *A Nightmare on Elm Street 4: The Dream Master*, 1987) which would allow the killer to enact a horrible fate upon them. They would die because they were some combination of young, brash, sexual or bold and the audience was primed to cheer for their demise.

In the 1990s Teen Horror Cycle many of these tropes would be turned on their head simply because the 1990s was a time of intertextuality, in which a form of media (i.e., a text) references another text. Intertextuality was being utilized in films and television shows such as *There's Nothing Out There* (Rolfe Kanefsky, 1991), *Reservoir Dogs* (Quentin Tarantino, 1992) and *The Simpsons* long before *Scream* (Wes Craven, 1996) made it popular in the minds of many. As Jonathan Rhodes writes of the new implicitness of intertextuality:

> Textual studies have a long history of fetishizing the text as a solitary, pristinely autonomous object, and this notion of textuality has exerted considerable pressure particularly on literary and film studies, but also on media and television studies.... In a world of seemingly infinite texts, genres help us to taste-test and select what to watch. Once we have selected, and are listening, watching, or reading, genre codes serve as a shorthand to tell us what is going on. There is never a genre-less moment, for to step outside genre is to step into a chaotic semiosis in which shopping lists and great novels are read alike.[8]

The 1990s were a time of political and economic advancement for America, which meant that those with privilege and power could continue to grow and maintain what they already had. But for the new generation, or Generation X as they would soon be known, that was not good enough. The trickle-down politics of 1980s conservative powerhouse former president Ronald Reagan were not enough. The youth of the 1990s decried the notion that they should have and want to achieve the same American Dream in the same way their parents did. By the end of 1991, Nirvana's rallying rock anthem "Smells Like Teen Spirit" was dominating popular music and at the same time the Riot Grrrl movement was starting to spread farther than the boundaries of its city of origin, Olympia, Washington. The bands that comprised the Riot Grrrl scene called out rape, abuse and assault in their songs and at their shows and attempted to make feminism as punk rock as it felt at the time. Third Wave feminism was coined by Rebecca Walker in *Ms. Magazine* after the Anita Hill hearings in Washington. Rodney King's beating by police and the guilty officers' subsequent acquittal, even though the beating was caught on tape, incited the Los Angeles riots and forced America to realize that even after the Civil Rights movement, America was not a post-race society as so many liked to claim. As the 1990s began, the Cold War, which had tepidly raged for decades, drew quietly to a close. America no longer had a looming destructive force, but only Americans themselves—something that the 1990s Teen Horror Cycle would learn how to tackle.

In this notion of relative international peacetime for America, it made sense that the hulking monsters of Jason Voorhees and Michael Myers were no longer as interesting as they once were. The conversations around feminism and girlhood and the fact that women continually made up half if not more of the audience who consumed culture helped switch horror's focus. As *Entertainment Weekly* reported in 2009:

> Name any recent horror hit and odds are that female moviegoers bought more tickets than men. And we're not just talking about psychological spookfests like 2002's *The Ring* (60 percent female), 2004's *The Grudge* (65 percent female), and 2005's *The Exorcism of Emily Rose* (51 percent female). We're also talking about all the slice-and-dice remakes and sequels that Hollywood churns out.[9]

The notions of survival in the face of trauma, fear and violence were part of the national conversation. As the once profitable slasher franchises were beaten by their own diminishing returns, few wanted to give up on the subgenre, but some element of it had to change. The development of youth culture in the 1990s would allow for this shift from "teenie-kill pics"[10] to young women fighting for their voice and their lives.

The central conflict and tension within the 1990s Teen Horror Cycle is between the generation coming of age and the choices of their parents. These films represent the idealistic rejection of morals of their parents' generation and often take pains to show the older generation's fallibility through the tropes of absent or deceased parents combined with a terrible secret that is revealed about the protagonists. As the notions of grunge and alternative culture became mainstream, they became commodified, and therefore Hollywood was tasked with creating commodities that critiqued themselves and their mass-culture nature.

The films written about in this book represent the height of the 1990s Teen Horror Cycle, meaning that they were produced within the Hollywood system with the overwhelming majority of them receiving large releases and marketing pushes. A "film cycle" as Stephen Neale states in his book *Genre and Hollywood* is "a group of films within a specific and limited time-span, and founded, for the most part, on the characteristics of individual commercial successes."[11] Richard Nowell further defines it in his book *Blood Money: A History of the Teen Slasher Film Cycle* as a "story structure that could be articulated differently and combined with content drawn from a variety of sources and which enabled filmmakers not only to provoke audience horror, but also to entice intrigue, thrills and amusement."[12] A film cycle by its very nature helps delineate themes, tropes and specific film advancements through a codified lens, which in turn helps articulate the fractured concerns and methodologies of texts within a specific period. The ideology and trends of the 1990s are what separates these films from the teen-oriented horror films that came before them, but this very ideology is what keeps these films in dialogue with the rest of the horror genre. The 1990s Teen Horror Cycle articulates the fears and concerns of an America which, for the first time in decades, was seemingly free of a major international conflict and was beginning to look at the horror within its own borders.

The teen horror films of the 1980s shared a codified and unified vision in many regards—down to basic elements like a masked or purposefully concealed killer, a Final Girl, a bevy of attractive young victims, a terrible place where a past trauma occurred and a weapon that can only be truly effective when in close proximity to a victim—which, in all fairness, yielded a diverse and wide-ranging group of films that are still beloved. The 1990s Teen Horror Cycle shares some of these traits but also reimagined them to reflect and refract the fears of a new decade. In 1990s teen horror films, many of the unifying elements were centered on the Final Girl who tended to hold a terrible or unknown secret, an internalization of what Carol Clover termed the "Terrible Place"—a physical location such as a house or specific room where trauma lives "in which victims sooner or later find themselves in."[13] The women who lead these films are often in one way or another the site of their own horror—a secret or an identity that has been covered up, repressed or normalized—which begins to take hold at the start of the film and attempts to overtake the narrative. John Kenneth Muir elaborated on the new protagonists of the 1990s horror film: "they are heroes, yes, but they are not without flaws. Not flawed necessarily in the vice-precedes slice-and-death fashion of the old slashers, where bad behavior—sex and drugs—promised conservative punishment, but something else. It's more than that in these films."[14] The films in this book all have a specific codified look that was evolving parallel to the mass market teen culture of the time in music videos and on televisions on stations like the WB, which was intent on creating savvy programming for the teens who thought they knew it all. Resistance to the 1990s Teen Horror Cycle is in part a resistance to the mainstreaming and mass marketing of horror films. These horror films are replete with young, recognizable stars who often do not fall victim to the killer(s) but rather become more ingratiated with the world of the film and with the audience who saw it. The audience was asked through the narratives of the films and through the recognizable stars to root for the Final Girls (and occasional Final Boys), not the killers.

When the Toronto International Film Festival's year-round programming director Jesse Wente programmed the retrospective *Back to the '90s* for the TIFF Bell Lightbox in 2014 he said of the films:

> The films are more female-centric.... The female characters are more fleshed out, and in a lot of cases they're not seen through the lens of the male relationship. In a lot of the '80s movies, the girls are often still objects to be obtained or to break into a circle of some kind and a lot of it still relational to the men.[15]

The 1990s Teen Horror Cycle was in many ways indirectly (and occasionally directly) feminist. Young women maintained their roles as protagonist Final Girls—as they had done in the 1970s and 80s—but often their complicated narratives, which made them complicit in the horror that befell them, created increasingly complex and inherently interesting characters that appealed to the young women and men who saw these films. These female characters were no longer just smart, kind, levelheaded or lucky, as they had been in previous horror film incarnations of Final Girls; they were navigating their own complex moralities in a society that no longer knew what to value itself. But these young women could control the narratives and enact varying amounts of change within them, bringing an unexpected critique to many of the films that came before them.

That is not to say that young men were not interestingly or complexly portrayed in these films. John (Josh Harnett) in *Halloween H20*, Anton (Devon Sawa) in *Idle Hands* (Rodman Flender, 1999) and Steve (James Marsden) in *Disturbing Behavior* (David Nutter, 1998) as well as Zeke (Josh Harnett) and Casey (Elijah Wood) in *The Faculty* (Robert Rodriguez, 1998) all must overcome some form of expected toxic masculinity that threatens their own personal relationships and narratives. Toxic masculinity, which has also become a touch point of cultural conversation over the last few years, denotes a culture that advocates for men's dominance, emotional detachment, and sexual aggression—traits that push the patriarchal agenda forward. Just as the 1990s Teen Horror Cycle utilized part of feminism and 1990s girl power to examine the role of women in cinematic narratives, it also critiqued the expected roles of young men. The discussion of toxic masculinity bleeds into the inclusion and discussion of feminism, which aims to see true equality achieved between the sexes. The characters within these films are not simply battling an unkillable killer, they are fighting against explicit societal norms and expectations.

On a more superficial level, these films were made by sizeable film studios, adding to the budget and therefore glossiness of the productions. In this cycle of films, star power was key; the casts were hip, young and recognizable mainly from their appearances on television shows such as *Party of Five*, *Dawson's Creek* and *Buffy the Vampire Slayer*. This layer added an increased familiarity to the brands of these movies and by extension indoctrinated to them an audience that was beginning to consume culture. Film studios bank on their stars' viability as recognizable faces to get teens to spend their money on movies, hence why the marketing of so many of these films feels the same—the same beautiful faces coolly gazing out at a potential audience. The posters, which are some of the first marketing pieces available for any film, set them in contradistinction to the posters that came before them. Horror fans, rightfully so, love the artistry of the 1980s horror posters, which often featured elaborate paintings over Photoshopped portraits. These posters became omnipresent in the 1990s. However, those from the 1980s were selling the look and feel of a film needed to secure international markets before the film itself was even made, while the 1990s teen horror films had a more marketable and tangible selling point—talent. Teen stars were pulled from television dramas marketed to teens, which created another layer to the intertextual understanding of these films as properties that operated within a larger culture. As Stephen Neale writes:

> [Film genres] do not solely consist of films. They consist also of specific systems of expectation and hypothesis which spectators bring with them to the cinema and which interact with films themselves during the course of the viewing process.... They offer a way of working out the significance of what is happening on the screen: a way of working out why particular actions are taking place, why the characters are dressed the way they are, why they look, speak and behave the way they do, and so on.[16]

In the 1990s, films were no longer just films; they were soundtracks, fashions, slang, award shows and identities. The film studios could cross-market enough of their products so much so that if an audience member enjoyed a film, they could purchase several other products to go along with it. The corporatization and merchandizing of films was working in ways it never truly had before, creating a vast cross-pollination of consumed youth culture. These films, just as any other youth cycle of films, represents, as Timothy Shary describes it in his book *Generation Multiplex*, "an ongoing cycle of generational adjustment and conflict."[17]

The 1990s, for some, offered a respite from harsh international realities that were becoming more present as the Internet became an everyday presence in most people's lives. Thus, looking inward, part of America was willing to admit it had a problem with its young women. After the Anita Hill hearings and the increasing conversations around rape and assault, horror films became a way to repurpose the young female figure in horror films and attempt to empower her. Now, keep in mind the female figure that American film studios had in mind was white, slim, cisgender, heterosexual and able-bodied. This limited view of the gender kept the discussion within certain boundaries. This emboldening of white feminism is inherently problematic as it skews the female experience one way. While the 1990s Teen Horror Cycle was able to take steps forward for some, it never went far enough for everyone.

While these films offer an imperfectly empowered view of one very specific type of womanhood, they do address the systemic and insidious ways in which power can be taken. Throughout many of these films, the antagonist feels something is owed to them; they have an unspoken privilege that allows them to attain whatever fame or relationship they feel is owed. For the heroes of these films, fame, fortune and conformity are all tied together and it is their ultimate rejection of these tenants that makes them heroes worth rooting for. For these media- and culture-consuming audiences, the 1990s proved that fame and fortune come at a cost. Whether it be the media circus surrounding the O.J. Simpson trial or the grim reality of the Columbine shootings, teenagers in the 1990s saw national tragedy narratives dominate the screen, and those who fall off the edge in these films see tragedy as a stepping stone to something more powerful—notoriety.

Beginning with an overview of America in the 1990s and the rise of youth culture, this book tackles films within themes, grouping them together by release dates in order to examine some of the industry trends and leanings as they developed. The first half of these films is not nearly as codified as the final half, as the first veers all over the Teen Horror map, showing teens as both heroes and monsters with the horror situated in first sexual encounters, stalking, and the attainment of power. After *Scream*'s massive success, the industry had a blueprint of a narrative that truly worked and that audiences wanted to see more of. The industry changed and players like Dimension Films released a relatively large amount of teen horror films within a three-year period that were all codified in similar ways. In this section, several films which were released in 2000 are included, as their look and feel are the further articulation of many 1990s trends and themes and were still technically produced and shot in the 1990s. The book concludes with an examination of the ends of some of the franchises that were released after 2000 and producers attempted one last cash grab off properties that may still have had some name value left.

Like any of the films discussed in this book, the cinematic depiction of the teenage years is used to intensify already life-changing moments. The filmmakers use of youth as a lynchpin or turning point for characters is not out of the ordinary within the larger scope of teen films. Take *The Breakfast Club* (John Hughes, 1985) for example; the entire film sees a group of different (but all white) high school students decide in an afternoon they no longer want what their parents want or what society wants, which yields enough content for one of the most popular teen films ever. When looking at teen horror films, it is important to note that the clichéd teen approach to life—that everything is life or death—is actually life or death for these characters. Teen horror films offer a place where mortality is real and tangible. Horror maestro Wes Craven said of teen horror films, "Kids today have fears and they need a way to process their terror in a positive and funny manner."[18] In the 1990s, it was no longer enough to just scare teens straight, they had to be confronted with the realities they were so hungry for.

1

They Never Had It So Good
America in the 1990s

America in the 1990s has earned a special place in our recent nostalgic collective memory. It was a time of prosperity, of youth culture dominance, and of social strife. For the majority of the 1990s President Bill Clinton led the country through a time when progressiveness seemed almost attainable. For some it was a time noted for the rise of Indie culture through movements like Riot Grrrl and Grunge music, yet there was also the creeping cultural shift for those who still felt like their voices were not being heard. From the Anita Hill hearings to the Los Angeles riots to the HIV/AIDS crisis and beyond, there was a feeling that even though America was a leader on multiple fronts, it was still overlooking its most vulnerable citizens and that an uncomfortable power dynamic was still in place even if the culture was willing to pay lip service to it.

In the 1990s, America's economy grew by an average of four percent per year, a still relatively unheard-of growth rate, with an average of millions of jobs added per year.[1] For the politicians who always wanted to save face, America never had it so good.

The 1990s began with George H.W. Bush as president, succeeding Ronald Reagan in the position. Bush had previously occupied the role of vice president and maintained a successful if, in the end, contentious term as president. In the early 1990s the Soviet Union fell, bringing an unexpectedly swift end to the Cold War, which had dominated the political landscape for decades. America had no true enemies at the time and therefore, politicians, and in turn, culture, could turn inwards, focusing on America itself and the rise of its youth culture. When looking inwards, America could begin to fix the economic woes of previous decades, allowing for the aforementioned growth, but it also led to uncertainty about what the country was becoming and how it served its population. As French historian Alexis de Tocqueville wrote, "I know nothing more opposed to revolutionary attitudes than commercial ones."[2] After decades of political and social distrust and uncertainty, America was beginning to claw back its ability to focus on itself as a commercial entity. William H. Chafe wrote of this shift in the American consciousness in his book *The Rise and Fall of the American Century*:

> The Cold War, which had anchored American history for more than four decades, was about to end in glorious victory for the cause of freedom. An era of unprecedented prosperity soon swept the land, marked by the power of information technology to create unheard-of fortunes in a dot.com world. Like a giant bestriding the universe, America seemed to reign supreme in the world, unchallenged in its economic energy, military strength, and its cultural hegemony.[3]

One of the first dynamic cultural shifts of the 1990s occurred in 1991 when a then 35-year-old law professor, Anita Hill, gave testimony to the U.S. Senate Judiciary committee about the sexual harassment she had experienced while working for Clarence Thomas, who was President Bush's pick to fill a space on the Supreme Court. The hearing was broadcast live on television, and the American public could view what became a defining moment for women and the black community for the coming decade. Hill testified to a committee comprised of men about the inappropriate comments and come-ons she had experienced from Thomas:

> After a brief discussions of work, he would turn the conversation to a discussion of sexual matters. His conversations were very vivid. He spoke about acts that he had seen in pornographic films involving such matters as women having sex with animals and films showing group sex or rape scenes... Because I was extremely uncomfortable talking about sex with him at all, and particularly in such a graphic way, I told him that I did not want to talk about this subject... My efforts to change the subject were rarely successful.[4]

Hill's testimony began an unwieldy national discussion about women in the workplace. In a national setting, a woman was coming forward to speak about experiences directed at her because of her gender, which made it extraordinarily difficult for her to come to work every day. The testimony incited women's rights activists as well as the black community, some of whom applauded Hill for coming forward and some of whom condemned her for impeding a black man from being elected into the U.S. Supreme Court. Thomas was sworn in October 23, 1991, with Hill's testimony having seemingly little to no impact on the decision, but it continued to ignite women across the country to speak out against the injustices they still faced.

Pulitzer Prize winning journalist Susan Faludi did not write about the Hill/Thomas testimonies in her 1991 book *Backlash: The Undeclared War Against American Women* as the events were unfolding in real time, but she may as well have. *Backlash: The Undeclared War Against American Women* examines a cultural fear, not of liberated women but of the idea that women may achieve equality. Faludi examines the ways in which society and popular culture creates scare tactics against women enforcing their preferred place within a patriarchal society. Faludi takes particular aim at films like *Fatal Attraction* (Adrian Lyne, 1987), which sees a potentially free woman in the form of Alex Forrest (Glenn Close) as a shell of a person, psychotically bent on the destruction of a happy family. Faludi's book breaks down the multiple ways in which women have been sold the idea of the new, ambitious career woman as a figure to be feared, directly confronting the backlash against Second Wave feminism in an effort to enforce women's roles as wife, mother and caregiver. Faludi wrote of Anita Hill's testimony in the preface to the fifteenth anniversary edition of *Backlash*:

> The television sexist spectacle of the Senate Judiciary Committee members mocking Anita Hill's allegations of sexual harassment against Supreme Court nominee Clarence Thomas proved one humiliation too many for female viewers to witness. After all this time, indignant women told each other across the nation, these men still "don't get it." Indignation led to anger, which led to mobilization, which, by the Spring of 1992, led to a massive pro-choice demonstration in Washington, the birth of dramatically effective feminist PACs like Emily's List, and a record number of progressive women running for national office. But women's political awakening provoked instant reprisal. The speakers at the Republican National Convention in the summer of 1992 couldn't get off the subject, and their panic was evident in their hyperbole. A feminist army, they wailed, had invaded our culture, our TV sets (where a fictional woman was "mocking the importance of a father," as Bush I's running mate famously seethed onstage).[5]

One of the most direct cultural actions of these events was the formation of Third Wave feminism, which began with Rebecca Walker's lightening-rod piece in *Ms. Magazine*, "Becoming the Third Wave."

> Thomas' confirmation, the ultimate rally of support for the male paradigm of harassment, send a clear message to women: "Shut up! Even if you speak, we will not listen." I will not be silenced. After battling with ideas of separatism and militancy, I connect with my own feelings of powerlessness. I realize that I must undergo a transformation if I am truly committed to women's empowerment. My involvement must reach beyond my own voice in discussion, beyond voting, beyond reading feminist theory. My anger and awareness must translate into tangible action. I am not a postfeminism feminist. I am the Third Wave.[6]

Third Wave feminism was an extension, a reimaging, a rebranding of feminism with increased conversation around sexual assault and violence against women. However, the new generation of feminists were far more aware of the media's impact on the popular consciousness and therefore sought to ingratiate themselves in the culture, making an impact through mass media and creating their own work with the goal of showing that activism and social work could be part of entertaining content. This engagement in culture was not only important, but also necessary. As mass culture was becoming more accessible and important than ever, the new wave of feminists were attempting to fight the mainstream media's social cooption of their movement. As journalist and author Andi Zeisler wrote in her book *Feminism and Pop Culture*:

> If feminism's relationship to popular culture had been uneasy since the dawn of the women's liberation movement, in the late 1980s and early 1990s it became downright hostile. Everywhere women turned, they were hit with indictments of women's gains: Magazine headlines purported to reveal "The Awful Truth About Women's Lib," newspapers suggested that feminism was responsible for everything from rising rates of divorce to higher incidents of rape, and movies offered images of women driven by feminism and its byproducts to misery, loneliness, and murderous insanity.[7]

One of the smallest movements with the biggest legacy to come from this revitalization of feminism was Riot Grrrl. Beginning in Olympia, Washington, Riot Grrrl was a feminist punk movement founded and partially organized by members of local bands Bikini Kill, Heavens to Betsey and Team Dresch, among others. The movement started with a focus on music but then grew into zine making (zines being handmade mini-manifestos). Author Marisa Meltzer wrote of the movement, "These women were reacting to issues within the relatively insular punk community, but also tapping into a larger cultural movement. The late eighties had been a particularly dark moment for feminism, and the decade became a kind of grab bag for feminist gains and losses."[8] Essentially Riot Grrrl preached that if mainstream culture refused to create safe spaces for women in popular culture, they would create them for themselves. This spawned women, perhaps most famously Bikini Kill lead singer Kathleen Hanna, to yell, "Girls to the front!" at the band's shows, ensuring that women would not be forced out by more aggressive male presences. Hanna spoke about her entry into feminism and the rise of Riot Grrrl to Vice's *Noisey* in 2016:

> I came out of the domestic violence, rape-crisis phone [center] communities. That was why I even started a band because everyone was saying "feminism is dead" and I had just found it. And I was like, if feminism doesn't need to exist anymore and we live in a "post-feminist" society, why is the shelter always too full? Why are two families sharing a room? And why is the rape crisis phone ringing off the hook all night long? That was the impetuous to get on stage.[9]

In tandem with Riot Grrrl grew the more generic, mainstream grunge/alternative rock movement. As the Hill hearings took place and as women around the country began to organize concurrently and separately as the next wave of feminism, alternative culture was about to go mainstream.

1. They Never Had It So Good

In 1991 the lead single "Smells Like Teen Spirit" from Nirvana's album *Nevermind* was released. Though little was expected of it, it quickly ascended the rock charts as well as entered into mainstream culture. All of sudden, a new generation had a rallying cry, one their parents did not understand, one that *Time Magazine* referred to as an "anthem for the apathetic."[10] The song would go on to launch the iconography of Nirvana's lead singer Kurt Cobain as the poster child for disenfranchisement and also spur a litany of similar bands with similar messages who decried the culture they were being sold and who questioned what the American Dream actually was. This was the moment when bands like The Pixies, The Melvins and Sonic Youth, who had started their careers in the 1980s, were about to go mainstream. This was when bands like The Smashing Pumpkins, Hole, Pearl Jam and Stone Temple Pilots went mainstream and brought with them iterations that offered a mix of Riot Grrrl sensibilities and grunge aesthetic with instantly catchy punk or goth tinged hits. Bands and artists like Alanis Morissette, Garbage, No Doubt, Salt-N-Pepa, Tori Amos, TLC, Bjork, Missy Elliott, Liz Phair, Fiona Apple, Destiny's Child, The Breeders, and Elastica, among others and to varying degrees of success, brought women to the front of the stage. The all-women music festival Lilith Fair did so, as well. As the 1990s progressed, so did women's voices in popular culture. Female singers were bringing what were previously thought to be female topics not ripe for mass-culture discussion, such as rape, assault, abusive relationships, female anger and female disenfranchisement, into mainstream culture and finding an audience who wanted to hear what they had to say.

One of the most potent brands of the mainstreaming of Riot Grrrl and Third Wave feminism were The Spice Girls, who garnered a massive number one worldwide hit with their first single *Wannabe*. A British all-female pop group who preached fun, friendship and girl power, but were somewhat secretly manufactured by a group of men who were hoping to make a quick pound, became a worldwide sensation—for a few years at least. There is no denying the overt commercialization of The Spice Girls but it is important to also acknowledge their brand of sex-positive feminism which was being passed on to a generation of girls just coming into their own.

> While [The Spice Girls'] message of girl power can be credited with giving feminism a sparkly sheen, they were also completely without political consciousness. Whether this brand of warmed over feminism was their own idea or something constructed by their handlers we'll never know—the Spices were never off-message when it came to their signature slogan—but based on the enthusiasm with which they preached it, it's safe to say they were operating of their own accord.[11]

The Spice Girls existed at first in distinction to the resurgence of boy bands such as The Backstreet Boys and *NSYNC, who encouraged and thrived off young female attention, even though the majority of performers in these bands were in their 20s and 30s. As Susan J. Douglas elaborated on the feminist impact of The Spice Girls in her book *Enlightened Sexism*:

> Negotiation was what The Spice Girls were all about: between sexual objectification and feminist politics, between female bonding and pursuing male approval, between self-respect and self-display. They tried to look like Barbie and sound like Gloria Steinem. They insisted that girls could have it both ways, to capitulate to—and even embrace—male fantasies about how young women should look and dress and, at the same time, defy and even conquer the dismissal of women as serious, independent beings that the Wonderbra-short shorts look typically evokes. They were the Roman candles of girl power, their message that feminism was necessary and fun sparkling through the culture before fizzling out.[12]

When Kurt Cobain sang "Smells Like Teen Spirit," it was a rallying cry for anyone who had ever wanted something more than a husband or wife, some children and a house in the suburbs. It was a moment that asked, was there more than what the Reaganism dreams had promised? This was the birth of Generation X, a generation that was derided for questioning the way things were at one of America's most prosperous moments.

The alternative and punk artists of the 1990s were beginning to see through the promise of the American Dream and like Dorothy looking behind the curtain of the Great and Power Oz, realizing that this was a pacification to keep the masses working, busy, and occupied.

The term Generation X was taken from Canadian author Douglas Coupland's 1991 book *Generation X: Tales for an Accelerated Culture* and the moniker quickly caught on. The book dealt with characters who were overeducated and under-stimulated, who could access more of the world than previous generations but were struggling with the inherent meaning of what any of it meant. This term and its ideas came to define teens and adults in the 1990s who were just starting to pave their own way through life, uncertain of the future and how to get there.

While the Grunge movement was overwhelmingly white, the 1990s was also a time when rap began to enter the mainstream with a mix of decadence and social commentary, which caused more hand-wringing from the conservative Right, whose racist policies were critiqued in the music. While the 1980s ended with NWA's "Fuck tha Police," the 1990s was marked by KRS-One's "Sound of da Police" in 1993. The 1990s not only saw rap cemented as a mainstream music genre but also as a rallying point for some black communities. In 1991 taxi driver Rodney King was severely beaten by Los Angeles police officers following a car chase. George Holliday, a witness, was nearby and documented the event with a video camera unbeknownst to the police officers. Holliday then handed off the footage to KTLA, a local television station, who ran the footage on their nightly news show. Author Gil Troy wrote of the vast differences in realities that existed for many Americans:

> The King beating shifted the national conversation abruptly. Explaining African Americans' fury, one twenty-four-year-old told reporters: "Every black man has a story." The "two Americas"—black and white—had fragmented further. Three black Americas emerged. A prospering black middle class was freer, wealthier, better educated, better positioned than ever, aided by affirmative action programs in education and employment. Racism persisted but opportunities abounded. A black working class was stagnating, suffering from the loss of good jobs due to America's deindustrialization, even as racism [was believed to have] diminished. And at least 1.5 million people constituting the black underclass were chronically impoverished, perpetually on welfare, and broadly illiterate.[13]

The footage caused an investigation and eventual trial for the officers' use of excessive force and assault with a deadly weapon. All four officers were ultimately acquitted and Los Angeles erupted into riots in 1992 as minority communities could no longer contain their frustration as the government and law enforcement continued to target their communities. As grunge and alternative culture grew, rap was continuing to not only make a case for itself and its cultural impact but also for the lives and experiences of specific communities.

The 1990s in America would in the West's collective consciousness come to be defined by one man, Bill Clinton, who was elected president in 1992, defeating George H.W. Bush and taking the office from 1993 until 2001. Forty-three at the time of his inauguration, Clinton was the third youngest man to ever occupy the office. Clinton ran his campaign with slogans like "For People, for a Change" and "It's Time to Change America" while Bush and his running mate Dan Quayle opted for slogans like "Stand by the President" and "Don't Change the Team in the Middle of the Stream." Clinton's campaign was one of youthful energy and promise. After 12 years of a Republican in the office of president—from Reagan to Bush—Clinton and his team were banking on his cool, easy-going, ladies' man image. In his sweeping treatise of the 1990s in America, *The Age of Clinton*, author Gil Troy writes of this Clinton promise:

> When Clinton was at his worst, he pandered. When he was at his most popular, he triangulated. But when he was at his best ... he synthesized, navigating with his centrist vision. His ability to fuse Reaganite conservatism and Great Society liberalism, the opportunities provided by many rights and the strong communities that emerged from a suitable sense of responsibility, the Hillbillies and the Yalies, Main Street and Wall Street, American's super-ego and America's id, reflected his and America's dueling legacies, impulses and beliefs. Balancing it all properly, constructively, he believed, was "the purpose of prosperity," and would, he vowed, help disoriented Americans, many of who felt "lost in the funhouse" of the 1990s.[14]

Clinton's first term was marked by national reforms and issues. While he was able to pass domestic legislation like the Family and Medical Leave Act which required employers to ensure employees had a job upon their return from a leave due to medical or family issues and the Violence Against Women act which provided $1.6 billion towards investigation and prosecution of violent crimes against women, the Clinton administration also suffered its first major setback when it came to health care. Clinton and his wife, Hillary Rodham Clinton, attempted to enact universal health care in America, but the plan died in 1993. The Clinton administration misread and mishandled its inaction, as they waited too long to bring the bill before Congress in an attempt to force a vote and weighed it down with bureaucratic lingo which no one had time to parse out. As *The Atlantic* reported in January 1995:

> The Clinton plan would have imposed sweeping changes on one seventh of the national economy, with consequences far greater than Congress could possibly consider before casting a rushed vote. It represented a regulation-minded, top-down, centralized approach at a time when the world was moving toward decentralization and flexibility—and when the supposed health crisis was solving itself anyway. The more people learned about this plan, the less they liked it, and it finally died a natural and well-deserved death.[15]

The bill was seen as one of the first great downfalls of the Clinton administration and its carcass was hung out to dry as to deter anyone who thought real and progressive health care reform in America was a tangible idea.

Clinton's second term was marked by technology and scandal. The Internet was now undeniably part of the world and its operations, with daily use of the Internet and computers on the rise and growing steadily as both a necessity at work and as part of a leisure activity. In 1998, the culture and politics of the 1990s would collide as news broke of President Clinton's affair with White House intern Monica Lewinsky. Clinton initially denied his involvement with Lewinsky, which exacerbated the scandal as more parties got involved and indisputable evidence was entered into the trial. Judge Susan Webber Wright was forced to rule that President Clinton had indeed given false testimony, perjuring himself and implicating himself in obstructing justice, bringing about the charges of impeachment. Ultimately all of the Democrats in Congress, as well as some Republicans, voted to acquit Clinton, allowing him to finish his time in office.

The Lewinsky scandal was notable for many reasons. It brought up all of Clinton's womanizing ways, which remained in the public's mind as the now nearly omnipresent 24-hour news cycle continued to grow its reach with outlets like CNN, MSNBC and FOX News all operating at capacity by 1996. The stories of Juanita Broaddrick, who accused Clinton of rape in April 1978, and Kathleen Willey and Paula Jones, who both accused Clinton of assault or harassment, were debated and rehashed repeatedly on news outlets. Outside of Lewinsky, Clinton himself had also admitted to an affair with Gennifer Flowers. Many questioned how the avowed feminist Hillary Clinton could stand by her man. In her writings, she claims to have forgiven her husband, shouldering some of the responsibility for the extramarital affairs because she was not available enough to him. She has never publicly commented on the other allegations other than saying in 1992, "You know, I'm not sitting here, some little woman standing by her man.... I'm sitting here because I love him, and I respect him, and I honor what he's been through and what we've been through together. And you know, if that's not enough for people, then heck, don't vote for him."[16]

Hillary Rodham Clinton has been a lightning rod of accusations, conspiracy theories and judgment. When she and Bill were first married and he became governor of Arkansas she was lambasted for keeping her maiden name and for continuing to work. She drew even more ire during the 1992 presidential campaign when she said, "I suppose I could have stayed home and baked cookies and had teas, but what I decided to do was to fulfill my profession."[17] Clinton has never outspokenly courted controversy herself, though some of her actions and choices have brought them on her. Her polarizing nature as one of the most highly visible women of the 1990s led to an interesting dichotomy. Who was this woman who could argue so passionately that "women's rights are human rights"[18] and stand by a man accused of rape? No one will ever truly know and Clinton's own defensiveness around these questions has led many to question her authenticity, the lack of which would become one of the great sins of the 1990s. She was derided and mocked for demanding a seat at the table when her husband was in the White House and then stepped back from that role in order to help him secure his second term in office.[19] After stepping back, the Lewinsky scandal broke out once again bringing into question her success as a wife and mother. For many women in the 1990s, Hillary Rodham Clinton faced the struggles all women faced: she was too brash, too assertive, too docile, too forgiving. No one seemed willing to admit that Hillary Clinton understood the political arena better than many and the choices she made and reneged on were designed to help her, one day, attempt to shatter that last, highest glass ceiling for women.

Under Clinton's administration several factors came into play: the increased recognition of the diversification of America; the Digital Revolution; the increased emphasis on finance and trade as local manufacturing died out due to the Digital Revolution; the cultural revolution on multiple platforms; and the cult of self-help feel goodness that promised to help everyday Americans achieve utter and total bliss. All of these elements were amplified as the 24-hour news cycle continued to look for anything and everything to broadcast. Each misstep of a celebrity or politician was turned into a disaster, national tragedies were insurmountable events which only turned around once the right pop song had been licensed and, perhaps more importantly, as artist Andy Warhol predicted, everyone was getting their 15 minutes of fame whether through national scandal or a segment on *The Ricki Lake Show*.

As the news and viewership grew with every national tragedy, national mourning became a pastime. There is no denying the very real impact that any of these events had on their local communities and the families affected by them, but the notion of national mourning became palpable with audiences all over America questioning what they could do to help until the next major story came along.

The Waco siege of 1993 was perpetrated by the Texas state law enforcement and the U.S. military. The country closely followed the story, witnessing one of the government's first true and unforgivable missteps. The cult known as the Branch Davidians was being investigated for illegally stockpiling weapons and for its leader David Koresh's alleged child abuse. But the storming Branch Davidians' compound was an unmitigated disaster with most of the Davidians dead and four federal agents killed and dozens more injured. For many, the government's involvement and handling of the Waco siege was a massive over-stepping of their jurisdiction with haphazard decision making carried out because the whole world was watching. One of the people now particularly weary of the government was Timothy McVeigh who in 1995 carried out the Oklahoma City bombings—another national tragedy for America in the 1990s.

Possibly the most contentious and iconic trial of the decade was the O.J. Simpson trial. Former NFL star O.J. Simpson was arrested and tried for the murder of his ex-wife Nicole Brown Simpson and her friend Ron Goldman. Before the court appointed trial, O.J. Simpson's public trial began with a slow-moving chase with authorities in pursuit of Simpson in his white Bronco, which was tracked by television crews in helicopters and broadcast live on CNN and Court TV with over 95 million viewers tuning in.[20] As the *Washington Post* reported of this coverage:

> Court TV and CNN had made the bold decision to cover every turn of the case, no matter how meaningless. Back then, this was revolutionary and maybe even a little risky; never had one news event been covered so continually. But rather than recoil, TV viewers barely noticed they were ignoring their soap operas and prime-time dramas because this one beat them all. Here was a celebrity on trial for murder—with race

1. They Never Had It So Good   23

and sex providing colorful sidebars—with a cast of newly familiar faces as its central characters. Suddenly the decision to carry the case around the clock seemed brilliant; in the days before live streams, constantly updated Web sites and social media, the two channels were feeding a national hunger.[21]

When Simpson was ultimately found not guilty it divided not only America but also the black community. One of the decade's reigning icons, Oprah Winfrey, held a live show as the verdict was being read and talked to the audience for their reactions. Some of the audience stood and applauded the verdict, feeling that this could be a turning point in race in America, while other women in the audience slumped in their chairs with their heads down, feeling that, once again, a man accused of domestic violence was more powerful than they. As one audience member said, "I'm very happy, I think justice was served." Another audience member countered with "I'm not happy, it's not fair. I feel so bad for [Nicole Brown Simpson], I feel like she's rolling over in her grave. She said if [O.J. ever killed her], he'd get away with it."[22] The Simpson trial for all of its antics and circus-like qualities affirmed that the race divides in America were still deep and that the power dynamics for women were still in flux.

As the millennium neared its end on April 20, 1999, Eric Harris and Dylan Klebold walked into their high school, Columbine, in Littleton, Colorado, armed with explosives and semi-automatic weapons and killed 12 students and one teacher with many more injured. The devastating shock of the tragedy wore heavily on America. Littleton was the kind of small town where the American Dream was supposed to thrive, leaving many to wonder, how could this happen? As with the other major tragedies and events of the 1990s, the days after, the weeks after and the months and years after were covered by every major news outlet, each one scrambling for anything that would point to a clear-cut reason for why these two teens would commit such atrocities. Some blamed Marilyn Manson's music, some blamed violent video games and movies, and some blamed the clique-based high school culture and bullying. Others perpetrated the notion of the Trench Coat Mafia, a clique group both Klebod and Harris supposedly belonged to. In Dave Cullen's book *Columbine*, Cullen interweaves interviews, texts and reporting to create one of the most cohesive timelines of the events and the shooting's effects on a small community.

> The Trench Coat Mafia was mythologized because it was colorful, memorable, and fit the existing myth of school shooters as outcast loner. All Columbine myths worked that way. And they all sprang to life incredibly fast—most of the notorious myths took root before the killers' bodies were found. We remember Columbine as a pair of Goths from the Trench Coat Mafia snapping and tearing through their high school hunting down jocks to settle a long-running feud. Almost none of that happened. No Goths,

no outcasts, nobody snapping. No targets, no feud, and no Trench Coat Mafia. Most of those elements existed at Columbine—which is what gave them currency. They just had nothing to do with the murders.[23]

While no one realized it at the time, the weight and narrative the media gave the Columbine tragedy overshadowed the actual events. Once parents, teachers and any other adult heard the proposed narratives coming from their televisions, youth culture was under suspicion. What were these performers encouraging our children to do? Ultimately in an era where information was supposed to be travelling faster and becoming more accessible than ever, the hardest lesson for the country to learn was that misinformation could still spread faster than facts if it made a more convincing narrative.

The 1990s was a time when concern over narratives was at a high and the ability to control one's narrative was at a premium. No one will ever truly know what exactly happened between Anita Hill and Clarence Thomas, but there are lots of opinions on it. Kurt Cobain was never able to truly articulate why fame, fortune and a family still led him to kill himself in 1994. Hillary Clinton is still trapped by her self-imposed censorship, demanding to talk about policy, reform and government initiatives rather than subjugate herself to the cult of personality, which in turn has led many to label her as untrustworthy. Bill Clinton said as he ran for his first term as president in 1992 that "there is nothing wrong in America that can't be fixed with what is right in America." The problem for America in the 1990s was that what was wrong and what was right changed depending on whom you talked to.

Historian William H. Chafe summarizes the haphazardness of 1990s in America as only one can, repurposing a quote from a British author about a French war:

> Ironically, America in the 1990s encapsulated the Dickensian paradox: it enjoyed the best of times yet also experienced the worst of times. Unprecedented prosperity brought a standard of living to millions unheard of in prior generations. The stock market soared above eleven thousand; high-tech start-ups soon sold for billions of dollars; and for countless people, there seemed to be no limit to potential growth, happiness and fulfillment. Yet for countless others, it was a time of coming apart. Life got worse, not better. Jobs fled the country. Families seemed to be falling to pieces. Children grew up in knowing only one parent. Worst of all, there seemed to be no common vision holding the country together, no glue that cemented people of different religious persuasions and cultural values. And in the middle of it stood Bill Clinton, himself the embodiment of the twoness—one of the brightest, most charismatic, most talented people to ever occupy the Oval Office, yet simultaneously, a person possessed of demons that hurled him back into defeat at precisely the moments when he was ready to score his greatest victories.[24]

2

Imitate Us
America's Youth Culture

Teenagers, as they are thought of today, are a relatively new concept to the modern world. Up until the 19th century, Western society consisted of children and adults. Before the Industrial Revolution hit America's shores around 1760 until about 1820 and its advancements carried Western society from there, life was rather predictable for many families due in large part to the nature of the reigning industry of the time—farming. Once industrialization took hold, jobs became uncertain as machines began replacing laborers. Families no longer knew what to teach their children, if they should be sent to school, or if they should keep working on the land alongside them.[1] Since there was no two ways about the job shortage, one way to circumvent this was to demand children attend school, thereby omitting them from the work force. While the nineteenth century did have youth advocates often known as child protectionists, the notion of the teenager was ostensibly designed to prevent labor competition within families.[2]

Teenagers, the term and the idea of them as a specified group, did not enter the North American consciousness until the early 1940s. The notion of the teenager as its own specific culture group with defining ages, rites of passage and eventually its own culture could not have existed before then. In essence, the notion of the teenager was waiting for technology and the economy to catch up. The teenager could not have existed before 1940 as America was still pulling itself out of the Great Depression. While America faced the atrocities of World War II, it was a prosperous time for the country because the war kept the economy moving.

The term "teen-ager" by all accounts made its debut in *Popular Science Monthly* in 1941 but was not fully popularized until the *LIFE Magazine* December 1944 article, "Teen-Age Girls: They Live in a Wonderful World of Their Own," which implied not only a life cycle of teenagers but also a potential market.[3] Interestingly, the *LIFE Magazine* article focused on the white-middle-class teenage girl, an almost crystal ball into the increased focus on them in the decades to come. As the *LIFE* article began:

> American businessmen, many of whom have teen-age daughters, have only recently begun to realize that teen-agers make up a big and special market.... The movies and the theater make money by turning a sometimes superficial and sometimes social-minded eye on teen-agers. Their new importance means little to teen-age millions. By their energy, originality and good looks they have brought public attention down from debutantes and college girls to themselves.[4]

From there teenage girls as an entity or an audience could make or break a grown man's career, from Frank Sinatra to Justin Timberlake. Teens were becoming the tastemakers, the haves over the have nots, because within this cultural context to mainstream America and all of its corporations, only white middle class teens existed to sell the news trends and fads to. Their dreams could be expounded, exploited and condensed into easily sellable merchandise and events. They were consumers without the mortgage or children but with their parents' money or money of their own from low-paying jobs allowing them to dominate the marketplace. Teens by all accounts have the wherewithal to understand their place in the world, make decisions and have opinions just as much as adults yet they exist within a society that often holds them back, forcing them to systematically jump through hoops decided upon in government legislature through the form of high school. Thomas Hines writes of this tension in his book *The Rise and Fall of the American Teenager*:

> We are more accustomed to thinking of contemporary teenagers as predators than as victims, but there are good reasons to worry about them. Far more of them are growing up in low-income households than was the case a few decades ago. They spend more time on their own: today's young people are able to be with their parents ten to twelve fewer hours each week than was the case three decades ago. They are likely to attend schools that are overcrowded, a condition that will worsen because few school districts expanded their secondary schools to accommodate the larger number of teenagers they will enroll during the next decade. Many school districts have little choice in the matter, because they are starved for money. Public schools, new taxes, and teenagers are three of the least popular causes in contemporary America and when you put all three together, it's a political loser.[5]

Part of using the growing youth culture as a capitalist movement was to begin creating content just for them. This took shape most notably in music where crooners and rock and rollers could sing about love or rejection of the establishment and garner the kind of attention most musicians dream of. Another format would be films. Films are the near-perfect blend of marketability when done right; they can tell a story but they can also sell you on the music, fashion and lifestyle within a film. They can create icons over an opening weekend and for a relatively reasonable price pull audiences out of the day-to-day mundaneness of their own lives. Colin McGinn writes of the emotional impact of films in our mind in his book *The Power of Movies*:

> Movies thus tap into the dreaming aspect of human nature. Moreover, they improve upon our dream life. They give us dreams we yearn for. It is a rare individual who is not fascinate by his own dreams, with their raw ability to reveal, their magical expressiveness; movies partake in this fascination. The impact of movies stems, then, at least in part, from the primal power of the dream. To be sure, the dream component of the movie experience is augmented by the special qualities of the medium, but the primary emotional hook originates in the evocation of the dream.[6]

While youth oriented film had existed since narrative cinema's inception, the concept of the teen film was relatively new and was not fully realized until film studios gave teens what they wanted, which was rebellion. Part of the youth oriented film's roots began with the film studio MGM and their Andy Hardy series. Andy Hardy was played by Mickey Rooney and involved an idyllic small town that Andy and his family inhabited. The films would involve Andy getting into minor forms of trouble which led to some kind of man-to-man talk with his father which ultimately helped Andy set things right. There were 15 films in the Andy Hardy series beginning in 1937 until 1946 with an attempted reboot in 1958 including titles like *Andy Hardy Gets Spring Fever* (W.S. Van Dyke, 1939), *Andy Hardy's Double Life* (George B. Seitz, 1942) and *Andy Hardy's Blonde Trouble* (George Seitz, 1944). These films, no matter how family-friendly and life affirming they were could not have prepared audiences with what they truly wanted. In 1953 Marlon Brando starred in *The Wild One* replete with a leather jacket and cigarette. Brando's Johnny Strabler is asked, "what are you rebelling against?" His answer—"what've you got?"—would set the stage for teenage attitudes and the fear of teenage attitudes for decades to come. The iconic figure of the rebel would continue to grow in films like *Rebel Without a Cause* (Nicolas Ray, 1955) while the female figure would be a fun-loving if chaste girl as seen in the *Gidget* (Paul Wendoks, 1959). As the 1970s arrived with the counter-culture promises of New Hollywood as seen in films like *Taxi Driver* (Martin Scorsese, 1976), *Apocalypse Now* (Francis Ford Coppola, 1979), and *Dog Day Afternoon* (Sidney Lumet, 1975), it would also show the flip side to mainstream femininity in Brian De Palma's *Carrie* (1976), which offered an alternative and soulful, if deadly, look at the inner-workings of a social pariah.

The 1980s, however, were a boon to mainstream teen films. The rise of the films of John Hughes, the Brat Pack and the teen-centered horror film offered a glimpse into what parents feared, and more importantly showed teens, albeit for a brief running time, a way out. This was all aided by the death of the American movie theatre and the rise of the multiplex in the

1980s. As Hollywood was able and more than willing to produce more and more films, single screens could no longer meet their demands, so multiplexes (cinemas with multiple screens) rapidly began to populate malls all over North America. The youth market is a fickle beast and film studios saw the way to ensure their popularity was to increase their output, not only capitalizing on any one trend but also milking that trend to death. Timothy Shary writes of this multiplex movement in his book *Generation Multiplex*:

> Hollywood revised its '50s formula by intensifying the narrative range of youth films through placing teenage characters in previously established genres with more dramatic impact (gory horror, dance musicals, sex comedies), and as a result, a new variety of character types grew out of this generic expansion.[7]

Hollywood and its studios are nothing if not calculating the worth of offering up multiple iterations of a popular theme until moviegoers move on to something else. Molly Ringwald was one of the most visible stars in the 1980s and was part of John Hughes' stable of actors. Her face came to define a version of white 1980s female teenagerdom: a girl with a reputation (bitchy, weird, etc.) who would ultimately find the means to reveal more of herself and in doing so would create a richer, fuller life for herself where she was accepted for who she was. Hollywood works to find the formulations for success and then mines them for all available profit. The rise of the multiplex created spaces for every kind of fan. On any given night, a filmgoer could see a drama, a comedy, a horror movie or a musical. The limitless possibilities were what kept Hollywood alive and what ingratiated them to youth culture.

Concurrent to the multiplex phenomena was the rise of VHS in the 1980s. As VHS tapes became more affordable, they became more profitable. Soon there were places to rent movies all over the Western world allowing consumers to stay home and watch movies. This allowed a generation of kids who were maybe not quite old enough to get into the multiplex to see the newest horror film a way to access them. The VHS culture was particularly important to horror films, as the audience that could readily and continually access VHSs created enough profit for these films to generate sequels—not sequels worthy of the glossy multiplex, but sequels that could continue the story on a tight enough budget to satisfy the fans.

Horror in the 1980s was popularized by the slasher film. The slasher film deals with a killer who targets victims based on some kind of past misdeed or trespass and dispatches with them usually one at a time by a handheld weapon, which necessitates proximity to victims to properly dispatch them. Killers in these films are usually stopped by the Final Girl. The Final Girl, as defined by Carol Clover in *Men, Women and Chainsaws* is "the one who encounters the mutilated bodies of her friends and perceives the full extent of the preceding horror and of her own peril.... She alone looks death in the face, but she alone also finds the strength either to stay the killer long enough to be rescued (ending A) or to kill him herself (ending B)."[8] Within this description there are almost always exceptions to the rules. For every instance of following the rules of the slasher film, there is almost always some kind of inversion, which challenges its audiences to keep up with the formula they believe they know so well. There is also a titillating aspect of it. The victims in a slasher film are almost all uniformly young, nubile and transgressive. In *Friday the 13th* (Sean S. Cunningham, 1980) Mrs. Voorhees attacks teens indiscriminately because her young son Jason drowned while two camp counselors were having sex. This rational set up in the early days of the slasher allowed filmmakers throughout most of the teen oriented horror movies of the 1980s to set up a sex scene in which a young actress at least shows her breasts, and on occasion even gets to have sex, before a brutal dispatch at the hands of the killer. As Robin Wood put it in his treatise on 1980s horror in his book *Hollywood from Vietnam to Reagan ... And Beyond*:

> The last survivor of the teenie-kill movies, endurer of the ultimate ordeals, terrors and agonies, is invariably female; the victims in the violence against women films are predominantly young. But the motivation for the slaughter on both dramatic and ideological levels is somewhat different: in general, the teenagers are punished for promiscuity, while the women are punished for being women.[9]

While those elements comprise the surface of slasher films, they also embody the elements of any great teen movie. Teens in these films have to confront parts of their sexuality, the sins of their parents and their communities, and looming adult responsibilities. As Shary writes of the teen slasher heyday of the 1980s:

> Consider that in the Reagan era (1981–1989), a new notion of America conservatism was sweeping the country, and horror films about wild youth were replaced by less metaphorical narratives about youth actually enjoying the pleasures of rebellion and sensuality; thus the teen sex film flourished in the early 80s. Later the public awareness of AIDS growing by the late '80s and a marked shift in the teen sex film from promiscuity to romance, the youth horror film again seemed to capitalize on the fears of sexuality and adulthood.... [Perhaps] the over-done violence of so many slasher films brought an entertaining glamour to more diverse terrors of the supernatural; perhaps the subgenre simply lost financial support from studios, given the theatrical failure of virtually all youth horror films from the late 80s to the mid 90s.[10]

While these films did predicate themselves on punishment for titillation, they still fall within Laura Mulvey's theory of the Male Gaze developed in her paper *Visual Pleasure and Narrative Cinema*:

> The film opens with the woman as object of the combined gaze of spectator and all the male protagonists in the film. She is isolated, glamorous, on display, sexualised.

> But as the narrative progresses she falls in love with the main male ... losing her outward glamorous characteristics, her generalized sexuality, her show-girl connotations.... By means of identification with him, through participating in his power, the spectator can indirectly possess her too.[11]

Mulvey articulates that the camera's gaze is inherently gendered as male subscribing to the supposedly normative male gaze of fetishizing any and all nubile female bodies. The gaze of the camera therefore negates a female character's agency rendering her subservient to the narrative, which, in these cases, is about the male character and/or viewer. As Mulvey concludes, "Woman, then, stands in patriarchal culture as a signifier for the male other, bound by a symbolic order in which man can live out his fantasies and obsessions through linguistic command by imposing them on the silent image of a woman still tied to her place as the bearer of meaning, not maker of meaning."[12]

Within these horror films, slashers as well as other iconic 1980s offerings like *Fright Night* (Tom Holland, 1985) and *The Lost Boys* (Joel Schumacher, 1987), the gaze of the audience was male, or believed to be male. These films, as beloved as they are by audiences all over the world, did not capitalized on the feminist implications of the Final Girl; they were marketed and talked about in mainstream media in regards to their gore and their sexualized elements. As Mulvey writes in *Visual Pleasures and Narrative Cinema*:

> In a world ordered by sexual imbalance, pleasure in looking has been split between active/male and passive/female. The determining male gaze projects its phantasy on to the female form which is styled accordingly. In their traditional exhibitionist role women are simultaneously looked at and displayed, with their appearance coded for strong visual and erotic impact so that they can be said to connote to-be-looked-at-ness.[13]

In the coding of these horror films, the male gaze was always established and even encouraged by the reoccurring trope of the camera adopting the killer's gaze and spying on young women. This is only one of many techniques that code the female characters as objects to be looked at. Women were attractive and attracting before they were fully formed characters. As Wood says, "The violence against women movies have generally been explained as a hysterical response to 60s and 70s feminism: the male spectator enjoys a sadistic revenge on women who have begun to refuse to slot neatly and obligingly into his patriarchal predetermined view of the way things should naturally be."[14] As the cultural discourse around women was changing and women were demanding change, horror films were easy to point to as misogynistic dinosaurs that were a regressive force rather than a progressive one. Producers of horror films would eventually use their tradition of casting women for leading roles

2. Imitate Us 31

as a rebuttal against this perception. From *Psycho* (Alfred Hitchcock, 1960), to *The Haunting* (Robert Wise, 1963) to *The Ring* (Gore Verbinski, 2002), horror films have often offered a respite for female filmgoers who are tired of their gender conforming roles, where, as stated by Laura Mattoon D'Amore, "women often find their potential as smart and independent is overshadowed by plot lines about their beauty, madness, or romantic interest."[15]

The increased public discourse around the HIV/AIDS crisis emboldened concerns about the seemingly reckless sexuality that was being portrayed in mainstream films. By the 1990s, the Anita Hill hearings, the rise of the Third Wave of Feminism and Riot Grrrl, young women were being placed at the center of a national discourse. The concerns around their bodies and their rights were at the forefront of a cultural discourse. While women could see President Bill Clinton enact legislation to aid survivors of domestic assault, the act was tainted with the knowledge that he had been accused by multiple women of rape and assault. Young women continued to struggle to come forward and deal with instances of sexual assault, abuse and a variety of other terrifying realities. As Anita Harris wrote in the *Feminist Review*:

> Since the early 1990s, young womanhood has become a topic central to debates about culture and society.... Girls, including their bodies, their labor power and their social behavior are now the subject of governmentality to an unprecedented degree. The cultural fascination with girlhood and the modes of governmentality by which their bodies, labor and behavior are regulated have been organized primarily around two images: "girl power" on the one hand, and "girls as risk-takers" on the other. Through each of these representations young women emerged as their own phenomenon.[16]

Through all of this, it became apparent that the youth culture of the 1980s had to shift; it had to mean something again to young women whose realities were changing. All of the meaningful youth culture had gone underground and would resurface with Nirvana's *Nevermind*, which would spark the commodification of alternative culture. The album's first lead single did not just appeal to those on the outside of culture, but also to those within, with its undeniable rifts, chord progression and its almost-pleading narrative that everything was not okay. Shortly after 1991, grunge, indie, alternative culture was a marketable and quantifiable quality to have. In 1992 designer Marc Jacobs was still making a name for himself and succeeded in making headlines in 1992 for his Perry Ellis Grunge Collection. The collection was comprised of flannel, knitted hats and baby-doll dresses, all which signified that alternative culture could be commodified despite the fact that the majority of grunge style developed out of students and artists wearing what they could afford in an effort to ward off the chilly damp of the home of grunge—the Pacific Northwest. Almost overnight, grunge aesthetic, as well as Starbucks, hit malls all over America, ensuring that any cultural connoisseur could buy the best flannel they could afford, get a designer coffee and see *Singles* (Cameron Crowe, 1992) or *Reality Bites* (Ben Stiller, 1994), all within the indoor mall.

The summer of 1995 saw the release of Amy Heckerling's *Clueless*, a sweet teen romantic comedy based on Jane Austen's *Emma*. *Clueless* stars Alicia Silverstone as Cher, an affluent LA teen who takes it upon herself to make over a new, less fortunate student, Tai (Brittany Murphy). As Tai's transformation takes shape Cher realizes that popularity is not everything she had once thought it to be and that she can actually use the resources at her disposal to help people. *Clueless* was a sleeper hit of the summer, well-reviewed overall and eventually was made into a television show. The *Clueless* effect proved to Hollywood that the youth market was still there, but it needed to be revitalized because teens perhaps knew more than Hollywood was willing to admit. As *Clueless* begins with a classically filmic montage of Cher and her friends doing "typical" teen girl activities, Cher's voiceover breaks through, saying, "Okay, so you're probably going, 'Is this like a Noxzema commercial or what?' But seriously, I actually have a way normal life for a teenage girl." Cher's own self-effacing charm is part of what makes this privileged character so likeable. Using *Clueless*' template, Hollywood had a new way to reach a youth market that had begun to seem unreachable after its 1980s heyday.

Clueless was so successful because it incorporated a variety of teen problems, including sexuality, class and friendship, into its narrative. Cher's main friends in the film, Dionne (Stacey Dash) and Tai, each have a different experience and expectation of sexuality and drug use and none of them are made to feel particularly bad about themselves for their choices. Journalist Laura Cohen wrote of this exceptional aspect to *Clueless*:

> *Clueless*' central theme of female friendship is completely critical to the point of the entire movie… And when Cher and Tai fight, their teary-eyed and love-filled make-up shows the strength of their bond (only true friends go down a "shame spiral" if they feel like they've been unsupportive of the other). These kind of real-life woman-to-woman friendships are still largely underrepresented in the media, but *Clueless* shows what other movies still don't reflect today.[17]

A film to consider in contrast to *Clueless* is Larry Clark's *Kids* (1995). Distributed by Miramax, *Kids* tells the story of a group of teens in New York City who use drugs and indiscriminately have unprotected sex with each other, passing around STIs, including HIV. Tom Doher, who wrote for *Cineaste Magazine*, critiques the two films:

> No wonder the polar rift in directorial sensibilities (Heckerling and Clark represent two diametrically opposed attitudes to filmmaking no less than towards adolescence)

was seized upon as emblematic of American culture's own ambivalences towards the permanent subculture in its midst. Are the kids alright or all screwed up, budding citizens heading into a better tomorrow or pretty vacant punks with no future?[18]

Kids felt like the fear mongering tactics of an older generation who were trying to shock their children into submission, while *Clueless* offered a bright happy world where good things happen to good people—particularly good women.

Clueless worked in tandem with the advent of The Spice Girls, where fun and friendship ruled and some boys drooled. Mainstream culture grew more concerned with young women through the rise of books such as *Reviving Ophelia: Saving the Selves of Adolescent Girls* (1994) by Mary Pipher, which discusses young women dealing with self-harm, STDs, drug and alcohol abuse, and anger, particularly towards their parents.

While parents of these girls wrung their hands over their daughters, other women got to work making music (as with Riot Grrrl) and magazines, such as *Sassy Magazine*, for them. *Sassy* was made by real girls (or women) for real girls. Addressing everything from sexuality, to fashion, to politics, to music, to makeup, *Sassy* was part of a movement that recognized young women's complexities and interests outside of imposed gender and encouraged culture to catch up. As is the case with any major cultural movement, its tenants will always be homogenized. From Riot Grrrl to the Spice Girls, culture for young women was being commodified, but at least it was presenting them with options.

This is where the 1990s Teen Horror Cycle intersects, as male run studios were willing to recognize the powerful intersection between women, horror, youth and films. The heyday of the 1980s slasher film had died at various stages with killers at the forefront and now it was time to focus on the Final Girls.

3

Co-Deads
Buffy the Vampire Slayer (1992) and *My Boyfriend's Back* (1993)

Before *Buffy the Vampire Slayer* (Fran Rubel Kuzui, 1992) became synonymous with late-90s WB Television culture, it was a film—a film that has been derided by its writer and future television series show runner, Joss Whedon. Directed by Fran Rubel Kuzui, who would go on to be a producer on both *Buffy the Vampire Slayer* the television series and its spin-off *Angel*, the film seems like a blip on the cultural radar—especially when viewed through the long shadow which the beloved television series casts on it and within the realm of Whedon's other work. The film, however, is a perfect emblem of its time, a story that laid the groundwork for many other films, television series and comics that would come after it. It was released in 1992, the same year Carol Clover's foundational text on the horror genre, *Men, Women and Chainsaws: Gender in the Modern Horror Film*, and Rebecca Walker's *Ms.* article, "Becoming the Third Wave," which helped galvanize the young feminist base who did not fully agree with second wave feminism or found it lacking, were published. *Buffy the Vampire Slayer*, a gateway film that seems harmless on its surface, laid the groundwork for the California Valley girl with a soul, taking the female character who would usually be coded as an early victim of whatever malevolent force was besieging the characters on screen and turning her into the film's hero.

For many, the film is fluffy and trite when viewed in contrast to the television series, which ran from 1997 to 2003. While the television show would go on to explore the intricacies and intimacies of friendship, sexuality, violence and death, the film was a teen oriented romp within none of subtleties that a television show could explore. The comparison between the film and television formats is unfair since it generally overlooks the easy shorthand with which the film conveys multiple themes and viewpoints. *Buffy the*

Vampire Slayer is a deceptively fun film, working on multiple feminist levels, as well as a satire of the overwrought vampire tropes of the 1980s, marking a refreshing break from the gothic romance of vampiric figures.

The film, which most fans of the television series prefer to forget about, is an introduction to many of the themes and storylines that make up the seven seasons of the television series. Part of the derision towards the film is Whedon's own open derisiveness towards it, which he has spoken candidly about several times. In a 2001 interview with *The AV Club* Whedon explained:

> WHEDON: I had major involvement [with the film]. I was there almost all the way through shooting. It didn't turn out to be the movie that I had written.... Not that the movie is without merit, but I just watched a lot of stupid wannabe-star behavior and a director with a different vision than mine—which was her right, it was her movie—but it was still frustrating.[1]

At the time of the film's release, *Buffy the Vampire Slayer* received a mixed review with the *New York Times*, which called it "a slight, good-humored film that's a lot more painless than might have been expected."[2] The film would go on to recoup its $7 million budget with a domestic box office of just over $16 million in North America.[3] *Buffy the Vampire Slayer* was not popular enough to be part of the larger upcoming teen girl cultural movement but it made just enough impact to retain a low-level cult status.

The film follows high school senior Buffy Summers (Kristy Swanson) whose main ambition is to "graduate high school, go to Europe, marry Christian Slater and die." As she approaches her final months in school she is found by her Watcher, Merrick (Donald Sutherland), who tells her that she is the Chosen One, the Slayer, a young woman whose destiny is to fight the vampires that stalk our world. Buffy's ambivalence toward her destiny comes from wanting to lead her own "normal" life with her vapid friends and her equally vapid jock boyfriend. The more Merrick convinces her of her own natural power, ability and the realities of the vampire forces, the more Buffy believes and is determined to fight an evil elder vampire, Lothos (Rutger Hauer), and his minion, Amilyn (Paul Reubens). While trying to balance her high school popularity with her newfound responsibilities, Buffy grows close to Pike (Luke Perry), who, once socially beneath her, eventually becomes her greatest ally.

The film has been billed as a comedy, a romantic comedy, a satire—its closest filmic relative—and, on occasion, a horror film. *Buffy the Vampire Slayer* is indebted to all the female victims of the slasher films of the 1980s, as well as the Anne Rice vampires who bled gothic aesthetic and the pseudo-punk vampires of the 1980s who grew in popularity after *The Lost Boys* (Joel Schumacher, 1987).

As Whedon has stated many times over the years, his inspiration for Buffy came from wanting the young women who were repeatedly victimized in horror films to be able to fight back and develop characteristics beyond that of victimhood.[4] *Buffy the Vampire Slayer* is a high-level realization of the need for maturity and ability in the face of great evil and consequence. The film also taps into many of the tenants that Third Wave feminism was beginning to develop and extol—namely that power, respect and rights do not have to come at the cost of selfhood. As The Gossip lead singer Beth Ditto wrote in her foreword to *Riot Grrrl: Revolution Girl Style Now*, a compilation of essays and artifacts from Riot Grrl's heyday in the early 90s:

> For the first time in history valley girls were feared.... Riot Grrrl was by far one of the most undeniably effective feminist movements, turning academia into an accessible down-to-earth language, making feminism a trend for the first time in history. Before the riot grrrls, feminism was only available to kids lucky enough to go to college, but riot grrrl gave a name, a face, a sound to feminist frustration.[5]

Third Wave feminism and Riot Grrrl were movements that sought to break down the walls between discourse and action and attempted to show women of every age that there was a place in feminism for them. *Buffy the Vampire Slayer* realizes these very notions practically in real time, illustrating that feminism can be fun, accessible and not tragically five minutes ago.

The film takes its time developing the character of Buffy as an internal and external force, one that can occupy one space in one way and another space in another way. The lesson Buffy must learn is that learning and growth lead to responsibility and change—ideas that are of little interest to her at the beginning of the film.

An early scene in the film shows Buffy and her friends shopping at the mall and going to see a film at the multiplex—a display of Buffy's performative persona. The shopping mall is not an accidental setting and Timothy Shary explains its importance in his book *Teen Movies*:

> The mall became a scene of teen congregation where arcades and food courts replace the pool halls and soda fountains of the past. Furthermore, since the 1970s, following the dramatic decline of the American movie theaters, Hollywood has come to depend on the centralization of multiple theaters in large retail centers to increase the number of screen venues and to offer moviegoers a greater variety of convenience. Thus the multiplex was born. With the relocation of most movie theaters into or near shopping malls in the 1980s, the need to cater to young audiences who frequented those malls became apparent to Hollywood, and those audiences formed the first generation of multiplex movie goers.[6]

Buffy and her friends are stand-ins for the audience watching the film. The characters (Buffy and her friends) deciding to go see a film in a multiplex are not unlike the majority of the film's audience. Their own ambivalence and apathy toward how they while away their time has an impact on the economy that, in turn, breeds a seemingly apathetic culture.

The mall and the multiplex are also places where social classes can clash. As shown in the movie theater scene, Buffy and her friends talk throughout the film, much to the irritation of Pike and his friend Benny (David Arquette). The two groups trade barbs with each other, parting ways. It is not until the vampire threat is felt by both Buffy and Pike that their social pretensions begin to drop away.

Beyond Buffy's economic power (the film implies that she has disposable cash because her parents are always out of town and they remain well-off) is her social capital. She is attractive and sensible enough to surround herself with likeminded friends on the cheerleading squad and a jock boyfriend, Jeffery (Randall Batinkoff). Buffy is determined to revel in her lack of responsibility to anyone or anything. As the threat of vampires grows more real, she's forced to cut classes (not to shop, but to train) and skips out on social time with her friends (the biggest taboo for her). As Buffy spends time in a more private sphere outside of her social capital, her life at school becomes increasingly problematic. Early in the film Jeffery's friend Andy (Andrew Lowery) asks if he can "borrow" Buffy from Jeffrey and later in the film, as Buffy is beginning to embrace her role as Slayer, Andy slaps her butt, at which point Buffy pushes him against the nearby lockers and Jeffrey admonishes his friend with "Hey, keep your hands off my *thing*." Buffy's social capital is based on her perceived adherence to a patriarchal order—her role as a "thing." Buffy's transformation into the role of the Slayer does not define her, per se, but it does help her perceive a world outside of the patriarchal order.

Early in the film, Buffy laments a teacher telling her that she has "no sense of history" then laughs with her friends about when she would ever need it. However, Merrick is able to convince her of her destiny and abilities by detailing the dreams she has:

MERRICK: Do you ever dream that you were someone else, Buffy?
BUFFY: Everybody does.
MERRICK: Someone in the past, someone real. A peasant girl? An Indian princess, perhaps? A slave?
BUFFY: I was a slave.
MERRICK: In Virginia?
BUFFY: I don't know, there was this big farm or something. There was this one where there were knights and I'm...
MERRICK: A servant girl, a bar maid.
BUFFY: Oh my God. I never told anybody about this. There's this one with this man, and I'm fighting him. Well, I'm always fighting him, but he's so strong.
MERRICK: His name is Lothos.

Buffy's ties to history are not through avenues approved by high school classes, but through past lives that detail not the male dominated world history but that of an often lower class woman (slave/servant). Through the film, Buffy must join her past, her destiny and her reality marking her as different and a new woman who, like the past Slayers, is willing to fight back.

Buffy's main conflict is established when in her first encounter with Lothos, Merrick sacrifices himself to save her. In this scene, Buffy realizes there are consequences to her actions and that she may never be ready to face a vampire of Lothos' power. Pike tries to persuade her that fighting Lothos and the vampires is her calling and that she can do it but Buffy is reticent of letting go of her past identity/identities to create a new one.

Buffy attends the senior dance to find her friends shunning her and sees that Jeffrey has now started dating one of her former clique members. As Buffy's past life falls away, Pike (suitably cleaned up for the occasion) arrives and they slow dance.

PIKE: You're not like other girls.
BUFFY: Yes, I am.

In this simple exchange, the film acknowledges the place for many varied experiences within girlhood and womanhood. Though Buffy's friends (the only other notable women in the film) have deserted her, this exchange implies that they are as worthy and capable as she is, that Buffy has simply been forced to reckon with her responsibilities and prophetic destiny before the rest of them.

Buffy the Vampire Slayer goes even further to embrace the tenants of feminism by exploring the way multiple characters are trapped by assumptions. By the end of the film, Merrick is not a "dirty old man" but a teacher and mentor who cared for Buffy and Pike is not a wastoid burn-out, but a capable partner to Buffy. The vampires in the film can take on multiple meanings but their most interesting metaphorical value is that of a hedonistic, unthinking force looking only to consume. Initially, Buffy and her friends are trapped by the tenants of the mall and all that it promises; vampires, once they are turned, have no autonomy and only function to feed, create havoc and do Lothos' bidding. Buffy's liberation from the mall, school, and her friends allows her to see the world for what is it, and moreover she does not have to create a new world order but can exist within it on her own terms—like going to the dance in a fancy dress while still defeating an elder vampire.

Johnny Dingle (Andrew Lowery) only needed to fall in love once in his brief life. He and his crush, Missy (Traci Lind), have grown up in a small town together, though she barely seems to notice him. He has held on to a

3. Co-Deads

gift he has wanted to give her since the first grade and now that she's broken up with her jock boyfriend Buck (Matthew Fox), Johnny sees his opportunity to ask Missy to the prom. Johnny plans a fake heist at the convenience store where Missy works in order to show off his bravery and win Missy's affection. As these situations tend to go, there actually is a heist, which Johnny attempts to foil, but instead he is shot. With his dying breath he asks Missy to prom. She complies because he is dying, not knowing that this promise will bring Johnny back from the dead to continue their relationship. *My Boyfriend's Back* walks an awkward line between romantic comedy, supernatural comedy and an EC Comic (a genre-based brand of comics which produced classic titles such as *Tales From the Crypt* and *The Vault of Horror*) that ultimately serves to tell the story of a high school senior, his belabored crush and the power of love.

The film was written by Dean Lorey, whose other screenwriting credit in 1993 was *Jason Goes to Hell: The Final Friday*, one of the many supposed "finals" in the Jason Voorhees mythology. *My Boyfriend's Back* was directed by character actor Bob Balaban, whose most famous credits as an actor include *Close Encounters of the Third Kind* (Steven Spielberg, 1977) and a variety of appearances in Christopher Guest movies such as *Best in Show* (2000) and *A Mighty Wind* (2003). Balaban, however, is not primarily known as a director and in a 2014 interview with *Buzzfeed* he said of his experience with *My Boyfriend's Back*:

> *My Boyfriend's Back*, a teenage comedy about a boy who becomes a zombie and takes his girlfriend to the prom, is a middle-of-the-road Hollywood product thing. It sort of had vaguely cute potential…. It was very, very diminishing, that experience. I learned after it that I had really better only do things because I like them, and not because it sounds like a good idea because I'll get a career from it.[7]

The film opens with an animation sequence that closely mirrors the EC Comic format and style, at once highlighting the film's oddity, apparent through the film's marketing materials, while also attempting to make it non-threatening to teen audiences. The comic book interstitials make appearances throughout the film, but in its opening moments they serve to set up the film as a hero's journey that goes through mythic proportions to achieve an end goal or prize. Ultimately, as is the case with most romantic comedies, the hero(s) must learn something about themselves, apply it, and self-actualize. *My Boyfriend's Back* is that hero's journey in which Johnny attempts to circumvent this journey by pre-planning a fake heist in order to impress Missy. What follows when he returns from the dead is an actual hero's journey as the town begins to turn on him and see him as "other," which is a thinly coded metaphor for prejudice against perceived outsiders in small towns.

My Boyfriend's Back romanticizes innocent love against all odds—even death. But as contemporary society has slowly become more accepting of diversity, the classic love story, which pits two would-be lovers from opposing forces to prove that love can conquer anything, has become more of a metaphor—and what better metaphor than refusing to die for the promise of a date. As James T. Dowd and Nicole R. Pallotta wrote in "The End of Romance":

> In romantic fiction, then, love invariably thrives where it is forbidden. It is a convention of the romantic genre that lovers risk crossing social boundaries of all types to be with one another. However, as in the story of Romeo and Juliet, or in the earlier tale of Oedipus and Jocasta, the socially ill-suited lovers must separate in order for the social order to be reestablished. In actual social life, the tragedy that usually befalls the lovers to effect this end is rarely encountered as the forces of custom, socialization, and social segregation conjoin to minimize the chances of love developing at the wrong time or with the wrong partner.[8]

The film begins and is continually framed with Johnny's narration as well as the comic book motif, which works its way into the overall film through a haphazard tone and Balaban's preference for exaggerated camera angles. Johnny begins the film by informing the audience via voiceover that this story is about the "beginning of the end" of his life. This plays tonally into the film through its use of the over dramatization of teens in general, but also through the literal end of Johnny's life, which allows him to actually live.

The film sets up Johnny as a regular teen with wants and desires who also is content to hide behind formalities and social boundaries. The film shows him applying concealer to a zit and biking to school, mechanically waving at neighbors and passers-by in a show of small town niceties. The style of these shots seems most overtly cribbed from Tim Burton's *Edward Scissorhands* (1990), which also elaborates on the impact of a supernatural or unnatural being taking up residency in a small town community. The town's deep normality stands in contrast to the films hyper-metaphorical tale. While the town is covered in an eerie niceness, the townspeople also readily and willingly accept that Johnny has and can return from the dead. This heightened filmic world of the small town mirrors Burton's own obsession with small communities, allowing *My Boyfriend's Back* to use the macabre themes of reanimated corpses to pose a pointed commentary on the sedated lives enclosed within small towns.

While Burton's film oscillates between fantasy and gothic, Balaban's picture is more concerned with the inner-workings of the average teen, as the film dives into several of Johnny's dream sequences, which not only involve sex but also performance anxiety. Johnny's first dream is depicted shortly after the film introduces Missy and Johnny falls asleep in class. The dream begins with a sexualization of the classroom sequence and then transports Johnny and Missy to the middle of the gym where a cheering crowd prevents Johnny from performing sexually. Missy looks up disappointedly from underneath him. The referee calls out the inadequate size of Johnny's member, Missy looks sad, and the crowd stops cheering. All of this plays in tandem with Johnny's laments over Missy's perfection. The film sets up and frames Missy as the tantalizing pin-up that she is but eventually succumbs to her apparently innate goodness, which trumps her physical beauty. The film looks at Missy through the male gaze, sexualizing her at every turn, but also take pains to illustrate her humanity and compassion, making her more recognizably human and fallible as her attraction to Johnny grows.

In Johnny's fantasies, Missy is purely a sexual entity, but as the stigma around Johnny grows after his return from the grave, so does Missy's character. Once Johnny is no longer viewed as a person, the film depicts Missy as a fuller character—one who stands up for Johnny. In Johnny's dream sequence later in the film, after he comes back from the dead, Missy visits him in his bedroom and as things begin to get hot and heavy, various appendages of Johnny's begin to fall off. This is a more complicated dream sequence because Johnny and Missy have already gone on a successful date, meaning the possibility of sex between them could create a tension between reality and fantasy. Johnny faces the clearest reality when he is forced to reconcile his fantasy setup of the heist with the reality of being shot. Johnny's real-life dream scenario of being the hero is foiled as he actually dies. When he realizes he has been struck with a bullet and is dying, he murmurs, "I'm not dreaming," before succumbing to the wound. Johnny's fantasy life has overtaken and begun to corrode his real life.

In the tonally morbid but satirical funeral scene, Johnny's father (Edward Herrmann) says, "be nice to God" as his son's casket is lowered into the ground. Johnny comes back to life and crawls out of his grave, which a nonplussed gravedigger (Bob Dishy) tells him he must stay in lest he start decomposing. But Johnny has returned for a very specific reason—to take Missy up on her promise of a date. Simply by leaving the graveyard Johnny has begun the process of his own re-demise but cares not as he is sure that he and Missy will inevitably fall in love.

As Johnny returns into society, no one seems all that fussed or concerned over the apparent necromancy that has taken place, but they are concerned about his status as "other." Buck and his friend Chuck (Philip Seymour Hoffman) mock and threaten him, which results in Chuck's inadvertent death. Johnny, not wanting to let a good body go to waste, promptly eats him. In turn, the town goes haywire and a mob replete with pitchforks and torches comes after Johnny. There is a subplot with a mad scientist (Austin Pendleton) who can cure Johnny, but ultimately the scientist just wants more of his DNA to sell and become rich from. The film coalesces into a mélange of a zombie film, a redemption film and a satire of both genre and small town films. *My Boyfriend's Back* plays out the archetypes codified in teen films but sets them against the backdrop of Johnny, a decaying body that has no place among the healthy and virile high school. The closer Johnny and Missy get and the more she falls in love with him, the more his body decays and he is unable to act on their physical love, which has been at the forefront of his mind. In this way, Johnny's love for Missy must be realized through emotional means so that when he gets the chance to live again and be with Missy, he values their relationship rather than just his or her body.

My Boyfriend's Back details a teen love story that, tinged with horror, focuses on the corporeal body. Through a teen relationship pitted against the odds of social norms, the film looks at death as the ultimate taboo to cross for love. A love powerful enough to raise one from the dead must ultimately be real.

4

First Blood
The Crush (1993) and *Fear* (1996)

Alan Shapiro's *The Crush* (1993) is about two characters at a crossroads. In order to successfully transition to a new stage of life these two characters flirt with and use each other, testing how far they can go to achieve their desired ends. Shapiro's film was initially centered on a young girl named Darian and her methods of seduction, playing with the taboo of young female sexuality. When the film was released, its production company was successfully sued by a family who felt the events were a little too close to what had happened between their teenage daughter, who was named Darian in real life, and Shapiro.[1] Upon the film's subsequent release on home video and television, the name Darian was changed to Adrian.

The film begins with would-be magazine journalist Nick (Cary Elwes) zipping around Seattle looking for an apartment in which to establish his bachelor life before he begins work at the prestigious Pique Magazine. After a near car accident with a teen, who is later revealed to be 14-year-old Adrian (Alicia Silverstone), Nick stops his car and glances over at the beautiful house which has a "for rent" sign. Adrian's family is renting out the guesthouse, which Nick thinks is perfect. Upon moving in, Adrian's fascination with Nick grows. They become friends and he is charmed by her precociousness and beauty.

Events take a turn for the worst when Adrian breaks into Nick's house and rewrites Nick's first big article for the magazine, which, it turns out, is much better than what Nick wrote. Nick teases Adrian with sentiments like, "If you were ten years older…." This lingering tension between the two characters is quickly stamped out when they share a kiss and Nick begins to understand what he has done. While Nick tries to distance himself from Adrian, Adrian's obsession grows and she flaunts her budding sexuality in front of him and attacks the other women—including Nick's girlfriend and colleague Amy (Jennifer Rubin) and Adrian's own best friend Cheyenne

(Amber Benson)—in his vicinity. The events of the film culminate in Adrian stealing a used condom from Nick's house and framing him for rape and assault. His life in shambles, Nick begins moving out of the house while Adrian and her family go to the country to recover from the supposed incident. Adrian escapes her family and returns to the house to kidnap Cheyenne. While Nick tries to free Cheyenne from the large, classical merry-go-round in the family's attic, Adrian, convinced that Nick is in love with Cheyenne and not her, tries to attack him. Nick turns around as Adrian rushes him and he punches her, sending her flying and knocking her out. The film's final scene in a mental institution sees Adrian pay lip service to her bad behavior while she is in fact setting her sights on her new doctor. Director/writer Shapiro described the film to *Fangoria Magazine* in a set visit:

> I would say it's more psychological [than recent suspense thrillers]. It's more in the mode of *Fatal Attraction*, in which, if you remember, no one really dies until the end. There are no murders, but there are a lot of scares. The film deals with an obsessive personality, and any character who's very intense—be it Travis Bickle or Glenn Close in *Fatal Attraction*—is always interesting. She's not just a one-dimensional, evil girl. It's not like *The Bad Seed*, even though she gets very bizarre. It's a really compelling, three-dimensional character piece.[2]

At its core *The Crush* is about two people looking to advance their station through the easiest means necessary. Ultimately, Nick wants to be a successful writer in his own right while following in the footsteps of his grandfather, a well-known writer who also worked for Pique. Adrian is trapped in her upper-middle class bourgeoisie lifestyle. She is so smart and precocious that she has skipped ahead two grades at school, making it hard for her to find friends. She's a piano prodigy, a very adept writer and the apple of her parents' eye. All of those elements coalesce into creating a young woman who is being pushed ahead in some areas of her life while held back in others. The film does not shy away from showing Adrian's girlhood existence, which clearly is not of her choosing but rather one that has been forced on her. It is replete with a full-size merry-go-round, refurbished by her father, that lives in the family's attic, casting an eerie, childlike shadow across the homestead. Adrian sees Nick as her escape from this patriarchal nightmare of "good-girl-ness." Using her emerging feminine wiles to seduce and secure Nick as a romantic partner would, in her mind, allow her the agency to leave the family home and exist without prior expectations.

Nick, however, is able to navigate the world unfettered and unimpeded. The only thing that causes worry or anxiety for him is perhaps too much attention from women such as Adrian, Amy and other colleagues. Nick, in this way, easily represents and embodies the bachelor/playboy aesthetic and

4. First Blood

Adrian's goal is to make him more established so that he can be a more suitable partner and lift her out of her current lifestyle. Adrian has achieved all she can with doting parents by her side. Skipping ahead in school and playing piano concertos that are warmly received at parties is all well and good, but these acts do not speak to Adrian's true capabilities. She is told to wait until she is old enough to perhaps live her own life.

Even if Adrian is a psychopath, she is a bored psychopath confined by the expectations of being a "good girl" and her upper-class lifestyle. In 1994 Mary Pipher's *Reviving Ophelia: Saving the Selves of Adolescent Girls* was released. Pipher, a psychologist herself, was concerned for the health and wellbeing of young women—namely those she felt were struggling against societal oppression and demands on their bodies and their mind—in the 1990s. While the book focuses on several case studies of real girls, Pipher also makes several overarching assessments:

> As a therapist I often felt bewildered and frustrated. These feelings led to questions: Why are so many girls in therapy in the 1990s? Why are there more self-mutilators? What is the meaning of lip, nose and eyebrow piercings? How do I help thirteen-year-olds deal with herpes or genital warts? Why are drugs and alcohol so common in the stories of seventh graders? Why do so many girls hate their parents? But girls today are much more oppressed. They are coming of age in a more dangerous, sexualized and media-saturated culture. They face incredible pressures to be beautiful and sophisticated, which in junior high means using chemicals and being sexual. As they navigate a more dangerous world, girls are less protected.[3]

Pipher's ideas and conclusions speak to the double-parenting that can happen to any child coming of age in a contemporary Western society, while the majority of parents preach to their daughters the importance of pride, consideration and achievement, they are often absent due to the demands of their work. These daughters are not always privy to work satisfaction and achievement so they turn to their "second" parent, popular culture. This second parent goes against what many parents tell their children, focusing on the glamour and satisfaction of fame and emphasizing the importance of the female body as an object to be idolized and gazed upon. To achieve this level of success, certain standards must be met. Within this duality, children, teens and young adults are left to make decisions for themselves as they become increasingly independent and the lines between practicality and glory can become muddied. As Pipher continues:

> Parents who grew up in a different time with a different set of values are unhappy with what their daughters are learning. They feel like they are trying harder than their parents tried, and yet their daughters are more troubled. The things that worked when they were teenagers are no longer working. They see their daughters' drinking, early sexualization and rebelliousness as evidence of their parental inadequacy. They see

their own families as dysfunctional. Instead I believe what we have is a dysfunctional culture.[4]

Adrian embodies this dichotomy as she begins to become increasingly obsessed with Nick. After their kiss, which alerts Nick to his inappropriate behavior, he attempts to cease any unnecessary contact with Adrian, which only emboldens Adrian to work harder at her seduction. Throughout the film, she is content to lie out on the lawn between the houses in a variety of swimsuits, drawing attention to her body and willingly objectifying it. In fact, the camera becomes Adrian's perceived or desired gaze as the events progress. The camera lingers on her body, documenting its curves, then cuts to Nick peering out of his window to quickly backing away. Within this space, the audience is able to view Adrian's intent.

In *The Crush*'s most telling sequence, Nick goes into the main house on the search for more clues about who Adrian is. As he looks through her things, Adrian arrives home and runs a bath. Nick hides in her closet as Adrian enters her room and takes off her clothes. She becomes aware of his presence and tempts him with her naked body before going to her bath. Nick then quickly exits the house but runs into her father, Cliff (Kurtwood Smith). Lying, Nick tells her father that he was just returning a book Adrian had lent him. Cliff gets Nick to help him take some boxes up to the attic where he reveals the carousel he built for his daughter. Adrian arrives on the scene to see what the two men are up to when Cliff asks Nick what book Adrian lent him. Adrian lies and covers for Nick saying, "*Wuthering Heights*." A later scene shows Adrian on her swing. Shapiro points his camera underneath her, ensuring that as she swings forward wearing a skirt, her underwear is visible. The camera cuts to Nick watching Adrian but from the side, unable to see this under-the-swing shot. The camera's under-angle is not only a hypermale gaze, but also one that is expected when an attractive young girl in a thriller is on a swing. Simply placing the shot from the side would not have been enough. As Nick approaches her, Adrian plays coy content with the power she has amassed through that earlier exchange about the book.

NICK: I don't know where to begin. I guess what I want to say is, I really like you, Adrian.
ADRIAN: I really like you too.
NICK: No, I mean, as a friend. I mean, let's face it, you're 14, I'm 28. That's a big difference.
ADRIAN: Whatever you say.
NICK: Seriously, Adrian. I want you to know you can always count on me and I'll always be your friend, no matter what.
ADRIAN: Like that night up at the lighthouse when we kissed?
NICK: Now that was a mistake, Adrian.

4. First Blood 47

ADRIAN: Was sneaking in to watch me undress a mistake too? Mm?
[Nick walks away]
ADRIAN: Nick! Ever do a virgin?
NICK: What?
ADRIAN: I know you want to.
NICK: Now look! Let's avoid any confusion here. I'm going to make this very simple for you, you're too young for me. There's nothing between us, nothing!

Through this exchange, Nick's own feelings are challenged by Adrian's refusal to accept them and the audience's expectations are challenged because they have been part of Adrian's sexualization through the camera's gaze. In not behaving like an adult and taking responsibility of the situation from the get-go, Nick has put himself and everything he cares about in jeopardy. But, as John Kenneth Muir has pointed out, it is exactly Nick's actions in this situation that have compromised him.

> By this point, Nick has hung by his own petard and failed to follow his girlfriend's sage advice. "You have to be the adult," Amy informs him. "You can't blur the line." That's exactly what Nick has done, blurred the line and though he is hardly guilty of a crime, his behavior encourages Adrian in her delusion.[5]

As Nick continues to reject Adrian, she becomes more aggressive and begins outwardly attacking Nick's belonging and the people he cares about. Nick sets the scene with Amy, excited to show her the new paint job he got for his car with money from his hit article—the one that Adrian ultimately wrote. As Amy and Nick pull off the tarp, Amy's face drops, as it is revealed that someone has scratched the word "cocksucker" on the hood of his car. Clearly, it is Adrian who has done this but no one believes Nick—least of all, Adrian's parents. The irrationality of Adrian's rages—cover-ups for her fear that she is not actually all that special, mature or high-minded—manifests itself in this case as a slur and hate speech. Her controlled outward self is merely a mask for the petty rage that simmers within her. Throughout the film she attempts to prove her virility by telling Nick she got her period so she's not pregnant and commenting on Amy's small breasts. Adrian is keen to prove herself as woman and as an adult.

Her attempts to take charge of Nick's career and his gaze of course go horribly wrong for both of them when in a final act of anger, she accuses Nick of rape and assault, landing him in jail and her further in the care of her concerned parents. This not only feeds into the fears and stigmas surrounding rape and assault charges but also the fear of women's desire and ambition.

Adrian returns to her family home in hopes of being reunited with Nick as he packs up his life, but Adrian cannot handle the rejection any further and her mask slips enough so even her father, who has come to retrieve her, cannot deny who she really is. Nick's punch to Adrian is meant as a crowd-pleasing moment, similar to Alex's (Glenn Close) fate in *Fatal Attraction*. The uncontrollable woman will be controlled either through death (Alex) or institutionalization (Adrian), but as the film hints, walls are not enough to contain Adrian.

The Crush was a modest hit with a $13 million box office gross on a $6 million budget.[6] It did propel Alicia Silverstone to the stardom she would soon know through her true breakout role in *Clueless*. For *The Crush* she won Best Villain and Best Breakthrough Performance at the MTV Movie Awards and director Marty Callner decided Silverstone had the perfect look for the Aerosmith video *Cryin'*, which he was about to direct. From the Aerosmith video, director Amy Heckerling noticed Silverstone and eventually cast her as the lead in *Clueless*. While the lasting cultural cache of *The Crush* has been overshadowed by other films of the same ilk, it does provide a glimpse into the suffocating façade of the life of teenage girls.

From *Love Story* (Arthur Hiller, 1970) to *Say Anything* (Cameron Crowe, 1989) to *Save the Last Dance* (Thomas Carter, 2001) teen films have always had a soft spot for romance. Romance in teen films has become a marker— a space where teen characters can enact their own choices and ultimately set themselves on the path for creating the next generation—as they imply that the relationships at the end of the story are steadfast, unbreakable and certainly impervious to the distressing differences that going to university can breed. These relationships can change the world of the film, often overcoming class and social barriers, which in turn elevates these relationships to the cinematic realm. Love in film, especially youth centric films, is a sign of its time. It was not until the 1950s that culture began to bend to the desires of teens to see themselves on screen when, as writer Jon Savage puts it, "the spread of American-style consumerism, the rise of sociology as an academic discipline and market research as a self-fulfilling prophecy, and sheer demographics turned adolescents into Teenagers."[7] As Thomas Hine describes the power of romance within popular culture:

> While romance had always been part of both movies and popular music, both media became markedly more "romantic" than they had been during the more openly energetic 1920s. A 1935 study of motion pictures found that winning another's love was the chief goal of the main characters in 70 percent of moves, marriage for love in 36 percent and illicit love in 19 percent. And that these three goals accounted for 45 percent of all characters' motivations.[8]

But what happens when love—not just a crush, but true intimacy— begins to spin out of control? James Foley's *Fear* (1996) explores that notion.

The film initially centers on the Walker family and its patriarch, Steve (William Petersen), as all his fatherly nightmares are realized. Steve's daughter Nicole (Reese Witherspoon) has recently decided to live with him over her mother whose own instability was forcing Nicole to be a parent rather than a child. Steve and his new wife Laura (Amy Brenneman), along with her son Toby (Christopher Gray), attempt to form a nuclear family. While Toby seems to thrive in this new familial stability—even calling Steve "Dad"—Nicole begins to rebel. She does so first in small ways like wearing short skirts and makeup and then, after Steve's work interferes with a family outing, by dating David (Mark Wahlberg).

Nicole meets David during a night out with her friend Margo (Alyssa Milano) who is more wild and boy-inclined than Nicole. Nicole and David quickly strike up a romance but Steve begins to suspect something more sinister about David. Steve is first wary of David's casual possessiveness and ordering around of Nicole. Then after an altercation in which David beats up his friend Gary (Todd Caldecott) for hugging Nicole, David inadvertently strikes Nicole, giving her a black eye. Steve and Laura soon discover what has gone on and worry about their daughter's safety. However, Nicole relents and lets David back into her life when he pleads with her to give him another chance. David soon becomes more terrifying as he frames Steve for assault, rapes Margo, and destroys Steve's sports car. *Fear* culminates in Steve breaking into David's squat house, which he shares with his friends, discovering a bizarre shrine to Nicole, and then promptly smashing many of the possessions laying around the house. David and his friends retaliate by breaking into the Walkers house, where the Walkers battle David and his gang. David almost manages to kill Steve, ensuring his possession of Nicole, but Nicole stabs David and Steve pushes him out a window where he falls to his death.

Fear is, as John Kenneth Muir succinctly describes, "a pissing contest: a battle between two swinging dicks to determine which is longer."[9] This seems in keeping with Foley's previous efforts as a director for the film adaptation of David Mamet's *Glengarry Glen Ross* (1992)—an exploration of toxic masculinity. *Fear* is a more interesting case study because of its focus on Nicole's first love and first relationship, which goes horribly wrong, leaving it to the patriarch of the family, Steve, and David to determine her fate. *Fear*'s ultimate message is that women, particularly young women, lack the resolve and the wherewithal to see the true nature of love and romance. In short, *Fear* is a good father's worst nightmare.

Fear owes a debt to another film—Adrian Lyne's *Fatal Attraction* (1987)— which sees an unhinged woman, Alex (Glenn Close), become dangerously obsessed with Dan (Michael Douglas) after a brief affair Dan engages in when his wife and young daughter are out of town. The film's antagonist, Alex, is a successful book editor who is ultimately unfulfilled and psychotic because she does not have a husband or child. While the film works as an entertaining and well-made thriller, it is also a condemnation of the professional woman in the 1980s—a piece of male propaganda, if you will. Women, heed the warning to bear children lest you too become Alex.

In Susan Faludi's book *Backlash: The Undeclared War Against American Women*, she centers much of her discussion around the media of the 1980s and its importance in American popular culture. Faludi writes of *Fatal Attraction* and its pre-production:

> To inspire this modern vision of the Dark Woman [Close's Alex], Lyne says he "researched" the single women of the publishing world. "I was mostly interested in their apartments," he says. He looked at Polaroids of dozens of single women's studios. "They were a little sad, if you want me to be honest. They lacked soul." His "research" didn't involve actually talking to any of the inhabitants of these apartments; he had already made up his mind about unmarried women. "They are sort of overcompensating for not being men," he says. It's sad, you know, because it kind of doesn't work."[10]

If *Fatal Attraction* was a man's fear and suspicion of unmarried women, then *Fear* is a warning to young women to trust their fathers and cut them some slack. Throughout *Fear*, Steve is shown to be deeply concerned and therefore caring towards his daughter while grappling with the demands of his job as an architect, which appears to be the family's only (though very lucrative) source of income. When David and Nicole first meet and become attracted to each other, the film adopts an almost progressive tone which sees Nicole and David engage in standard teen activities such as playing pool, hanging out at Nicole's house and going to a local amusement park. When they meet, Nicole is forthcoming about her virginity and David seems respectful of it. As they begin to fall in love (or obsession in David's case), Nicole begins her sexual awakening. When they ride a rollercoaster at the amusement park, David fingers Nicole until she reaches climax and Foley trains his camera on Nicole's face as she orgasms, highlighting the pleasurable experience. Shortly thereafter, Nicole implies to David that she is ready to have sex and invites him over while Steve and Laura are out of town. David comes over and the two have consensual and intimate sex. Then David attacks Gary, leaving Nicole with a black eye. Laura comforts Nicole while she cries and Steve enters the scene deducing that it was David who gave her the black eye. Steve also notices a condom wrapper on the floor of her bedroom and decides to confront his daughter:

> STEVE: Nicole, I want you to understand that whatever you think I've done to disappoint you is no reason for you to go and screw up your whole life.

4. First Blood

NICOLE: What? Dad, I don't know what you're talking about.
STEVE: That's what worries me.
NICOLE: Look Dad, this may come as a big shock to you but every move I make does not have to do with you. Turns out I'm living my own life.
STEVE: Not yet you're not. As long as you live in my house, you'll follow my rules.

The film firmly aligns Steve's views of the events from this point and insinuates that Nicole's agency is clouded by her feelings towards David. Every time Steve warns or confronts David, he becomes more dangerous. Nicole continues to go back to him, more resolutely each time. Between the two men, it is a confrontation about possession. Steve believes that he can still be the gatekeeper to Nicole and continues to prove that point as Nicole's decisions become increasingly compromised. After the interaction in Nicole's bedroom, Steve is petrified that not only is his daughter in love with a psychopath, but she might also become pregnant, despite her use of contraception. In *Fear*, there is no open or generous discussion about sex—only shame. Having sex invites a world of unwelcome opportunities and Nicole's lack of experience makes her an easy target.

These exchanges between father and daughter serve to illustrate the discrepancy between parent and child in the 1990s. As Mary Pipher wrote in *Reviving Ophelia*:

> Parents are not the primary influence on adolescent girls. Instead girls are swayed heavily by their friends, whose ideas come from mass media. The average teen watches twenty-one hours of TV each week, compared to 5.8 hours spent on homework and 1.8 hours reading. The adolescent community is an electronic community of rock music, television, video and movies. The rites of passage into this community are risky. Adulthood as presented by media, implies drinking, spending money and being sexually active.[11]

Not only can it be assumed that Nicole is well aware of this media, but so is Steve, who can visualize a clear course from Nicole's first ill-fated love to her ultimate destruction.

Within the Walkers' family dynamic, Laura oscillates between a foil and an ally to Nicole, deriding her for being a "slut" when she wears makeup and comforting her when she fights with David. In essence, she is distilling those notions of what a "good woman" is—someone who stands by her man but does not abide the flashy feminine qualities of make-up and short skirts. A woman is natural and a support to the family, not a detriment. Nicole's own relationship with her mother is only mentioned when she first meets David.

NICOLE: I stayed with my real mom in LA when my dad moved up here. I was nine years old. It was just the two of us all alone in this big house. She was so sad most of the time, I kind of felt like I was the one taking care of her.

DAVID: It must've been tough.
NICOLE: Yeah.

As Pipher writes of this dichotomy of relationships to fathers and mothers:

> Western civilization has a double standard about parenting. Relationships with fathers are portrayed as productive and growth-oriented, while relationships with mothers are depicted as regressive and dependent. Fathers are praised for their involvement with children. Mothers, on the other hand, are criticized unless their involvement is precisely the right amount.... Daughters are as confused as mothers by our culture's expectations. Girls are encouraged to separate from their mothers and to devalue their relationship with them. They are expected to respect their mothers but not to be like them. In our culture, loving one's mother is linked with dependency, passivity and regression, while rejecting one's mother implies individuation, activity and independence. Distancing from one's mother is viewed as a necessary step toward adult development.[12]

The brief picture Nicole paints of her relationship with her mother is that of a sad woman who becomes increasingly and stiflingly dependent on her daughter, a fear no doubt passed on to Nicole. It would make sense for Nicole to leave the situation and look for a partner who is strong and caring—two things David purports to be. Through her relationship with her parents from a very early age, Nicole has learned that there is no joy to be had being alone— that even her father is fallible, which paints him as a contaminated source when it comes to giving relationship advice. If her father could upend her life through divorce, surely David can be forgiven for his trespasses.

The two women in Nicole's life also seek to shelter her from the potential danger of David by normalizing his actions. When Nicole comes home with the black eye, Laura sees it and Nicole tells her she got it in gym class. Immediately, Laura sees a bonding opportunity with Nicole and teaches her how to cover up a black eye with makeup. While Laura does not intentionally mean to normalize domestic abuse, she does want to cover up Nicole's black eye, knowing what it could imply, and does not question her further about the "gym class" incident until later when Nicole reveals what actually happened.

Margo, played by Alyssa Milano, who grew up acting on *Who's the Boss?*, may be the film's most tragic character. Milano was looking to break away from her clean-cut tomboy image and an edgy role in a film was a great way to do that (see also Elizabeth Berkley's transition from *Saved by the Bell* to *Showgirls*). Margo is sexually charged, free-spirited and the inspiration for Nicole's flirtation with short skirts and makeup. She is the one who gets Nicole out of the house, wherein she meets David. After the black eye incident, Margo says to Nicole, "[Hitting you] is their asshole way of saying they love you."

Margo's own life is punctuated by an absent mother who leaves her daughter to spend time with men who give her money and gifts, which seemingly allows her to support herself and Margo. Early in the film, Margo and Nicole look at an adult magazine and Margo says in reference to a nude photo of a woman, "That's power." Margo's life has revolved around the way men view her body as a sex object, and what she thinks she can get out of them through that gaze. This culminates in an incident at David's flop house where he rapes Margo, which Nicole sees part of and blames them both for. In the shared blame between David and Margo, it is clear that the film sides with the sexist notion that Margo's sexual availability means she was "asking for it." As author Sadie Doyle writes of this archetype in her book *Trainwreck: The Women We Love to Hate, Fear, and Mock, and Why*:

> There is an undeniable cruelty in our need for stories about wounded women. We do sometimes seek them out for reasons of pure schadenfreude, or internalized misogyny. We can use them as projection screens for our own fears and failings, or look to them to confirm that we're doing our own gender correctly.... We can look to the trainwrecks in order to tell ourselves, *well, at least I'm not that girl*.[13]

The terrifyingly clear apathy with which the film treats Margo's rape is made all the more absolute when Nicole eschews Margo from her life. After the assault, Margo appears in baggy clothes, looking haggard and tired and is constantly on the verge of tears. She is the filmic martyr for a young woman exploring her sexuality and occasionally enjoying that sexuality. When Nicole tells Margo to stay away from her, inferring David's rape of Margo was somehow Margo's fault and was more about cheating than assault, Margo yells back at her, "You're my only friend!" *Fear* makes it painfully obvious that Margo is not the girl to be.

The film's treatment of Margo's and even Nicole's own early sexual exploration always comes at a price. There are no true moments of intimacy, pleasure or enjoyment because they are all clouded by David's motives, which none of the women realize until it is too late. This way of thinking is in line with much of the media's portrayal of female sexuality, particularly in the 1990s. As Pipher writes:

> Girls face two major sexual issues in America in the 1990s: One is an old issue of coming to terms with their own sexuality, defining a sexual self, making sexual choices and learning to enjoy sex. The other issue concerns the dangers girls face of being sexually assaulted. By late adolescence, most girls today either have been traumatized or know girls who have. They are fearful of males before even as they are trying to develop intimate relationships with them. Of course, these two issues are connected at some level and make the development of healthy female sexuality extraordinarily complicated in the 1990s.[14]

Fear is a call to arms for women to continue to be fearful of sex and intimacy. That young impetuousness, even when it involves pleasure and contraception, is always something to be weary of. The film implies that women are always in servitude to a patriarch but a woman must choose between a "good" and a "bad" one. There is no alternative, only safety and the dark unknown. *Fear* quickly veers from Nicole's journey as a young woman to a father's journey to keep his almost-adult daughter safe from a man who is dangerous. While on the surface that may be fine fare for a thriller, the dynamic becomes increasingly twisted as the fights between the two men go beyond control of Nicole to control of property, such as cars and homes, thereby conflating women and property.

When Steve enters David's home and finds a shrine to Nicole, he also finds a bracelet he gave her which originally inscribed with "Daddy's Girl" now reads "David's Girl," once again confirming that no matter what happens, Nicole is supposed to belong to someone; it just happens that Steve's relationship is the more socially acceptable one. While *Fear* may assume father knows best, the eerie regressive quality of the film, which supposedly ends on a high note of "the family that kills together stays together," seeks to imply that this new world order of sexuality and empowering women to make their own decisions is ultimately a doomed one.

5

Generation Hex
The Craft (1996)

For as long as there have been horror movies, there have been witches in them, though the place of witches as a figure within them has mutated, evolved, and, for some periods, disappeared. The witch is an enigmatic figure in history, literature and film with none of the apparent consistency of the vampire or zombie. The figure of the witch reflects and refracts the concerns of the time in regards to women and women's place in the world. Benjamin Christensen's 1922 silent documentary/horror film *Häxan* (1922) explores and dramatizes the persecution of witches but is not above highlighting the titillating elements that link sexuality and Satanism. Disney's *Snow White and the Seven Dwarfs* (David Hand, 1937) and the Technicolor world of *The Wizard of Oz* (Victor Fleming, 1939) helped cement the witch as an old crone out to harm young women and their beauty. In the comedy *I Married a Witch* (Rene Clair, 1942) the beautiful Veronica Lake plays a witch who returns from the dead to seek vengeance on those who wronged her. *Rosemary's Baby* (Roman Polanski, 1968) sees a coven of witches as the enfeebled neighbors next door who can bestow immense amount of wealth and success upon those who do their bidding. Dario Argento's 1977 cult classic *Suspiria* again sparks concern about how a coven of witches uses their power to run a German dance academy. The late 1980s saw *The Witches of Eastwick* (George Miller, 1987) portray witches as both strong and independent yet continually drawn to the devil himself. Nicolas Roeg's *The Witches* (1990), adapted from Ronald Dahl's book of the same name, presents witches as purely malevolent, plotting to rid all of England, and eventually the world, of children.

The suspicion of witches is as old as the suspicion of women so it should come as no surprise that with the rise of Third Wave feminism and Girl Power that the witch as a cinematic figure would be reopened. The late 1990s saw television shows such as *Buffy the Vampire Slayer*, *Sabrina, The Teenage Witch* and *Charmed* all tackle young women who can gain and lose power through the apparent slippery slope of witchcraft and magic. At the end of the 1990s the *Harry Potter* books would present a sedate view of growing up through metaphors of spells and magic making. Andrew Flemmings' *The Craft* (1996) would presuppose these more mainstream depictions of witchcraft, witches and magic and present an, albeit flawed and problematic, representation of what it was to be a young woman in the mid-1990s—a portrayal that, if anything, illuminates that the same fears and anger towards women which caused the widespread witch hunts in Europe is still present in the modern era.

The witch hunts and "trials" that spread through Europe through the fifteenth and eighteenth centuries were a broad-based attack against "undesirables"—women and anyone else thought to step outside of Christianity's dictated moral code. Following the Medieval era, the European demeanor was pessimistic at best, having lost an approximate 20,000,000 lives[1] to the Black Plague. Faith in the church was waning and, in the church's mind, needed to be restored. This fear and panic would present itself in a way that would harm society's most vulnerable. The church and its believers needed to prove that the devil existed. As historian Walter Stephen put it, "Without proof of a devil, there can be no proof of God."[2]

One of the easiest ways evoke the importance of the church was to invoke the devil as an agent of sex and transgression who would directly harm, isolate and seduce women, enticing them to become witches. At this time, the church looked to a specific text, *Malleus Maleficarum* or "Hammer of the Witches" (1487), as a manual to hunt, persecute and question any supposed witch. As author Jack Holland writes of the handbook in his book *A Brief History of Misogyny*:

> It is not that *Malleus Maleficarum*, or "Hammer of the Witches" (1487), has anything original to say about misogyny—it has not; it merely repeats all the abuse heaped on women in the Bible and the Classical authors. But what it does do for the first time is explicitly link the supposed weaknesses of women's nature to their propensity to fall for the Devil, and thus become witches. Its influence was hugely augmented by a new invention—the printing press. There is more than a little irony in the fact that the invention that would revolutionize people's access to information should be so instrumental in spreading one of the most lethal forms of ignorance, fear and prejudice to ever manifest itself.[3]

But why were women and certain groups targeted either overtly or subconsciously? The answer, as is almost always the case, has to do with power and those who are unwilling to let go of it. As Leo Braudy writes of witchcraft in his book *Haunted*:

> [One] of the most intriguing aspects of witchcraft, astrology, clairvoyance, and other forms of initiating contact with the invisible world is the way each of these types of unofficial knowledge potentially contradicts the imperatives of institutional religion,

class structure, and genealogy authority.... [It] ruptures their system of social hierarchy and perhaps becomes a tactic admission that whatever inherited authority they have is fragile at best.[4]

The Craft tackles the ways witchcraft was perceived to threaten the autonomy of the clerical belief system, which dominated the times, through the pseudo-empowerment of four young women. The film begins with Sarah (Robin Tunney) moving to California with her father and stepmother. She transfers to a Catholic high school where she quickly falls in with Chris Hooker (Skeet Ulrich). He seems charming, initially, but begins spreading rumors about Sarah after she refuses to have sex with him on their first date. She then becomes friends with a group of outsiders who are all facing their own challenges: Nancy (Fairuza Balk), a girl from the wrong side of the tracks who flaunts it; Bonnie (Neve Campbell), whose body is covered in scars, marking her as unattractive and undesirable; and Rochelle (Rachel True), a black student who is bullied relentlessly because of her race by one of the popular girls, Laura (Christine Taylor).

While each of the girls faces their own problems, they wind up becoming fast friends when they realize Sarah is a natural witch (a skill she inherited from her mother, who died while giving birth to Sarah). Sarah helps the other three realize their potential as a coven by calling the corners (North, South, East, West) and invoking their all-powerful deity Manon. The girls soon become more powerful and seek retribution against their ill fates. Sarah casts a love spell on Chris, Nancy causes her abusive stepfather to have a heart-attack and die, triggering a massive life-insurance policy for her and her mother, Rochelle causes Laura's blonde hair to fall out in clumps, and Bonnie's scars disappear with help from Sarah. While these spells aid the girls in their stigmas and traumas, they rarely work to address the real issues.

Early in the film, the girls realize their initial power as Sarah casts "glamours" on herself, changing her eye and hair colors. While the more significant spells they cast (i.e. the love spell and the hair spell against Laura) change their circumstances, they come at a price. As Lirio (Assumpta Serna), the owner of the local Wicca shop, warns them, "Whatever you cast out will come back to you times three," echoing the Christian sentiment of, do unto others as you would have them do unto you. In this case, Chris' love becomes obsessive and scary, Nancy becomes mad with power and Bonnie and Rochelle become Nancy's minions.

Sarah realizes that the spells have gone too far after Chris attempts to sexually assault her. Nancy gets revenge by killing Chris at a party. Sarah wants out of the coven but the other three won't let her leave. Sarah seeks to use her natural powers to bind Nancy, only to have the three of them attack her in her home. Sarah then invokes the deity Manon for herself, scares Bonnie and Rochelle into running away and drives Nancy insane. The film ends with Bonnie and Rochelle visiting Sarah in an attempt to make amends. When Sarah rebuffs them, Bonnie and Rochelle laugh about Sarah not having powers anyway, to which Sarah causes a large tree branch to fall, almost hitting them. She leaves them with the warning, "Careful, you don't want to end up like Nancy." The film ends with Nancy strapped to a gurney in a hospital claiming she can fly as the screen fades to black.

In *The Craft* magic, spells and power are all woven together. Once Chris corrupts Sarah's potential social capital, she joins the outsiders who also have something to gain by obtaining power in an environment that prevents them from naturally doing so. For Sarah, Rochelle, Nancy and Bonnie, being a good student, athlete or friend is not enough to prevent them from the torture and accusations of high school; they must resort to otherworldly powers to tip the scale in their favor. As *The AV Club* wrote on the film's twentieth anniversary:

> In *The Craft*, the witches' collective powers are a way to silence those who demean and subjugate them—whether it's the men who threaten their safety, peers who judge them, or beauty ideals that restrict them… The unity of the women is the source of their power and when that disappears, their coven dissolves. There's a reason they practice their spells in the sanctified space of the sleepover: It's a place where young girls can safely forge new identities away from those who trivialize them.[5]

The element that binds the young women together outside of their magic is their similarities as undesirables in the society of high school. It is important to note the mise-en-scène of the film, which, particularly at the beginning of the film, highlights the setting of the Catholic St. Bernard's High School— a contemporary witch's unsafe space. As Sarah enters the school for the first time, eager to get away from her new home, she wears her street clothes, marking her as new to the predatory gaze of Chris. She passes under a statue of Jesus on the cross—a shot that informs not only the school as a relic of the past, but the students who subscribe to its social rules as dusty and passé as those rules.

Beyond just the high school experience, which can be traumatic in and of itself, *The Craft*'s use of a Catholic school serves to highlight the disparity between the coven and the other students, not simply through their differing ideologies but also through their social statuses. As Murry Milner writes in his book *Freaks, Geeks and Cool Kids: American Teenagers, Schools and the Culture of Consumption*:

> Religiously-oriented schools were founded to impart to their students a particular religious perspective and commitment to the values and beliefs associated with that world-

view. Parents sometimes send their children to these schools because they share the world-view of the school and they want their children to also. Just as often they send their children to these schools in the hope that they can help protect them from being corrupted by what they see as some of the worst aspects of contemporary culture: drugs, alcohol, sexual promiscuity, incivility, violence, secularism, and low academic standards.[6]

While this may be a common belief among parents, *The Craft* works to point out that these elements do exist in a Catholic high-school setting and, if anything, are more ingrained in its culture. Chris' sexual frustration first exhibits itself in the rumors he spreads about Sarah as a "lousy lay." These frustrations are further drawn out as Sarah's love spell works on him. At first he is a lovelorn suitor desperate for any of Sarah's attention; soon, though, he transforms into someone whose love becomes obsessive to the point of attempted rape. In perhaps one of the most telling moments in the film, Sarah does not go to her family or the police after the assault, but instead goes to her coven of Bonnie, Nancy and Rochelle. Sarah feels, and is, somewhat responsible for Chris' obsession with her, but her inability or unwillingness to seek help through channels of authority further serves to clarify the stigma of fear and unfairness with which a larger system handles the concerns of young women. These scenes play out in the shadow of the Anita Hill and Clarence Thomas hearings, which saw a woman testify to her superior's inappropriateness only to be dismissed and Thomas awarded a seat on the Supreme Court. The witches of *The Craft* must revert to vigilantism (which in turn goes awry) if Sarah is to be avenged. As the film's producer Douglas Wick said at the time of the film's release:

> [Female empowerment] is particularly important in high school where guys take up most of the space and the girls are squished into whatever corners are leftover. I thought it might be interesting to tell a story using witchcraft as an analogy for the boundless yet untapped inner resources available to teenage girls.... We wanted the journey into witchcraft to feel true emotionally, as the girls travel from total impotence to intoxicating power.[7]

The film's firmest grasp of intoxicating female empowerment comes from Nancy, the film's charismatic anti-hero. The film focuses on Nancy outside of the coven, emphasizing her sudden ascendency from lower class, "white trash" to the trappings of the nouveau-riche upper class after her stepfather's death. Nancy seems to gain the most from the sudden influx because she is the hungriest for it. When the group sits together and asks for varying things (Sarah asks for Chris to love her, Rochelle asks for tolerance toward her racist classmates), Nancy asks for all the power of Manon. The power comes to her through abilities to change traffic lights, fly, create elaborate illusions and essentially become the cinematic witch that audiences have feared for decades. As actress Fairuza Balk says of her character, Nancy:

> She's an addictive person and has gone through just about every kind of chemical abuse there is. For her, witchcraft is just another form of addiction, another way of dealing with her deep emotional scars. It becomes her obsession.[8]

Nancy's character is a warning about the consumption of power and how it can infect anyone. Nancy's power, and addiction to said power, quickly spreads to Bonnie and Rochelle, who are happy to subscribe to her way of thinking. It is only Sarah who can suspend her own desires to see how the group's antics are spiraling out of control. No longer the most powerful in the group, Sarah has the ability to recognize how power comes and goes.

Ultimately *The Craft* is about these witches' aspirations to have power over things they have no control over, only to find that changing those elements forces them to subscribe to a hive-mind way of thinking, essentially putting them in line with those antagonists who act out of fear of losing their social power and privilege. The women of *The Craft* must learn that, as Lirio says, true power comes from within. That power, as the film insinuates, is the ability to walk away from class/social/gender/racial power structures that confine and control the women. Sarah is able to walk away with knowledge and power from within and not subscribe to any values except her own, while the others will always live in the shadow of others' values. Misogyny, sexual violence and racial prejudice will still exist in the world. As Wick goes on to say about the message of the film, "The most unexplored territories in a civilized world are the ones inside us. The supernatural genre, with wolf or witch, can be a powerful expression of that inner life."[9] Sarah is allowed the privilege to embody this sentiment, which is on one hand satisfying enough to justify the film's conclusion, but on another, still fails to address the concerns and traumas that remain part of the world.

This concern is most explicit in the figure of Rochelle. Rochelle's narrative throughout the film is her struggle with her racist bully Laura. Laura hates Rochelle because she is a "negroid," and Rochelle's presence as a student in the school and a member of the diving team, which they both belong to, seems to be an affront to Laura. Writer Dianca Potts prefaces an interview with Rachel True with:

> When I was the only black girl in my private suburban religious school, I connected with Rachel's iconic role as Rochelle because, like me, she was bullied by racist classmates and teased for having "nappy hair." In an era where onscreen depictions of black adolescence were few and far between, her character's story validated my own narrative and made me feel less alone.[10]

Potts' point touches on one of the very real problems in film in general—a lack of diversity, both racially and narratively. Rochelle's story is the only one in this book to explicitly and directly address the problems of racism and intolerance—issues that exist in the world outside of film. It is also a narrative that writer Ashlee Blackwell notes in her piece *20 Years of the Craft: Why We Needed More of Rochelle*:

> Unfortunately, Rochelle's score to settle ... was played as superficial comeuppance for Laura's racial intolerance. A spell was cast on her to lose what we are to assume was one of Laura's most cherished assets and core of self-worth; her hair. But it is interesting how her straight, blonde locks were a symbol in itself of an idealized status of social capital, supposed racial superiority and prosperity.[11]

Rochelle's narrative arc in *The Craft* is important on the two levels identified by Potts and Blackwell. While the film discusses racism and the insidiousness of the bullying associated with it, it feels too easily dismissed. At the end of the film, Sarah can walk away from the power and the horrors that she has just experienced, but other characters cannot. Her ability to walk away highlights her privilege while also undermining the very real issues that a character like Rochelle faces.

The Craft did decently at the box office. While it did not reach the heights of *Clueless* or *Scream*, it did earn $55 million worldwide on a $15 million budget.[12] The critical reception was lukewarm at best with *The Toronto Star* critic Carole Corbeil writing, "The need for fantasy as a way of compensating for general feelings of powerlessness is probably the same for both sexes, but while boys of all ages have always had fantasy films at their disposal, girls have had to make do with leaner and stranger fare,"[13] and *Variety* writing, "The story [of *The Craft*] becomes very Christian and very conventional, with the pretty, middle-class girl winning out over the angry, out-of-control, poor girl. This fails to be exhilarating because the enemy is not properly located. The last image is so disturbing and so depressing that it indicts the whole movie."[14]

In early 2016, there were rumblings of a remake of *The Craft*. Wick stated later that year that the film would not be a remake but be more in line with a sequel.[15] While *The Craft* is an imperfect movie, it capitalized on a time and place that leaned towards female narratives that could be embraced by the outsider Goth culture that was becoming mainstream. *The Craft* reached for greatness and for some women achieved it. However, the cracks beneath the mainstream feminism ideology of the film cannot be hidden. Though it attempts to address the problems inherent for young women—similar prejudices faced by women during the witch-hunts—the film falls prey to its own need for classical narrative closure, ignoring the realities that many women cannot simply walk away from. *The Craft* brings up many issues and narratives that are often only addressed privately, but it cannot escape its need to find heroes and villains within a main narrative, that one must fall for another to rise. The true magic of *The Craft* is its forward narrative steps, made through young women working together to find and use power.

6

Bowling for Woodsboro
Scream (1996), Scream 2 (1997) and Scream 3 (2000)

Wes Craven and Kevin Williamson's *Scream* is the epicenter of the teen horror movie movement in the 1990s. *Scream*'s runaway, unexpected success marked turning points in the careers of many and, for a brief while, allowed a discourse about horror films to take up significant space within popular culture. *Scream* is an important film, not just because of its financial success—though that does elevate above much of the fare talked about in the rest of this book—but also because of its adherence to, attention to and ultimate rejection of elements of the slasher film formula, allowing the slasher film to revive in popularity for a new audience. *Scream* is a film that both acknowledges and challenges what horror films are, and in particular what slasher films were. While the narrative of *Scream* is a fascinating intersection of popular culture, horror films and mainstream third wave feminism, its story begins with two brothers.

After struggling on the outskirts of the film industry for years, Miramax Films was basking in the revelation of the mainstream indie film after finding massive success distributing and marketing films like Quentin Tarantino's *Reservoir Dogs* (1992) and *Pulp Fiction* (1994) alongside more oddball fare like Kevin Smith's *Clerks* (1994). The company was founded in 1979 by brothers Harvey and Bob Weinstein with the name Miramax coming from their parents' first names Max and Miriam. Miramax was always a decidedly family affair with the brothers unable to draw little differentiation between their business and their personal lives. Everything that Miramax touched was going to be a hit at any cost because to them, their business was their lives. By the mid–1990s, Harvey, who oversaw the Miramax brand, was generating a reputation in Hollywood as a bully. He would bully directors on sets, in their homes, and at events and harass voting members of the Academy Awards to secure nominations and wins for his films. The problem was, Harvey's tactics seemed to work—for a while anyway. In the 1990s Miramax was synonymous with a brand of indie films that were guaranteed to tug at the heartstrings of mainstream America while being faux-highbrow enough to appeal to film fans. Harvey recognized that the Oscars represented legitimacy in an unstable industry—legitimacy he craved since getting into the film world. Miramax was a formidable presence at Oscar ceremonies throughout the decade with films like *The Crying Game* (Neil Jordan, 1992), *The Piano* (Jane Campion, 1993), *Sling Blade* (Billy Bob Thornton, 1996), *Good Will Hunting* (Gus Van Sant, 1997), *Life Is Beautiful* (Roberto Benigni, 1997) and *Shakespeare in Love* (John Madden, 1998). While Harvey was the toast of the town (at his own request), his brother Bob was toiling with the other Miramax property, Dimension Films.

Before 1996 Dimension Films was known for releasing schlocky, straight-to-video genre fare such as *Hellraiser III: Hell on Earth* (Anthony Hickox, 1992), *Children of the Corn III: Urban Harvest* (James D.R. Hickox, 1995) and *Halloween: The Curse of Michael Myers* (Joe Chappelle, 1995). Though Dimension did generate the occasional legitimate interest from genre fans with films like *The Crow* (Alex Proyas, 1994), it was primarily thought of as a dumping ground, but that was all about to change. As author Alisa Perren notes in her book *Indie Inc.*:

> The general neglecting discussing Dimension and other commercially minded genre divisions can be attributed in part to their status as low culture. Their content is often visceral, including a great deal of sex, violence, highly stylized action, explicit language, and, crude humor. Like their distant antecedent the exploitation film, genre films often have been viewed as artistically bankrupt, produced mainly in the interest of making a quick buck.[1]

Hollywood agent Cary Wood who was decidedly not a horror fan brought Kevin Williamson's screenplay originally titled *Scary Movie* to Bob saying, "Don't worry, it's not horror, it's really funny. It makes fun of the genre.... You gotta buy it." Which Bob did for the price tag of $500,000.[2] Prior to Bob obtaining the script, Williamson was just another struggling screenwriter in Hollywood, shopping around scripts that were generating interest but no actual deals. The inspiration for *Scary Movie* struck immediately as Williamson recalls:

> I got the idea from watching a Barbara Walters special on the Gainesville murders. I was broke, house-sitting for a friend to pay him back for the money he'd lent me for groceries, and I was scaring the hell out of myself. I thought I heard a noise. I walked the house with a butcher knife and a phone, and called my friend while I searched the place. We got into this huge discussion, testing each other on horror movies. And that's how *Scream* was born.[3]

Woods then quickly got the script into the hands of Drew Barrymore who was planning her own Hollywood comeback after several years of raising hell in the Hollywood party scene and wanted to be taken seriously as an actress. With Barrymore interested in playing the lead, they were able to secure horror legend Wes Craven as a director. Craven was averaging about a hit a decade with horror classics like *The Last House on the Left* (1972) and *A Nightmare on Elm Street* (1984) with a smattering of cult classics like *Swamp Thing* (1982), *The Serpent and the Rainbow* (1988) and *The People Under the Stairs* (1991) in between. Though he initially passed on the film twice, he relented and signed on, lured by the star power of Barrymore and the challenge to parody horror films while still making one.[4] As Craven himself recalls of this process:

> I had heard about it before and was interested, but I had gone through this struggle of trying to separate myself from the horror genre and here was something with a strong, scary opening sequence. I thought, this is the kind of sequence that you can do and never be forgiven for. The critics will hate it and the audiences will be repulsed... As it turned out, these were all unfounded fears. When I heard Drew Barrymore was attached, it changed. I had meetings with Kevin Williamson and we found the script was generating its own heat and we were attracting the kind of cast I'd never worked with before. I had a great buzz on it. ... *Scream* confirmed my belief that horror films are great character pieces. They get deep under the skin of human psychology.[5]

Though Dimension Films invested only $15 million in what Bob retitled in pre-production as *Scream*, Bob saw the film not only as a way to make a mark in the industry but also as a way to step out of his brother's shadow.[6] While *Scream* got underway with its production, Barrymore opted to play the opening scene victim and the *Scream* team cast rising television star Neve Campbell of Fox's *Party of Five* as the film's Final Girl, Sidney Prescott. The rest of the cast filled up with more up-and-comers, including Courteney Cox, a veteran actress who was about to hit her stride with the soon to be omnipresent television series *Friends*. While *Scream*'s casting deck was filling favorably, Bob wanted assurance that the film would be everything it needed to be, though he himself seemed unsure of what the actual elements of success were. Bob hired noted producer B.J. Rack to watch the production alongside producer Cathy Konrad. Rack's role, as Bob saw it, was to insure the production did not go over budget and could save money where necessary.[7]

The production practically ground to a halt when Craven was nearly fired after Bob felt the daily rushes were not up to par. The production of *Scream* had to shut down while Craven and his team cut together the rushes to appease Bob. Finally happy that his supposed gamble was paying off, Bob quietly acquiesced and stopped making noise until the run up to the release.

Meanwhile Craven was battling back and forth with the Motion Picture Association of America (MPAA) editing the completed film to keep it from receiving the devastating NC-17 rating, a rating that ensured a limited release and would saddle the film as a persona non grata in Hollywood. As Craven recalled at the time:

> I was ecstatic [with the film]. It came out just terrifically. We got an incredible response from early press, media and test audiences, so I was very happy with it. We had to cut some stuff, but not that much. One thing the MPAA said was, "You cannot have any movement [of the innards]." We had a shot were the guts fall out, but had to just use the part were they're already out. We had to shorten the shots of people hanging. They objected to moments throughout the film. The worst part was the ending, which is very intense. The MPAA flatly announced, "You're miles from it. You'll probably never get an R rating." Well, we did, but it took endless screaming and crying and writing letters and paring it back somewhat. None of the test viewers said it was too gory, but the MPAA was just hysterical about it."[8]

Bob on the other hand was already wrestling with a controversial release date, December 18, 1996, in the middle of the Christmas season, which is usually reserved for Oscar hopefuls. As Peter Biskin writes of the decision in his book *Down and Dirty Pictures*:

> Bob had conceived the idea to open *Scream* Christmas week. "The [conventional wisdom] was, OK, Christmas—Christmas fare: the prestige pictures, the family-oriented movies, the softer, gentler kinds of things," [Bob] explains. Christmas is the "every Miramax quote unquote prestige movie comes out. My attitude was, There's nothing for teenagers to see. Great, I'm going against *The Piano*." Adds [Cathy] Konrad, "Bob was adamant about it, and he had done his tracking. That guy knew everything about every movie. He had looked at the competition and analyzed those numbers—his office was like the New York Stock Exchange. Counter programming, niche programming—no one was thinking that way at Christmas."[9]

Konrad would also elaborate on big brother Harvey's feelings towards Bob and Dimension saying, "Harvey didn't pay a lot of attention to *Scream*, honestly didn't believe in it. He would always say, 'I don't really know what Bob's doing over there. He plays in his sandbox, I have mine.'"[10] Bob got his way and *Scream* opened in time for the Christmas season. It opened with a box office of just over $6 million coming in second to *Beavis and Butt-Head Do America* (1996).[11] While a respectable box office it was certainly nothing to write home about initially. The reviews for the film were positive but measured, with Bernard Weinraub writing for the *New York Times*:

> In a sense, *Scream* reinvents the horror film, turning classic elements of the genre upside down. It is a chilling film as well as a spoof, a movie about a serial killer who uses his love of scary movies to outwit the police and terrorize a picturesque California town. On another level, the odd and complex story immerses itself almost totally in

the bleak universe of teenagers whose lives revolve around school, sexual anxieties, horror movies and tabloid TV.[12]

Owen Gleiberman at *Entertainment Weekly* wrote of the film:

> Scream revives the slasher films of the Reagan era in all their gruesomely, ritualized glory. There's one crucial difference though: The teenagers in *Scream* have been raised on endless VCR replays of those very same movies. And so the sudden appearance of a mad killer becomes a case of life imitating schlock.... Now they have to outsmart their own video-zapped fantasies.[13]

Soon word of mouth about the film began to spread and *Scream* maintained a position in the top 10 of the box office through the Spring of 1997 eventually gaining a world-wide total box office of $173 million.

As the critics above have accurately identified, *Scream* is about teenagers trying to survive in the face of a masked killer who seems to be targeting a small group of friends within the Woodsboro, California, community. The events begin with the elaborate murder of Casey Becker (Drew Barrymore) and her boyfriend Steve by a masked killer who would eventually be dubbed Ghostface in popular culture. The news spreads throughout the high school the next day and news vans show up with the single-minded Gale Weathers (Courteney Cox), a reporter for the trashy tabloid news show *Top Story*, in tow. The events feel all too familiar to Sidney Prescott (Neve Campbell) whose mother was raped and murdered almost exactly a year prior. Sidney's friend Tatum (Rose McGowan) worries about her and invites her to stay at her house, as Sidney's father is out of town on business and is seemingly unreachable. Sidney's boyfriend Billy (Skeet Ulrich) tries to be empathetic while competing with his own insatiable libido. More murders follow and the killer targets Sidney who continually fights back and escapes. The film culminates in an elaborate party at Stu's (Matthew Lillard) house where Tatum's brother and deputy sheriff of the town, Dewey (David Arquette), arrives with Gale Weathers. More characters are picked off or injured as Sidney realizes it is not a killer but *killers* in the form of Billy and Stu. The duo reveal they staged everything so Sidney will be murdered on the anniversary of her mother's death, which they perpetrated, and they plan to frame her father, who they have kidnapped. Billy and Stu take turns stabbing each other so it appears they are wounded but with the intention of miraculously surviving to plan a sequel. While the boys are distracted by their own self-inflicted wounds, Sidney grabs the Ghostface costume, and, using their preferred method of taunting victims, calls them over the phone with an altered voice and trivia questions. They attack Sidney and she fights them off, killing them both. Sidney and the remaining survivors, Randy (Jamie Kennedy), Gale and Dewey, live to see another day.

As author Stephen Neale writes in his book *Genre and Hollywood*:

> [Film genres] do not solely consist of films. They consist also of specific systems of expectation and hypothesis which spectators bring with them to the cinema and which interact with films themselves during the course of the viewing process.... They offer a way of working out the significance of what is happening on the screen: a way of working out why in particularly actions are taking place, why the characters are dressed the way they are, why they look speak and behave the way they do and so on.... Intertextuality can ensure that texts and textual meaning will stick to other texts, like a rumor, rewriting finished stories and told histories, placing them under a new light. If our text world is populated by intertextual ghosts, this is a system that allows for texts to haunt, target, and beleaguer others, and hence for counter-discursive struggles for both meaning and textual power.[14]

Scream's power comes from its ability to at once satirize the horror film, specifically the slasher film, as well as function as one. The irony is most evident in *Scream*'s mention of other horror films—most notably John Carpenter's *Halloween* (1978), which becomes a method for movie nerd Randy to relay the supposed "rules of a horror film" right before the harrowing climax of the film. Randy says,

> There are certain RULES that one must abide by in order to successfully survive a horror movie. For instance, number one: you can never have sex. [crowd boos] BIG NO NO! BIG NO NO! Sex equals death, okay? Number two: you can never drink or do drugs. The sin factor! It's a sin. It's an extension of number one. And number three: never, ever, ever under any circumstances say, "I'll be right back." Because you won't be back.

In 1992 Carol Clover's treatise on the horror film—particularly the slasher—*Men, Women and Chainsaws: Gender in the Modern Horror Film* was published. Within the book, Clover reiterates many of the rules that Randy details. She identifies the heroine of the these films as the Final Girl, a character who through virtue of her supposed chastity and purity is able to overcome whatever monsters are presented to her.[15] The monsters or killers are also defined by Clover as "emphatic misfits and outsiders"[16] The film needs to consist of several elements, such as a weapon used by the killer which necessitates close proximately for which to be effective and which represents a phallic symbol (i.e., a knife or machete)[17]; a set of pre-ordained youthful victims who make unwholesome choices such as engaging in sex, drugs or both[18]; the Terrible Place, a location which holds a history for the victims; and the Final Girl, who becomes a key to the killer(s)'s motivations.[19]

Scream's narrative encompasses all of these elements but plays with their importance. The victims (Casey, Tatum, Principal Himbry, notably) are not Reagan Era stereotypes of teens who play into conservative fears of popular culture; they are shown to be funny, smart, caring and resourceful. Casey is bright and relatable, Tatum is the best friend who is both honest and sensitive to Sidney, and Principal Himbry (Henry Winkler) is an intense but impassioned educator. They do not fit the slasher trope of teens who are too busy to see the terror coming; Tatum and Casey both spend a good deal of time fighting back and nearly getting away during their deaths scenes, which cause their deaths to be felt on a deeper level than in previous iterations.

But *Scream* is Sidney's movie and is ultimately about the struggle of a young woman to control her own narrative in the face of misogynist forces. *Scream* details Sidney's struggles in relation to films. Early in the film when Billy appears at Sidney's window hoping for an intimate make-out session and maybe more, Sidney stops him and Billy complains that their relationship is "edited for television." Sidney constantly faces pressure from those around her, Billy in particular, to lead a normal life—something she wants for herself as well. What holds her back is the grief of her mother's death and the knowledge that she was unfaithful to Sidney's father, having several affairs with men in Woodsboro. When Gale arrives on the scene shortly after Casey's death, it becomes clear that Sidney and Gale have their own fraught history, as Gale does not believe Sidney when she names Cotton Weary (Liev Schreiber) as her mother's killer. Sidney's mother's history is known throughout the town as evidenced in a conversation between two classmates that Sidney overhears:

> CHEERLEADER: She was never attacked. I think she made it all up.
> GIRL: Why would she lie about it?
> CHEERLEADER: For attention. The girl has some serious issues. What if she did it? What if Sidney killed Casey and Steve?
> GIRL: Why would she do that?
> CHEERLEADER: Maybe she had the hots for Steve and killed them both in a jealous rage.
> GIRL: What would Sidney want with Steve? She's got her own bubble-butt boyfriend, Billy.
> CHEERLEADER: Maybe she's a slut, just like her mother.

Once the Ghostface killings commence, Sidney must face not only her own uncertain memories of the night her mother was killed but also her mother's history. As Billy and Stu torment Sidney at the end of the film, Sidney asks them why they did it:

> BILLY: I think she wants a motive. Well, I don't really believe in motives, Sid. I mean did Norman Bates have a motive?
> STU: No.
> BILLY: Did we ever find out why Hannibal Lecter liked to eat people? DON'T THINK SO! See, it's a lot scarier when there's no motive, Sid. We did your Mom a favor, Sid. That woman was a slut-bag whore who flashed her shit all

over town like she was Sharon Stone or somethin'.... Is that motive enough for you? How about this? Your slut mother was fucking my father, and she's the reason my mom moved out and abandoned me.

Sidney's push at the end of the film is twofold: not only must she fight back against her attackers, her friend and her boyfriend, but she must also reconcile her own issues with her own narrative. Once Sidney has to face what her mother has done and who it impacted, she is able to not only fight back but also to subvert Clover's definition of the Final Girl finale:

> The image of the distressed female most likely to linger in memory is the image of the one who did not die: the survivor, or Final Girl. She is the one who encounters the mutilated bodies of her friends and perceives the full extent of the proceeding horror and her own peril; who is chased, cornered, wounded; whom we see scream, stagger, fall, rise and scream again. She is abject terror personified. If her friends knew they were about to die only seconds before the event, the Final Girl lives with the knowledge for long minutes or hours. She alone looks death in the face, but she alone also finds the strength either to stay the killer long enough to be rescued (ending A) or kill him herself (ending B).[20]

Engaging with sex is rare in the Final Girl trope, but when Sidney and Billy do have sex, Craven takes pains to emphasize that Sidney's decision is not one of titillation but of choice. Sidney and Billy are at the house party, where their kissing grows more and more intense. Sidney removes her top and the camera pans to show Billy's bare back and to focus on Sidney's expression of vulnerability, emphasizing the fetishism of the male gaze and rendering the shot of a female one—a reaction that women have experienced which does not distance them from the film, but perhaps makes it more relatable. The fact that Billy's bare back covers Sidney's chest in the shot allows it to focus on Sidney and her choices rather than titillate the audience. Craven even cuts back to the party downstairs where the group watches *Halloween* and Randy and Stu lament their heterosexual desire to see breasts bared to them on screen:

> STU: I wanna see breasts. I wanna see Jamie Lee's breasts. When do we see Jamie Lee's breasts?
> RANDY: Breasts? Not until *Trading Places* in 1983. Jamie Lee was always a virgin in horror movies. She didn't show her tits 'til she went legits.

Sidney's heroic ending destroys Billy and Stu's misogynist leanings towards the Reagan Era horror film—the kind of film they want to recreate. However the film and Sidney's journey are more emblematic of third wave feminism's sex positive leanings. In the 1990s a Final Girl could have consensual sex but also destroy those who do her wrong. Sidney is not saved as Clover posits for the Final Girl trope: "gender transference ... the moment at which the Final Girl is effectively phallicised is the moment when the plot halts and the horror ceases. Day breaks, and the community returns to its normal order."[21] Sidney dons the Ghostface costume, saves her father and friends, and turns the game on Billy and Stu, calling them using their voice modulator and pushing a television on top of Stu's head and stabbing Billy repeatedly with a long umbrella. The true turn in *Scream* comes at what would be the final sting of the film; it's the moment when Michael Myers disappears in *Halloween*, when Young Jason appears at the end of *Friday the 13th*, when Freddy's arm pulls Nancy's mother through a window in *A Nightmare on Elm Street*. Sidney, Randy and Gale stand over Billy's supposedly dead body as Sidney picks up their gun and Randy says: "Careful. This is the moment when the supposedly dead killer comes back to life, for one last scare." As Billy lunges toward them, Sidney shoots him: "Not in my movie."

Sidney's decisive shot ends the madness and chaos caused by two men who wanted to harm their generation, destroy a small community, then ride out their lives on fake celebrity obtained through the deaths of others. Sidney ends their plan and their control of the narrative, which would dictate that the killer is entitled to "one last scare"—but not in Sidney's narrative. As author Sady Doyle writes in her book *Trainwreck*:

> The privilege of controlling your own narrative is easy to take for granted. It's easy to confuse for a right; to assume that, of all the people in this loud and crowded world, you're the best person suited to tell the world who you are, or what you are, or what your actions and emotions mean in context. Yet we know that narratives can be stolen, and weaponized.... All too often, losing your story means that if you make a decision people don't like ... they feel entitled to hurt you. It means being subject to a hostile, unasked-for, all-consuming intimacy: having other people claim ownership over your body, your sexual history, your medical history, your emotional life, your future.[22]

The issue of narrative is not simply confined to Sidney Prescott, or the slasher film, or the horror genre, or even film in general. A female crafted narrative in popular culture that does not end in marriage or the birth of a child is a rarity. *Scream* not only tackles the problem of women's narrative, giving Sidney room to explore her self-doubt, guilt and sexuality all in the span of the film, but also allows her to come out on top and give her narrative new meaning in a context she subscribes to.

The film ends with Sidney walking out of the house into the sunlight as police arrive on the scene, where Dewey, who was injured earlier, survives and is taken out on a stretcher. The camera continues to pull back over the scene, revealing Gale set up with a new cameraman after Billy and/or Stu dispatched with her first one earlier on, doing an exclusive on the events that have just transpired.

Craven and Williamson's choice not to end on Sidney or the survivors or a killer's return from supposed death, but rather on Gale's own ambition, allows the film to deliver a final sting of its own. As Billy says earlier in the film, "Don't you blame the movies. Movies don't create psychos. Movies make psychos more creative!"—a fitting takedown of the conservative Right's hand-wringing over the state of youth. But Gale's scene of the film shows the culture's need and insistence for tantalization and gory details, which enrapture home audiences with the tawdry details of others—a fascination that the characters would have to reckon with in the sequel.

Scream's status as a sleeper hit in late winter 1996 and the early months of 1997 ensured sequels would follow. In December 1997, *Scream 2* was released and saw the survivors of the Woodsboro Massacre enter into the semi-adult world of university. Outlets like *Entertainment Weekly* were already covering the *Scream 2* set with the same kind of attention that journalists and editors reserved for big-budget, franchised, star-power movies. In essence, *Scream* had made horror mainstream in the late 1990s. As Entertainment Weekly put it at the time:

> With its cutting one-liners and to-die-for cast, last year's *Scream* spoofed its way to the top of the teen horror movie list. Its $103 million box office take puts it right up there with *The Silence of the Lambs* and *The Exorcist*. Now Miramax has an ambitious plan to put *Scream 2* on more than 3,000 movie screens Dec. 12. Spending $15–20 million on promotion alone—roughly the entire budget of the original—the studio is betting that a traditionally fickle teen audience will again part with their allowance simply to be terrified.[23]

However, the term "sequel" or even "franchise" can conjure up images and instances more terrifying than anything in an actual horror movie. The use of sequels in a horror franchise can be seen as a movement to discredit or monetize on the originality of the first film. Horror films, slashers in particularly, are seen as having abused the sequelizing or franchising of their own mythology in the horror industry machinery that pumped out the sequels to *Halloween* (1978), *Friday the 13th* (1980) and *A Nightmare on Elm Street* (1984). When talking about a great horror film with mainstream appeal, a discussion of a sequel is never far behind. Sequels present an interesting litmus test for any fan—there are often hopes associated with the continuation of a beloved story or mythology or the opportunity to see an expansion of a universe—but on the flip side, film studios see the potential for massive and easy box office revenue. Many film insiders are happy to site instances during the franchise heyday of *A Nightmare on Elm Street* when New Line studio was in pre-production of the fourth sequel (eventually titled *A Nightmare on Elm Street 5: The Dream Child*) and in order to pre-sell the film in multiple markets, the poster was completed before the film's script was.[24] As scholar Caetlin Benson-Allott writes, "Sequels [face] the challenge of extending commercially recognizable film properties without any of the original actors or directors. They had to offer viewers a new mode of identification with their series, indeed with their very seriality.[25]"

Scream 2 would be the rare sequel to rise to the challenge of creating an entertaining sequel that firmly builds on the mythos set out in the first film while still bowing to the pressure of its studio. When Miramax bought Williamson's initial script for *Scream* it also came with outlines for two sequels. As Craven noted at the time of *Scream 2*'s release:

> We had the briefest of sketches from Kevin for the other two films and we really didn't think beyond that while we were shooting it. We all like the premise and we had a lot of the good continuing cast returning, not just the villain, which is normal in these franchises. We did have worries about repeating the success of the first…. This film actually feels more like an element of a trilogy rather than a sequel. We're basically continuing the development of Sidney and the people around her as they face another threat. I'm proud to be a part of this, whereas I wouldn't have been proud to be a part of *A Nightmare on Elm Street 2*.[26]

Miramax was so keen to repeat the success of the original that the budget for *Scream 2* was increased, as was the marketing and promo budget. The shooting schedule was ramped up so the sequel could follow in its predecessor's footsteps and secure a Holiday 1997 release date. As Craven said of the production of *Scream 2*:

> It has been tougher than the last one. There has been very little time for mistakes and reshoots. We lost a whole day due to damage to the negative in Georgia [where *Scream 2* was shot], and there have been a lot of what I call technical reversals. We've had to go fast, it has been difficult physically and I didn't get much sleep.[27]

Scream 2 employs even stronger star power than the first film with Neve Campbell, Courteney Cox and David Arquette returning and Liev Schreiber reprising and vastly expanding his role as the wrongfully accused Cotton Weary. With a bigger budget comes an expanded cast, allowing the production to cast then-hot young actors like Sarah Michelle Gellar (from TV's *Buffy the Vampire Slayer*) Heather Graham (*Boogie Nights*), Jada Pinkett Smith (*The Nutty Professor*) and Jerry O'Connell (*Jerry Maguire*). The film also pays lip service and screen time to one of the biggest complaints of the original film— the lack of diversity on screen. Craven, not one for shying away from an inclusive cast with his previous films *A Vampire in Brooklyn* (1995) and *The People Under the Stairs* (1991), placed emphasis on a more diverse cast by having the opening kills feature a young black couple played by Jada Pinkett and Omar Epps. The opening ten minutes of *Scream 2* deal directly with the act of seeing a movie and the lack of diversity in general in mainstream films when Phil (Epps) and Maureen (Pinkett) discuss seeing a movie about the events of the first film entitled *Stab* as they enter the theatre:

> PHIL: We got these tickets for free.
> MAUREEN: It's some dumb-ass white movie about some dumb-ass white girls getting their white asses cut the fuck up, okay?

While Phil and Maureen are picked off by the new Ghostface(s), the audience of *Scream 2*, along with the members of the audience in *Scream 2* seeing *Stab* in the cinema, view the opening scene, which references Casey's (Drew Barrymore) death scene from the first *Scream*. In this scene, Williamson and Craven (who both returned to writing and directing duties respectively) play with the notion of a Hollywoodized, fictionalized universe. In *Stab*, Casey (now played by Heather Graham) is considerably sillier and has considerably less clothing at her disposal. The audience viewing *Scream 2* easily aligns with Maureen watching *Stab* as she complains and mocks the film while still jumping at a few of the scares. What *Scream 2* serves to do at the climax of this scene and in the rest of the film is to merge the fictional world of *Stab* or horror films with the supposed reality of Sidney and her classmates. This offers a continual emphasis of the *Scream* franchise engaging with its audience in a dialogue about horror films while still producing one. The introductory scene of *Scream 2* also hints at the villain of the third film— the film studio itself. The sequence with Maureen and Phil is all too happy to condemn the elaborate lengths a film studio will go to in order to promote its film. As Maureen and Phil enter the theatre they are presented with Ghostface costumes courtesy of the studio, and then during the screening itself an usher works a lever that propels effects in the theater to supposedly enhance the experience. Craven takes his time in the set-ups of this scene, ensuring the audience of *Scream 2* can see the mechanics that go into publicity and the chaos they can create.

After dispatching with Phil in the men's washroom, Ghostface kills Maureen in the cinema, stabbing her repeatedly during the screening. Maureen staggers amidst the unruly crowd to get help and finally stands in front of the screen, screaming and dying. Craven oscillates the camera between Maureen's point of view and the audiences'. In her final moments, Maureen has been subsumed by the fictional film, inadvertently playing into the demands of the audience. While this scene is coded as a wink and a nod to an audience's understanding and expectations of a studio on a highly-anticipated film sequel, the tone becomes much darker as Maureen dies in front of the screen and the crowd slowly take off their Ghostface masks in order to get a better

6. Bowling for Woodsboro   75

view and understanding of what is happening. The chaos and hype of the film have led them to take part in the murder of two innocent bystanders. Craven and Williamson are careful to plot the narrative that Billy and Stu set out in the original—that movies don't create psychos, they just make psychos more creative and Billy's very specific motivation against Sidney. On the surface, Maureen and Phil's deaths are par for the course set out in the first film—two recognizable stars picked off in the opening 10 to 15 minutes—but for the characters within the film, they will provide clues and an eventual modus operandi for the motivations of Ghostface this time around.

The film picks up with Sidney, now a theater student at Windsor College, and Randy, who studies film there. News of the Phil and Maureen's murders reaches Sidney, who is already experiencing increased attention from the media and obsessive "fans" with the release of *Stab*. Quickly it becomes clear that someone has once again taken up the mantle of Ghostface and is targeting Sidney. After the original team—including Dewey, Gale and Randy—assembles, they realize that the killer is following the pattern of the original, initially targeting victims with the same names as the victims in the first film and then targeting those Billy and Stu failed to kill. As Randy elaborates on the rules of a sequel:

> RANDY: Number 1, the body count is always bigger. Number 2, the death scenes are always much more elaborate—more blood, more gore, carnage candy! Your core audience expects it. And number 3, if you want your sequel to become a franchise never, ever…
>
> DEWEY: [interrupting] How do we find the killer, Randy? That's what I want to know.

In *Scream 2*, all the returning characters have grown deeper into their coping mechanisms—Dewey is more bashful, Gale is hungrier, Randy retreats further into film knowledge and Sidney has become more fearful. Both Randy and Gale are presented with interesting foils. Randy has a ying to his yang in the form of Mickey (Timothy Olyphant), another film student who is much more interested in making films rather than talking about them. Gale is plagued by an eager local reporter Debbie Salt (Laurie Metcalf) who seemingly one-ups Gale at every turn while knowing everything about her. This cast highlights *Scream 2*'s focus, which is on survivors and not victims. Craven and Williamson break up the narrative so the audience can follow two parallel stories that intertwine. The primary story centers around Sidney and maintains her status as Final Girl while not revolutionizing it in the same way the original did. She attempts to have a normal life attending college, engaging in some social outings and maintaining a serious relationship with nice-guy Derek (Jerry O'Connell), while dealing her deep seated trust issues. Through

Sidney, the film explores what it means to survive a traumatic event. Parallel to Sidney's story line is Gale and Dewey's. The two continue their flirtation throughout *Scream 2* and eventually act on it, though Dewey is weary of Gale's predatory ways. It is only through the nuisance of would-be reporter Debbie Salt, who casts Gale as part of the *Scream 2* narrative rather than an outsider reporting on it, that Gale no longer tries to report on her fellow characters. This break in narrative allows Craven and Williamson to present two killers who are linked but hiding their true identities.

In the climax of the film both Mickey and Debbie are revealed to be the killers working in tandem. Mickey is a garden variety psychopath who sees his claim to fame not in the act of killing but in the media circus trial that he is sure will follow:

> MICKEY: ...'cause these days it's all about the trial. Can you see it? The effects of cinema violence on society. I'll get Dershowitz or Cochran to represent me. Bob Dole on the witness stand in my defense. Hell the Christian Coalition'll pay my legal fees. It's air tight Sid. I'm an innocent victim.

Debbie however, presents one more final reveal as Sidney recognizes her as Mrs. Loomis, Billy's mother. In the climactic final confrontation, which involves Sidney, Mickey, Mrs. Loomis, Cotton and Gale takes place in the university's theatre stage, which is set for the play that Sidney is shown rehearsing earlier in the film. Though not directly stated, the play is *Agamemnon* from *Oresteia*, a trilogy of Greek tragedies written by Aeschylus. The play, like many classical Greek plays, deals with revenge, justice, injustice and, most interestingly, the idea of a punishment handed down through generations. In the production, Sidney plays Cassandra, a figure from Greek mythology who has prophetic abilities but is cursed with forever being disbelieved. The figure of Cassandra has been utilized across genres but can be easily applied to the role of the Final Girl, whom Carol Clover identifies as a figure who is able to "perceive the full extent of the preceding horror."[28] In Greek mythology Cassandra was at the mercy of men who cursed or raped her. Lutfiana Hermawati writes of Cassandra:

> A few, however, have taken pity on the Cassandra, portraying her more as the lost child that she was. For them, she is often shown on her knees with a helpless look that was meant to garner the pity she so richly deserved. However, she was rarely portrayed, however, as the intelligent heroine that she truly was; a victim of circumstance because she refused to play by the rules established by a group of sanctimonious and undeserving gods.[29]

Scream 2 frequently puts Sidney in situations that mirror horror tropes: being chased by a killer, receiving threatening phone calls, and coming upon the dead bodies of her friends. However, it is Sidney who is able to lead the killers (and her allies) away from their chosen genre of the horror film and into her world of Greek mythology, as Sidney's predictions about the safety of those around her is realized just as the new Ghostface(s) target her and her friends. As a Cassandra figure, Sidney effectively subverts the movie gods' plans by undermining the tropes of the slasher film to continually explore new narratives.

In the final shoot out, Sidney not only reaffirms her role as Final Girl, but also offers redemption to Cotton Weary, who she allows to take the spotlight and title of hero. Sidney, however, continues her role of not allowing the killer to control the narrative end of the film. In the final moments, Sidney and Gale arm themselves with handguns and prepare to shoot the supposedly dead killer, once again negating the antagonist's final scare.

> [Sidney, Gale, and Cotton look at the body of Mrs. Loomis, after being shot by Cotton]
> GALE: Is she dead?
> SINDEY: I don't know. They always come back.
> [as if to confirm what Sidney just said, Mickey leaps to his feet screaming, despite his injuries. Gale and Sidney shoot him. Mickey is knocked backwards and collapses, dead]
> COTTON: Woah!
> [Sidney approaches the body of Mrs. Loomis and shoots at her forehead. The body twitches a bit, then is still again. Gale and Cotton stare at Sidney]
> SINDEY: [shrugs] Just in case.
> [Sidney drops the gun and walks away]

Scream 2's production budget of $24 million was redeemed several times over with a worldwide box office take of $171 million—less than its predecessor but still respectable.

Scream 2 faced uncertainty up until its release with several reports of leaked scripts making their way around the Internet, which was still in its relative infancy in 1997. An initial leak revealed that Hallie (Elise Neal) was another killer working with Mickey while also in a relationship with him. This twist would have yielded yet another nail in the coffin for Sidney's trust issues, but the reveal was scrapped and Hallie became yet another supportive friend of Sidney's to meet a grisly fate. While no official version of this original script with a trio of killers is readily available, it would have created not only a more interesting dynamic for Sidney but also for the inclusivity which Williamson and Craven seemed to be reaching for. The emotional deaths of Maureen and Phil at the beginning of the film could have been more fully realized with a black character as part of the mayhem rather than as another token figure. However, due to no official version being released or even shot, Hallie will live on as yet another black character supporting an overwhelmingly white narrative.

After *Scream*, Williamson would be hot property writing, producing and directing films such as *I Know What You Did Last Summer*, *The Faculty*, *Halloween H20* and *Teaching Mrs. Tingle*, as well as in developing the television show *Dawson's Creek*. *Scream 3* would mark the only time in the series that Williamson was not credited as a screenwriter. In the brief three years between the release of *Scream 2* and *Scream 3* the political and social climate of America had shifted greatly, mainly due to the 1999 Columbine High School shootings. Dimension was already in development on the second sequel, based on an outline produced by Williamson that was being written by Ehren Kruger, who would go on to write *The Ring* (Gore Verbinksi, 2002). Following the Columbine shootings and by Kruger's own preferences, much of Williamson's draft was discarded in favor of focusing on the comedic elements of *Scream* and upping the ante of the film-within-a-film conceit, with the action taking place around the shooting of *Stab 3*.

Scream 3, released in 2000, was the most dubiously received by critics and set up the post-modern Holy Trinity of Sidney, Gale and Dewey in Hollywood. Kevin Williamson's outline and draft was scrapped with neither Williamson nor Miramax explicitly stating why. Williamson did state in a 2013 interview with *Entertainment Weekly* that his vision for *Scream 3* was vastly different than what wound up on screen:

> "In my original story for *Scream 3*, the killers were basically a fan club of Woodsboro kids that had formed because of *Stab 1* and *Stab 2*. They were all doing the killings and the big surprise of the movie was when Sidney walked into the house after Ghostface had killed everyone … and they all rose up. None of them were actually dead and they'd planned the whole thing."[30]

Scream 3 continues the trail of breadcrumbs started in *Scream 2* with the survivors of the second film transplanting to Hollywood and in one way or another overseeing their narrative, which was initially based on their lives but is now two sequels deep and subverting their own personal mythologies. Sidney, Dewey and Gale all have on set counterparts playing them: Angelina Tyler (Emily Mortimer) won the part of Sidney Prescott through a talent competition and is worried that the onset deaths will negatively affect her career, Tom Prinze (Matt Keeslar) plays a Hollywoodified version of Dewey, and Jennifer Jolie (Parker Posey) plays the on-screen version of Gale with the same unrelenting qualities of Gale herself. *Scream 3* does not name these characters subtlety. Angelina Tyler and Jennifer Jolie are clearly pulled from Angelina Jolie who was a rising star in the late 1990s, and the character of Tom Prinze owes a debt to then-hunk Freddie Prinze, Jr., allowing the film to once again give a culturally aware wink and nod to the audience.

Teen culture reached a zenith in 1999 and 2000 with the release of films such as *She's All That* (Robert Iscove, 1999), *10 Things I Hate About You* (Gil Junger, 1999), *American Pie* (Paul and Chris Weitz, 1999), *Cruel Intentions* (Roger Kumble, 1999), *Jawbreaker* (Darren Stein, 1999), *Bring It On* (Peyton Reed, 2000) and *Varsity Blues* (Brian Robbins, 1999) and the shows like *Buffy the Vampire Slayer*, *Gilmore Girls*, *Felicity* and *Dawson's Creek*, all expounding on the virtues and conundrums of teen culture, as well as referencing popular culture to make their points. It made sense for *Scream 3* to show the mechanics of the system that was so heavily invested in turning teens into consumers. While *Scream 3* may be the murkiest film of the trilogy in terms of execution and story, it is also admirably ambitious. It is a film that does not shy away from pointing its finger at the system that allows for the exploitation and rape of a young woman and then casts her aside. *Scream 3* resets some of the initial mythology of the franchise, illustrating that Sidney's story began not only before she was born, but also in back lots where the people who made scary movies were capable of much worse than the villains they put on screen.

Like the other films in the series, the opening scene begins with a gruesome kill—this time involving Cotton Weary and his live-in girlfriend. This scene also introduces a voice-altering device used by the killer that can mimic any of the characters' voices, casting even more doubt and suspicion and growing the circle of suspects even wider. *Scream 3*, mainly due to Neve Campbell's insistence that she only be on set for three weeks,[31] once again veers between two storylines that converge for the climax—Sidney on her own, grappling with the guilt of past events and the nightmarish fear that though she never truly knew her mother, she will wind up just like her, and Gale and Dewey reconnecting while trying to solve the murders on the back lot of a Hollywood studio. Once again, a killer begins striking almost at random on the set of *Stab 3* (now a franchise after its introduction in *Scream 2*), but as Sidney and the others know, there is no such thing as random. Randy, who predicted his own death in the second film, gives them a guide by way of prerecorded warning:

> If you find yourself dealing with an unexpected back story and a preponderance of exposition, then the sequel rules DO NOT apply. Because you are not dealing with a sequel, you are dealing with the concluding chapter of a trilogy.... It's a rarity in the horror field but it does exist, and it is a force to be reckoned with. Because true trilogies are all about going back to the beginning and discovering something that wasn't true from the get go.... The past will come back to bite you in the ass. Whatever you think you know about the past, forget it. The past is not at rest. Any sins you think were committed in the past are about to break out and destroy you.

Similarly to *Scream 2*, the film separates Gale and Dewey from Sidney for long stretches of time in order to advance certain plot points. This split is heightened as Jennifer Jolie becomes Gale's shadow, mimicking her tendencies and traits, again (as "Debbie Salt" did in *Scream 2*) highlighting Gale's own strengths and weaknesses. Gale and Dewey are thrust together, their personalities clashing but still drawn to one another. Once again, their purpose is to develop and elaborate on the intricacies of the mystery narrative, stacking the deck with multiple suspects and motives. As Dewey is working on the set of *Stab 3* as an advisor, he has intimate knowledge and access, and Gale barges in and insists on helping not just herself, but Sidney and Dewey as well.

Scream 3 elaborates on Sidney's mother's back-story and her failed attempts to become an actress in Hollywood. Once again for Sidney, the supposed sins of the parent are falling on her, as well as on Gale and Dewey. Craven employs on of his most notable tropes, the dream sequence, which he emphatically utilized in *A Nightmare on Elm Street*, in *Scream 3* to explore Sidney's psyche. In the dream, Sidney's mother rises from the grave and taunts her daughter, saying that everything she touches dies and that Sidney is just like her. The film then shows Sidney throwing herself back into the killer's fold, defending her life and sanity after she learns of Cotton's brutal murder. She works with Detective Kincaid (Patrick Dempsey) who veers between being a suspect and love interest to Sidney—another man who Sidney keeps an arm's-length away. While *Scream 3* tries to make good on Randy's warning, Sidney again subverts the expected narrative by ultimately walking away from the traumas of her past and freeing her from the sins of others, which she has been blamed for but has no control over.

Sidney's fear of her mother's sins is continually complicated by the driving force of this movie, which has to do with yet another reveal of Maureen Prescott's life—her seemingly undocumented time in Hollywood as a horror actress, which culminated with a rape and the birth of her first child, who is revealed be Roman (Scott Foley), the director of *Stab 3* and Sidney's half-brother. Roman tells Sidney that it was him who spurred Billy and Stu into killing in the first film and that all the previous events of Sidney's life have been leading to this. Roman's anger comes from Maureen's rejection of him in favor of life with her husband and Sidney. In essence, Roman's greatest work is that he views himself as the real-life director of the *Scream* series, one that has plagued and tormented Sidney because she was the supposed "chosen" child. This confrontation reveals Sidney's frustrations with the misogynist killers of the past films and with Roman:

> SIDNEY: God why don't stop your whining and get on with it. I've heard all this shit before.
> ROMAN: Stop.
> SIDNEY: Do you know why you kill people Roman? Do you?

ROMAN: I don't want to hear it.
SIDNEY: Because you choose to. There is no one else to blame.
ROMAN: Damnit fucking damnit!
SIDNEY: Why don't you take some fucking responsibility?
ROMAN: Fuck you!
SIDNEY: Fuck you!

Sidney's journey through the film, and indeed the whole film series, is rejecting the sins of her mother, which not only did she not know about (or chose not to know about), but which have also endangered her friends. As Roman lunges at Sidney in the climactic battle, Sidney yells at him, "why don't you take some fucking responsibility?" which is what Sidney must do as well. To let go of the past, Sidney must acknowledge it. In doing so, Sidney's journey throughout the *Scream* series elevates her beyond just the mantle of the Final Girl in a slasher franchise but a young woman who has faced adversity and become not only, as Laura Mulvey would define it in her filmic male gaze theory, the maker of her own meaning,[32] but also the driving force behind one of the most successful horror franchises of all time.

Scream 3 wound up being yet another hit for Dimension films, grossing $161 million on a $40 million production budget.[33] But the lukewarm audience and critical reception would put off another sequel for 11 years. The production of *Scream 3* suffered from the same issues as *Scream 2*: a fear of pages being leaked, multiple characters set up to be the killer before the story arc was settled on, three different endings filmed. However in 2010 prior to *Scream 4*'s release, actor Matthew Lillard (Stu in *Scream*) revealed an alternate plot for *Scream 3* on the Bob Bendick Podcast, which seemingly fleshed out Williamson's initial treatment:

> The funny thing is I was supposed to come back for the third one; nobody knows this but the third one, they had written me in, to be the killer in the third one.... The idea was, from jail I was masterminding this kind of—this attack against Sidney, Neve's character. So three weeks before we were supposed to start shooting, "Columbine High School" broke out. They changed everything. They kind of took the script and threw it to the side and they bought me out and I never did the third one.[34]

Many of the elements alluded to by Williamson and Lillard would make their way into *Scream 4*, a film that would see Sidney, Gale and Dewey become the generation that had sinned and that would have to face a reckoning all their own.

7

Hit and Run
I Know What You Did Last Summer (1997) and *I Still Know What You Did Last Summer* (1998)

I Know What You Did Last Summer has the dubious honor of being next in the series of slasher films. Released the year after *Scream*, *I Know What You Did Last Summer* was written by Kevin Williamson right before *Scream*'s theatrical release, as film studios were already clamouring to capitalize on any momentum that could materialize. As Williamson told *Fangoria Magazine* in 1997:

> When I sold *Scream* on the spec market, it kind of caused a flurry… It was like, "OK we didn't get *Scream*, so write something else for us. What do you have that's like *Scream*?" And I was like, "Well, I don't have a clue!" [Producer Neal Moritz] came up and said, "I've got this book by Lois Duncan. Why don't you take a look at it and see if there's something you can work with?"[1]

This led to a marketing push upon *I Know What You Did Last Summer*'s release to capitalize on Williamson's previous effort, stating in the first trailer that it is "From the creator of *Scream*." Miramax, who held the rights to *Scream*, successfully sued Columbia Pictures, the production company behind *I Know What You Did Last Summer*, and the company removed the tagline from other marketing initiatives. *I Know What You Did Last Summer* would be the last film of the 1990s to have Williamson's name on it and not be produced and distributed by Dimension Films, as Miramax would soon sign him to a $20 million deal after *Scream* and *I Know What You Did Last Summer*'s box office success.[2]

I Know What You Did Last Summer continues to develop the elements that would come to define a Williamson movie—one that seeks to revise the slasher narrative and demands that its characters be treated with respect. As Williamson said of the film to *Fangoria Magazine*, "what makes it different from [standard] horror movies in the vein of, say, *Halloween* or *Friday the 13th* is it's not plot-driven, it's character-driven. Even though you know the horror elements of the killer stalking victims, it's very much a character-oriented piece."[3]

The film begins with four friends—Julie (Jennifer Love Hewitt), Helen (Sarah Michelle Gellar), Barry (Ryan Phillipe) and Ray (Freddie Prinze, Jr.)—as they celebrate the end of high school and their last summer in the small town of South Port, North Carolina. Taking place on the Fourth of July, the group celebrates with the town's local festivities but, tiring of them, goes to the beach where they drink, talk and generally fantasize about the potential of their futures. On the way back into town they get in a car accident in which they hit and kill a man. With liquor in the car, they can't call the cops for fear that it will ruin any future they might have. The four agree to dump the body in the ocean and forget it ever happened.

A year later the foursome find themselves back in the small town where a mysterious figure in a fisherman's slicker and a hook stalks and threatens them with the message "I know what you did last summer!" They believe the person they hit was David Eagan who has returned and is now stalking them. Julie and Helen visit David's sister Missy (Anne Heche) who opines her younger brother's death and the toll it has taken on the family. She also reveals that David had been deeply depressed before his death, as the year before he had gotten into a car accident that killed his girlfriend, Susie. As the fisherman kills Barry and Helen, Julie figures out that he is actually a man named Ben Willis (Muse Watson), who was Susie's father. They had hit Ben with their car as he was coming home from killing David. Ray and Julie fight off Ben and eventually throw him once more into the ocean from a boat. The police arrive on scene but all they can find is the hook.

Before Williamson sold his script to Columbia, *I Know What You Did Last Summer* was a young adult book written by Lois Duncan, published in 1973. Duncan was never a fan of the film, citing her experience going to see it in theaters:

> It's just plain more commercial to have things happening as they did in the movie. The movie was a shock to me. For one thing, this book was written in 1973, and I had almost forgot I had written it, so it was very exciting to learn that it was going to be a major motion picture. I could hardly wait to see it. I went to the theatre, bought my ticket and my popcorn, and found a seat. Then onto the screen came an insane fisherman carrying an ice hook. He wasn't in my book. I thought, you know, maybe I've walked into the wrong theater. So I was preparing to leave and then, no, up from the below rolled the words *I Know What You Did Last Summer*, and I thought, That is my book, but who is that man and what is he going to do with that ice hook? Well, I soon found out. He was going to decapitate my characters. Their heads were flying off and

blood was spurting, and everyone was screaming and I was screaming. I was so horrified I couldn't even open my popcorn. It was quite a shocker.... They kept me as far away as possible. I think they were afraid of how I might react if I realized what my little masterpiece was going to turn into.[4]

While *I Know What You Did Last Summer* follows the same trajectory of Duncan's book—the lives of a group of friends are threatened after a hit-and-run car accident—Williamson adpated the story into a more traditional slasher narrative. In Duncan's book, none of the characters die (though Barry is shot), Helen has far more success in her career than in the film, and a mysterious, potential romantic figure, who would factor into the film's sequel *I Still Know What You Did Last Summer*, appears in Julie's life. Williamson spoke to *Fangoria* about his process of developing the story into an R rated slasher from a young adult novel:

> Lois Duncan set up a really cool mystery, but... In the book the killer appears in three different places. He's dating the main character. And he's also a roommate, a secondary character, and the murderer doing all these things, they never interfaced with each other... To do that [visually], you would have to disguise him in some fashion, have him wear a mustache or something silly like that... So I came up with another mystery.[5]

I Know What You Did Last Summer works as an effective slasher that sees its trauma and terror rooted in the actions of its protagonists, further complicating the story. As John Kenneth Muir writes of the film:

> Kevin Williamson has updated [the tropes of 1980s slashers] to seem meaningful again. Available technology had changed a great deal since 1978–1985, the heyday of the slasher, so tropes like the "library of doom" have been recast using web searches and the Internet. More meaningfully, there's something at play here beyond the depiction of superficial, partying youth that was evident in the old slasher films.... The teens of this era are indeed bright, able to integrate a slew of new technologies into their lives, from the internet to cell phones, but, it seems, they have difficulty when it comes to making moral choices. Inevitably, when we look at the Columbine killers, Melissa Drexler, or other teens of the decade, they seem to choose wrong. *I Know What You Did Last Summer*'s teens are knowledgeable, whip smart and have veritable degrees in pop culture references, and absolutely no governing sense of what is right or wrong.[6]

As the 1980s raged and the moral majority influenced the no sex, no drugs policies that would trickle into slasher films, it was also a time of heady capitalism with young families driving themselves further and further towards capital gains. By the time the 1990s came around the young children of these families were nearing adulthood and as the nuclear family was corroding and evolving, there was yet another generation of teens who had been raised by television, films and music looking to understand the world through the lens of corrupted politics, unfulfilling jobs and a need to achieve. As the foursome sits around a campfire on the beach just prior to the accident, they swap stories of how they want to stay together as couples. Helen tells Barry that she'll have his children as she gets lucrative contracts on daytime soap operas and he becomes an NFL star between stints at rehab.

> HELEN: By that time, I'll just be finishing my two year contract with Guiding Light, coinciding with your first year as starting quarterback for the Steelers.
> BARRY: Cowboys.
> HELEN: Whatever. Then we can elope to Europe, or the Caymans, wherever, where I'll let you impregnate me with the first of three children before you head off to rehab. Then we can live happily, blah blah blah.

Julie tells her boyfriend Ray that she worries he'll go off to college in a different city from her and fall for a girl who wears all black and spouts poetry all day. Even though Ray assures Julie there is no one for him but her, there is a pervasive sense of moroseness to these dreams and ambitions. This generation had seen their heroes and public figures reach the highest of highs, just to be taken down for their personal misdeeds. For each of their goals there is a downside, something that must be acquiesced, an imperfect dream. *I Know What You Did Last Summer* was released at the height of tabloid news shows such as *Hard Copy* or *Inside Edition*, which documented celebrity and politician downfalls with breathless anticipation. Part of the public's fascination with these shows began and grew with OJ Simpson's trial—broadcast live—for the murder of his ex-wife and her friend. For those growing up within this culture it feels only natural that the characters would dream of success tinged by realities like rehab. Even when the foursome decides to cover up the murder, it is because they know how bad the accident will look and can practically anticipate the media coverage.

In the year after the accident, Barry and Helen both become shell-shocked to different degrees and regress. Julie nearly flunks out of her first year at university, while Ray begins to work the docks, becoming a fisherman just like his father. Interestingly, Julie's concerns about Ray falling for someone else partially come true. After Julie and Helen speak with Missy, they discover another of their classmates, with whom Missy had a brief relationship, has been visiting her. This is later revealed to be Ray. While Missy is not clad in black, she does possess a soulfulness that Julie does not. While Julie easily occupies the role of the Final Girl in the film, her one secret about the accident has brought about the near collapse of her life. Missy on the other hand has suffered immensely and constantly but has not acted out through her pain. She is shown to be kind and considerate but ultimately of much lower status than the other middleclass teens. Missy comes to represent the unknown— the lower-class existing on the outskirts of South Port, a town that clings to the notion of the American ideal and white picket fences. As Williamson says of the characters:

> I thought it was very compelling because you see these four beautiful, bright, incredible kids who, one year later turn out to be these suicidal, manic-depressive, Prozac-popping alcoholics. It was a nice dynamic. That wasn't in the book, but when I read it, that's what I envisioned.... So I like to think that I sort of made it a 90s morality tale as opposed to a 70s morality tale.[7]

I Know What You Did Last Summer focuses its horror on the actions of these teens and the terrible secret that is tearing them apart; but for the young women, the actions impact both their careers and looks, which is evident through the film's spotlight on their lives. Ray and Barry are hard done by, as well, but have nowhere near the interior lives that Helen and Julie are given.

While Ray and Julie are seemingly destined to take academia by storm and Barry is determined to pummel the NFL into submission, Helen's ambitions to go to New York and make it as an actress are the most visible. The film opens with her competing and winning the local beauty pageant and her death coincides with her ending reign as beauty queen, having failed in New York after only a brief attempt. Helen is constantly framed in doorways and mirrors, lending to the notion that she is an object to be looked at and that her looks are her most indelible quality. After the accident, Helen begins work at her family's local department store and remains a joke to her older sister Elsa (Bridgette Wilson). Her only other family member is a father who barely acknowledges her presence. Director Jim Gillespie makes it clear that Helen is completely and utterly alone with no true connections, so much that she appears almost relieved when the notes that say, "I know what you did last summer" begin appearing, as it gives her an excuse to reconnect with her friends. Her death is equal parts tense and tragic. The killer appears as she is about to give up her crown and kills Barry from the balcony where he sat the year prior. Helen screams, but no one does anything until it is too late. The killer chases Helen, who makes it past several obstacles including her family's store and Elsa, but she ultimately meets her demise as she sees her salvation. Helen runs toward the town parade from a back alleyway but is ambushed by the killer, who stabs her repeatedly with his hook. Helen's screams are muted by the sounds of the parade and lying only steps away from safety, she dies much the same way as she lived—alone and unnoticed.

Julie begins the film as a fresh-faced girl next door. After the car accident and as the film picks up a year later, Julie is finishing her summer semester. The scene begins with Julie's roommate calling her name and the camera panning in on the back of Julie's head as Julie dramatically swivels in her chair to reveal a slightly haggard looking girl replete with greasy hair and dark circles under her eyes—practically as good as any other jump scare in the film. In this moment, it is clear that the torment and trauma Julie has dealt with in the past year has taken a toll on her looks, creating an easy visual shorthand for Gillespie and Williamson to illustrate the taxing nature of secrets. Julie's stringy hair and sallow skin indicate a darker secret—one that, based on her appearance, the audience knows has torn her apart. As the film continues Julie looks less haggard and returns to form, taking charge and fighting back. The fight is ultimately one to reclaim their youth and their ambitions, which were lost after the accident. In one iconic scene Julie spins in a circle and screams, "What are you waiting for?" to the killer, which could very easily have been said to any of the foursome, who have all stagnated in their careers and life.

In this world of *I Know What You Did Last Summer*, nothing and no one is innocent. The dream of small town America has died and been covered up by secrets that invade and corrode the lives of the best and brightest of the small town. These teens know that one misdeed, one mistake, one accident is enough to end their lives and ambition, making them famous to the 24 hour news cycle audience if all is revealed.

Early in the film, before the accident, the foursome sit around the fire at the beach and each tell different version of the "Hook" urban legend. Each one has a slightly different twist to the story and a different interpretation of its meaning.

> JULIE: Please, it's a fictional story created to warn young girls of the dangers of having premarital sex.
> RAY: Well actually honey, you know how terrified I am of your IQ but it's an urban legend, American folklore and they all usually originate from some real life incident.

As other characters in this cycle of films will discover, the most terrifying thing about these legends is not falling prey to one, but becoming one. At the end of the film Ray and Julie attempt to end the cycle of madness, which they almost do, but that would be too easy for Hollywood. The film ends with Julie and Ray embracing one another, indicating some kind of reconciliation, but only as Ben's hook is pulled from the water. The final coda of the film allows for one final jump scare as the Fisherman comes back to haunt Julie.

I Still Know What You Did Last Summer, like its predecessor, strives to keep one foot rooted in slasher tradition and the other foot manifesting the concerns of 1990s teens but finds itself in an infuriating state of advancing discourse while also falling prey to its own narrative trappings. Set a year after the events of *I Know What You Did Last Summer*, Julie is back at college and still struggling with the post-traumatic stress disorder taking a hold of her life. While she is still dating Ray, tensions seem to overcome them as Ray pressures her to settle down for a nice quiet life in South Port. Julie is drawn to her classmate Will (Matthew Settle) who is bright, charming and clearly very attracted to her. Julie's other friends Karla (Brandy Norwood) and her boyfriend Tyrell (Mekhi Phifer) constantly try to get Julie out, taking her to clubs to ensure that she enjoys at least part of her college experience. Out of the blue, Julie and Karla win an all-expenses paid trip to the Bahamas for the Fourth of July weekend for four from a local radio station after answering the skill testing question, "what is the capital of Brazil?" to which Karla answers, "Rio de Janeiro." Julie invites Ray, but he refuses to go, still hurt over her dismissal of South Port. Karla invites Tyrell and Will in the hopes of Will and Julie getting together.

Ray confesses to his co-worker and friend Dave (John Hawkes) that he was going to ask Julie to marry him. Dave convinces Ray to surprise Julie and propose to her on the trip. Dave drives Ray to meet the group, but stops when he sees a car pulled over on the side of the road. Dave goes to help but is killed by the Fisherman. Ray gets badly injured but is able to escape.

Meanwhile Julie, Karla, Tyrell and Will make their way to the Bahamas and the resort, only to find it nearly abandoned as hurricane season is due to begin. Having the resort almost completely to themselves outside of a few employees—Mr. Brooks (Jeffrey Combs), Estes (Bill Cobbs), Nancy (Jennifer Esposito), Darick (Benjamin Brown) and Titus (Jack Black)—the group decides to make the best of their trip. But soon Julie sees the message "I still know what you did last summer" and begins to panic. No one else in the group sees it and it is not until Julie is almost seriously injured in a tanning bed and Karla is attacked that everyone begins to believe something is amiss. A hurricane bears down and the group is stranded on the island. The Fisherman makes his presence known, quickly dispatching with much of the hotel staff and Tyrell. The group is separated and attempts to survive the storm, hoping they can radio for help.

Ray wakes up in a hospital and knowing Julie is in danger pawns her engagement ring for a gun. He makes his way to the Bahamas and takes a dangerous boat journey to reach the island. It is revealed that Will is actually Ben Willis' son and the two have been working together to finally get revenge on Julie and Ray. In fact, it was Will who pretended to be the Radio DJ who let the girls win with the wrong answer (the correct answer being Brazilia). Ray appears and he and Julie kill Ben and Will. Karla has also survived the night and the three are rescued. In a brief stinger scene, some time has passed and Ray and Julie have married and settled in South Port. While enjoying the quaint banalities of marriage (Ray is enamoured with an electric toothbrush), Julie senses something is amiss and is attacked once more by the Fisherman.

I Still Know What You Did Last Summer is, if anything, a valiant attempt to capitalize on the initial film's success and utilize a blueprint that was working for the *Scream* franchise—focus on the survivors and the trauma inherent in violence rather than the villain who may or may not make an appearance in his or her original form but will certainly cast a long shadow over the proceedings. *I Still Know What You Did Last Summer* also utilizes the emerging star power of Jennifer Love Hewitt (who was trying also to break into the music world; the film featured her single *How Do I Deal?*), as well as bona fide pop star Brandy. This focus on female characters as central to the film's narrative is once again playing to the strengthening market of the day—teen girls.

I Still Know What You Did Last Summer's writing duties were passed on to television writer Trey Callaway after Kevin Williamson was locked in pre-production for a variety of Dimension Film developments. Its plot is driven by characters' reactions to extraordinary circumstances. It offers an examination of trauma, violence and guilt with a specific focus on the challenges that young people face. One of the more evident narrative pushes comes from Julie's trauma, which had, as previously mentioned, shown itself through unwashed hair and dark circles under her eyes to full blown PTSD with a variety of manifestations through nightmares, anxiety and a general withdrawal from everyday activities. When the film begins, Julie is confronted with a choice: to make a life for herself and overcome the trauma, or to overcome the trauma by settling down with Ray in the town where they grew up. Julie seems hell-bent on making college work for her, though she constantly struggles. The film opens with Julie confessing the accident and the events of the previous year in a church confessional. The priest is revealed to be Ben Willis, who attacks her. Julie wakes up screaming in the middle of a lecture. She runs out and Will follows her.

JULIE: I had another dream, Will.
WILL: The one in the shower?
JULIE: No, in a church. God, it was so real, I mean I could feel his breath on me. I thought that the dreams were over, I really did. I mean, I hadn't had one for months.
WILL: It takes time Julie; you'll do better.
JULIE: Well, it can't get much worse. That's not the first time I've freaked out in class, Will. I can't study, I don't get any sleep and I'm this close, this close to failing.... It was one year ago.
WILL: It's the anniversary, that's what it is. You've just got to take it easy on yourself.

JULIE: I'm really trying Will, but you know what? Sometimes I even wonder why I came up here in the first place.
WILL: To get out of South Port?
JULIE: Right. Now I remember.

I Still Know What You Did Last Summer focuses even more clearly through Julie's PTSD on the notion of memory—what is remembered, what is forgotten and what is repressed. In the film, Julie must come to terms with not only her involvement in her own trauma, but the repercussions of it on her mental health—the pain that gets in the way of "normal" life making it hard to conform and perform every day. The U.S. Department of Veteran Affairs, which has a mandate to focus on the effects and treatment of PTSD, notes the tremendous impact of trauma when it occurs during developmental years:

> Children and teens that go through the most severe traumas tend to have the highest levels of PTSD symptoms... Events that involve people hurting other people, such as rape and assault, are more likely to result in PTSD than other types of traumas. Also, the more traumas a child goes through, the higher the risk of getting PTSD. Girls are more likely than boys to get PTSD.[8]

AnxietyBC further explains the implications of PTSD in youth:

> Intrusive symptoms include distressing and vivid night and day dreams (also called *flashbacks*), and becoming highly distressed when exposed to reminders of the event. Youth can also avoid or try to stay away from any reminders of the event, report inability to recall significant details of the event, experience a range of negative emotions such as sadness, guilt, shame, and confusion, and lack interest or desire to participate in important activities.[9]

Julie exhibits all of these symptoms at one time or another. Karla and Tyrell are sympathetic to Julie's plight but ultimately unmoved as she attempts to warn them of their impending doom. The symptoms of PTSD cloak and confound Julie's reliability as a witness to her own events. When she is proven correct and after several more people die, Julie finally gets to confront her nightmare in person. When it is revealed to be Ben Willis and his son Will behind the killings, Julie must not only face her initial trauma, but also the fact that Will used her trauma to manipulate her.

WILL: I mean, look at the bright side Jules, we finally get to spend some quality time together.
JULIE: Why are you doing this to me?
WILL: Me, me, me, it's always about you—I'm having bad dreams, I can't sleep, I'm not doing well in school, I'm having trouble with my boyfriend.
JULIE: I trusted you!
WILL: You're so much like the rest of them! You never take responsibility for anything you do! And you think you can get away with murder!

The introduction of Will (whose last name is Benson or Ben's Son) into the film nods back to Lois Duncan's original text, in which the killer was the victim's half-brother who was dating Julie throughout the book. In this scenario, Will dictates the privilege Julie has, not just as a survivor, but as a supposedly innocent survivor. The opening dream in the church reveals that Julie has not told anyone about the true nature of the crime.

> Bless me father, for I have sinned. It's been a year since my last confession. I've never told anyone about this. Not my mom, not the police, or not even my friends, except for the ones who were there, well, they're not around anymore. You see I, I killed a man, but it was an accident.

Will's goal is to hold Julie accountable for her actions at any cost. Julie cannot play the innocent victim, as she ultimately planted the seeds of trauma that would overtake her life and continually refuses to publically acknowledge her role in it, even at the end of the sequel. In her confrontation with Will and Ben, she must finally begin to reckon her true self with her perceived self. When Ben goes to kill Ray, who has arrived on the scene, Julie picks up Ray's gun, which stalled, and manages to fire it. She shoots Ben, saying, "Just. Fucking. Die." After several shots he falls, dead, into the grave meant for Julie.

Once again, Julie and Ray stand victorious in the face of Ben Willis and have a chance at reclaiming their own lives. Karla, who disappeared for the climax, also survives. It is unclear what Julie and Ray have told the police—whether they confessed to everything, finally unburdening themselves, or once again chose to keep the secret. The final scene, in which their quaint domestic bliss is invaded, hints that they have once again chosen to keep the secret that will continue to haunt them until it ultimately destroys them, either through a physical presence like Ben or Will or in their own tortured minds.

8

Circulate Widely
Urban Legend (1998) and *Urban Legends: Final Cut* (2000)

Jamie Blanks' 1998 slasher *Urban Legend* may be the film most indebted to *Scream's* lineage. Financed and produced by Sony's TriStar Pictures division and Phoenix Pictures, *Urban Legend* follows a parallel storyline to *Scream*, aping on several character types, but moving the focus from murders inspired by horror movies to those inspired by urban legends. While horror films can be inaccessible due to expensive theatre tickets and video store rental fees, urban legends are ingrained in Western culture, passed down through friends, schoolmates or older siblings. Urban legends are often our first taste of the thrills of a good scare.

Jan Harold Brunvand investigates the contemporary urban legend in his book *The Vanishing Hitchhiker: American Urban Legends and Their Meaning*, describing the term thusly:

> The juxtaposition of the terms "modern," "contemporary," and "urban" and the word "folklore" may seem contradictory to those who think folklore as charming, obsolete, unsophisticated traditions passed along by wheezing old gaffers and cackling crones in backwood villages of bygone days. Urban Legends, on the contrary, are realistic stories concerning recent events (or alleged events) with an ironic or supernatural twist. They are an integral part of white Anglo-American culture and are told and believed by some of the most sophisticated "folk" of modern society—young people, urbanites, and the well-educated. The storytellers assume that the true facts of each case lie just one or two informants back down the line with a reliable witness, or in a news media report…. [Urban] legends are told seriously, circulate largely by word of mouth, are generally anonymous, and vary constantly in particular details from one telling to another, while always preserving a central core of traditional elements or "motifs." To some degree—again like much other folklore—urban legends must be considered false, at least in the sense that the same rather bizarre events could not actually have happened in so many localities to so many aunts, cousins, neighbors, in-laws and classmates.[1]

The central conceit plaguing the characters in *Urban Legend* is a serial killer on the loose who uses elaborate urban legend set-ups to pick off and murder a loosely tied together group of friends on a college campus. At the center of the story is Natalie (Alicia Witt), the Final Girl of the film who is, on the surface, composed and serious. Her more vibrant friends Brenda (Rebecca Gayheart), Parker (Michael Rosenbaum), Sasha (Tara Reid), Damon (Joshua Jackson) and potential love interest Paul (Jared Leto) all seem to be the targets of the killer. Set on the campus of the fictional Pendleton University, *Urban Legend* follows the trope set by the seminal film on urban legends, *Candyman* (Bernard Rose, 1992), of utilizing a setting focused on academia to disseminate the urban legend phenomena.

While *Scream* utilized its small-town setting to highlight certain characters' dependence on physical media, *Urban Legend* utilizes its college setting to mock those who still believe in urban legend, preventing them from seeing the real danger inherent in their situation. The film also makes rather clever use of several red herrings, setting the audience up to expect the killer's motivation to stem from an incident at the university rather than from one Natalie brings upon herself.

The film's opening kill uses one of North America's most familiar urban legends, the Killer in the Backseat. Michelle (Natasha Gregson Wagner) is driving on a dark and stormy night when she notices she is running low on gas. She stops at the nearest service station, where a stuttering and ungainly service attendant (Brad Dourif) helps fill her tank. After Michelle gives the attendant her credit card to pay, he tells her there is a problem with the card and the bank is on the phone. Michelle reluctantly follows the attendant who tries to prevent her from leaving, but, because of his stutter, cannot make out the sentences in time to stop her. Michelle is shaken by the incident but continues driving, realizing too late that the attendant was trying to warn her of a killer in the backseat of her car. She is decapitated. This simple opening is taken directly from many iterations of this popular urban legend[2] and sets up many of the motifs not only in the film but also within the study of urban legends— namely that all societal safe guards and contracts are not enough to keep one safe. As Brunvand writes of the legend *The Killer in the Backseat*, "sometimes the pursuer is a burly truck driver or other tough-looking character, and in several of the stories the supposed would-be attacker (the perusing rescuer) is specifically said to be a black man. Both motifs clearly show white middle class fears of minorities or of groups believed to be socially inferior."[3] *Urban Legend* sets up several characters to misdirect and subvert the audiences' expectations, offering a confounding sense of social order—*Urban Legend* suggests that those who society fears and deems unworthy are not the ones to fear, as they are continually used as scapegoats and warnings to the white-washed middle class group of friends.

The film picks up with Natalie and her friends at school learning of Michelle's death. Paul is all too keen on murder, utilizing the tragedy for the front page of the school newspaper. The school officials, represented by the security guard Reese (Loretta Devine) and Dean Adams (John Neville), are attempting to shut down the newspaper to stop widespread panic and remove any negative publicity about Pendleton from the minds of the students. While Dean Adams is a straight-laced academic with a clipped British accent, three-piece suit and white hair, Reese is a black woman who is hungry for adventure (as depicted in her multiple rewatches of *Foxy Brown* films) and wary of students and their motives. After learning of Michelle's death, Natalie becomes detached and withdraws from the group. Brenda is determined to cheer Natalie up and remains steadfastly by her side. Frat boy Damon invites Natalie out for a drive in his car to talk. Shortly after making up a story about a dead girlfriend, Damon makes a pass at Natalie who rebuffs him. Damon agrees to drive them home but goes to urinate before doing so. The killer sets up a trap inspired by The Hook—an urban legend in which, after making out with his girlfriend in the car, a boyfriend is killed by an escaped lunatic from a local asylum—and attacks Damon. Natalie flees in the car, but when she reports the incident, there is no evidence of any murder. The rest of the school and Natalie's friends tell her that Damon has played an elaborate prank and to forget about it. In short succession Natalie's other friends and acquaintances meet their demise in the same way; Dean Adams is killed, Natalie's roommate Tosh (Danielle Harris) is killed in a similar fashion to The Roommate's Death urban legend, Parker is killed through a mix of the Hot Dog urban legend (an animal being microwaved to death) and the pop rocks/soda urban legend (the killer pours pop rocks and bathroom cleaner down his throat) and Sasha is stalked and killed while doing her live on-air radio show. In the final third of the film, Natalie and Brenda believe that Professor Wexler (Robert Englund) is the killer, as he is believed to be the only survivor of the local campus urban legend, The Stanley Hall Massacre, which saw entire floors of students in dorm rooms murdered by a crazed professor exactly 25 years prior.

Urban Legend utilizes intertextuality in setting up Professor Wexler as a suspect. The characters learn that the massacre did in fact happen and that Wexler was the only survivor of the dorm attack; they assume he has snapped due to the anniversary and is now wreaking some kind of revenge on the campus. The rationale behind this assumption is paper-thin, but the cast makes it more convincing.

8. Circulate Widely

Robert Englund, playing Wexler who appears in only a handful of scenes, is by far best known for his portrayal of undead killer Freddy Krueger in the *Nightmare on Elm Street* franchise. In *Urban Legend*, Englund plays up any possibility of menacing malevolence, even in banal lecture hall scenes. The film employs Wexler early on to give a synopsis of the relevance and culpability of urban legends with a sneering contempt for the young people barely paying attention to him.

> PROFESSOR WEXLER: Last week we discussed folklore as a gauge for the values of the society that created them. Today—today, we get more specific.... A babysitter receives menacing phone calls, and, upon investigating them, she realizes that they are originating from an upstairs bedroom, the very room where she's left the children under her care to sleep. Now, who's heard this before? Hmm? [everyone raises their hand]
> BRENDA: Well, that really happened to a girl in my home town.
> PROFESSOR WEXLER: Oh, yes, I'm sure it did. I'm—I'm sure most of you grew up thinking that this happened to girls in—in all your home towns, but it didn't. You see, the babysitter and the man upstairs is what we call an urban legend. Contemporary folklore passed on as a true story. Now there are variations of this one going back to the 1960s, all of them contain the same cultural admonition: Young women, mind your children or harm will come your way.

"Mind your children or harm will come your way," may as well have been a tagline for *A Nightmare On Elm Street*, but hearing the words come from Freddy himself gives them a different weight and meaning. As John Kenneth Muir writes of *Urban Legend*:

> The point of such references is to forge a connection between aspects of pop culture, between urban legends and horror movies. Their history is interconnected and the movie seems to acknowledge that point. Modern folklore and horror movies both serve the same function in 1990s America, as stories that scare through often subtextual contexts or situations but which nonetheless hold power over their audience.[4]

While Englund's elongated cameo may be the film's most poignant reference to horror films, there are callouts to *I Know What You Did Last Summer* and a larger intertextual callout when Natalie and Damon are in his car and the radio turns on to Paula Cole's *I Don't Want to Wait*—the theme song to the television show *Dawson's Creek*, starring Joshua Jackson, who plays Damon. Damon immediately turns the radio off remarking that he "hates that song."

Brenda and Natalie run into Paul who is also trying to get to the bottom of the killings. The three of them drive from campus in search for help. They stop at a gas station and when Paul goes to pay for the gas, Natalie and Brenda investigate a strange smell coming from the car. They discover Wexler's corpse, implicating Paul as the killer. They make a run for it but get separated. Natalie hears Brenda scream and fears the worst. She is picked up by a janitor from the college (Julian Ritchings) who has popped up throughout the film, supplying Natalie and Paul with tidbits of information regarding the school's actual, covered-up history. A car passes them with its lights off and the Janitor flashes his high beams, triggering the gang initiation legend. The other car runs them off the road and they crash. Natalie makes a run for it back to the campus and hears Brenda's screams coming from the dilapidated and boarded up Stanley Hall. She runs into the building determined to save her friend only to discover that Brenda is the killer. Brenda ties Natalie up and reveals her motive.

> NATALIE: You're fucking crazy!
> BRENDA: I prefer the term eccentric ... but, yeah, I guess you could say I'm a little nutty.
> NATALIE: Why?
> BRENDA: Why? Why? Why?! You still haven't figured it out, have you? Well, lucky for you, Miss Thang, I got a visual aid. [presents a slideshow on a projector which she has set up] There I am, Natalie, with my boyfriend, the love of my life. Have you found the love of your life yet, Natalie? Of course not, you're too self-involved to bother. Pic ring any bells, Nat?
> NATALIE: Oh, my God.
> BRENDA: DING! DING! DING! DING! DING! His name was David Evans, the one you and your friend decided to have a little fun with.

Natalie's pre-college indiscretion involved her and her former friend Michelle playing out the gang initiation urban legend and inadvertently killing Brenda's fiancée. Paul and Reese arrive on the scene and are able to free Natalie and subdue Brenda, who intended to carry out the organ transplant urban legend on Natalie. When Paul and Natalie go for help, Brenda appears in the backseat, causing Paul to crash the car. Paul and Natalie survive but Brenda's body is not found. The final scene of the film reveals students at another college campus telling this story as an urban legend. The camera pans to reveal Brenda sitting among them. She admonishes the storyteller, saying, you're telling it wrong; here's what really happened. The final scene signals why the title of the film is singular and not plural; *Urban Legend* is not a movie about a serial killer using urban legends to kill people, it is an urban legend itself. This distinction codes the characters within the film as archetypes and tropes operating within a pre-existing set of limitations and at the end it is Brenda who is allowed to be the film's antagonist and narrator, spreading her own version of the legend.

Within *Urban Legend*, the male characters are cause for the female characters to act. The death of Brenda's fiancée at the hands of Natalie and Michelle sets the story in motion. Paul is an object of desire for both Brenda and Natalie but is ultimately just a tool to further cast them into conflict.

Peripheral characters like Professor Wexler, Dean Adams and the janitor provide bits of knowledge representing various levels of institutional knowledge, but none of them truly matter in the narrative of Brenda versus Natalie. This battle between the two girls comes from a crucial time in any young woman's life—leaving home. *Urban Legend* plays this out simply, utilizing the setting of a college campus to emphasize both young women making decisions for themselves. While Natalie seems more headstrong and realistic, Brenda plays up her "girlishness" by going to parties, acting like an air-head and lamenting her crush on Paul—none of which Natalie would ever give credence to. When Brenda's true motivations are revealed, it is possible to draw a parallel between a more traditional female role for Brenda and a modern one for Natalie. David was not only the love of Brenda's life, but a key to it, as well. When Natalie and Michelle took that away from her, Brenda not only had to come up with an elaborate scheme but enroll in college to do so. When her true motivations are revealed, none of them involve anything more than marrying David. Scholar Beverly Crane described this contradiction:

> In our culture, women have traditionally gone from the protection and care of their fathers to the protection and care of their husbands. The traditional notions of a woman's place therefore tend to produce cultural attitudes which expect women to remain "innocent" as well as "home," "together" with their families and with other women, and "silent" when men discuss important or intellectual matters. When the circumstances surrounding the "victim" and the "defenseless survivor" are examined in this light, it is apparent that the girls in the story have forsaken the tradition represented by the initial-positive grouping in order to become "intellectual," which is presumably why they are now a victim and a survivor. The significant experience which creates a need for this story lies in the changing role of women and the inappropriateness of the traditional attitudes and stances of women themselves in more egalitarian situations.[5]

David's death has forced Brenda to self-actualize in a way she may not have previously. She has a life and a purpose beyond her romantic relationship and her wedding, even if it is a psychotic one. Though *Urban Legend* keeps within the same feminist leanings as *Scream* through its focus on the Final Girl—in this case, Natalie, who winds up being a straightforward, guarded, strong female character—it has some fun engaging with Brenda's dramatic tendencies, such as the slideshow set up used to explain her inclinations. For Brenda, urban legends and folklore signaled a spiritual death for her, but she was reborn with a purpose.

As the 1990s drew to a close, the self-referential aspects of these films, used to attract a culturally hyperaware audience, was growing. No longer were characters just aware of movie genres and using said genres' tropes to navigate through the world of the film in which they found themselves in, they were also making films. Director John Ottman's follow-up to Columbia Pictures moderate success *Urban Legend*, titled *Urban Legends: Final Cut*, sees a group of film students once again entangled with a killer determined to use the titular urban legends against them. While the characters contentedly refer to urban legends throughout the film, *Urban Legends: Final Cut* is far more indebted to the works and tropes of Alfred Hitchcock than to modern folklore.

The film begins with the commencement of the Spring semester at Alpine University, which is home to the most prestigious film production program ever, as one professor so brashly puts it. Amy Mayfield (Jennifer Morrison) is still settling on her final thesis film—the film she will make in her final semester that could lead to a career in the industry. Alpine awards the best film of the graduating class with the Hitchcock award—an award almost guaranteed to open the door to Hollywood for the aspiring filmmaker. One snowy night Reese (Loretta Devine), from the first film, helps Amy to the campus library and tells her about the events of the first film and the security guard who refused to go along with the cover up at the university, causing her to get fired. Amy laughs, saying that she heard that happened at Pendleton University but that it is just an urban legend. Reese, having lived through the experience, just tells Amy to be safe. Amy takes this idea to Professor Soloman (Hart Bochner), who tells her to run with the idea. Once production gets underway, her crew begins disappearing and strange accidents occur. Amy is sure that there is a real-life killer after her after the apparent suicide of one of the school's most promising students Travis Stark (Matthew Davis). Travis's twin brother Trevor (also played by Davis) soon arrives on campus, increasing Amy's suspicion of foul play.

Amy and Trevor begin a covert relationship as Amy tries to finish her film. Trevor and Amy finally get their hands on Travis's film, which he submitted for the Hitchcock award and barely received a passing grade on; this is believed to have led to his suicide. The two watch the film and, as it ends, comment on how awful it was. Amy then notices a hard splice on the film reel, indicating that someone attached a different film to Travis's credits. Amy realizes killer has been targeting everyone who worked on the film, killing them so they could pass it off as their own. The only person left alive from the crew at this point in the film is Toby (Anson Mount), who has had a tempestuous relationship with Amy and sees her as competition. Amy and Trevor kidnap Toby and call in Professor Soloman to reveal Toby as the killer. Toby denies the accusation and Professor Soloman reveals himself to be the killer. Once a former student of Alpine's film program Soloman was denied the Hitchcock award the year he submitted because of one vote on the jury, which came from Amy's father who was an esteemed documentarian. Soloman plans to frame Amy for the murders and head to Hollywood, passing Travis's film off as his own. Amy, along with Trevor, Toby and Reese manage to kill him and the penultimate scene of the film reveals that Amy continues working on her film. The final scene shows Soloman in a mental institution. A nurse arrives to wheel the heavily sedated Soloman to another location and the camera pans up to reveal that the nurse is Brenda (Rebecca Gayheart) from the first film who says to Soloman, we have a lot in common. As she wheels him through the institution the theme music to *Alfred Hitchcock Presents* (1955) plays as the credits begin to roll.

Ottman's film relies far more on classic filmic tropes than its predecessor, attempting to elevate the film above what might be considered yet another standard fare urban legend horror movie. Several urban legends are used, most explicitly in the first kill of the film when Lisa (Jacinda Barrett) is drugged at a bar and wakes up in a bathtub full of ice and her kidney removed. She tries to escape but the killer decapitates her with a windowpane. The murder of Amy's director of photography Simon (Marco Hofschneider) occurs when Amy films students screaming at midnight to relive stress, which inadvertently covers up the real murder. When Amy asks her crew to fix up an amusement park ride for her horror ride urban legend scene, the killer meets Amy's request by killing two of her crew members.

The urban legends in the film are conflated with "movie magic," causing Amy's remaining friends and even Amy herself to doubt her perception. The film utilizes movie sets and practical effects, such as Amy's crew pranking her early on in the film, to cast doubt on the events taking place. This takes a turn, though, when the crew assembles to view a rough cut of one of the scenes in Amy's film featuring Sandra (Jessica Cauffiel), who gives an atrocious performance take after take. The first reel ends and is replaced by another reel that shows Sandra's actual death at the hands of the killer. Soloman has managed, however, to shoot the death so artfully that the rest of the crew believes it to be part of the film and Sandra's best performance, even though Amy tries to convince them otherwise. Sandra's death is less of an urban legend and more so tied to the history of snuff films. The snuff film has existed in a collective consciousness for some time and supposedly once duped the actor Charlie Sheen into contacting the FBI over what he believed to be a real death captured on film. Upon investigation it turned out to be part of a Japanese horror franchise, *Guinea Pig*.

> Since the early seventies rumors have persisted that murders are routinely filmed and circulated among a shadowy clientele hungry for the most extreme forms of "entertainment." However, time and again, these claims are proven false; or, if a movie is

located, the execution is quickly exposed as a fake.... Though the persistent belief in the existence of snuff suggests pessimism about the human condition, there is something oddly optimistic at the base of the hysteria.[6]

The events that take place in *Urban Legends: Final Cut* are not urban legends told around campfires, harkening back to simpler times or cautioning women against being sexually active; they are stories presented as walking the line between real and fake, depending on what the camera captures. Even though Amy's crew bears witness to Sandra's bloody death, they still assume Amy or someone else shot it as part of Sandra's acting reel. Because *Urban Legends: Final Cut* skews the entire narrative through the lens of Amy's camera, the majority of the characters do not believe the threat is real until it is too late. These characters, like the others of the 1990s cycle, have embraced metafiction and see themselves as commentators and spectators in their own lives rather than as actors with agency.

Professor Soloman, by contrast, offers the exception to that rule, though he is presented as a charming teacher who the students like; he is a man consumed by a sense of rage and injustice that causes him to lash out at Amy.

> SOLOMAN: You think this is what I wanted? FUCK TEACHING!
> AMY: What are you talking about?
> SOLOMAN: When I was a student here, the faculty was deadlocked for the Hitchcock between my film and a piece of shit by Chip Volker. So they asked a guest filmmaker to cast the deciding vote. Taylor Mayfield, documentary hack. In that one vote, your father robbed me of the career I should have had in Hollywood and I've been trapped here ever since. But then, Travis made a brilliant film and I saw my way out but I needed an alibi. Then bingo, you walk in my office with that twisted little movie idea giving me just the cover I needed.

Soloman's career has been a sort of educational purgatory. Denied his own opportunity at greatness, he must watch others pass through the halls of Alpine and on to the real world. While he had never seen urban legends as an opportunity for death and destruction, he needed to use in order to secure his opportunity. The story of the first film being passed on to Amy, triggering her film idea, was just enough. *Urban Legends: Final Cut* is essentially a sequelized version of itself. It is not just a sequel to its predecessor but a story that is caused by the very disbelief in the authenticity of *Urban Legend*'s narrative, which causes it to all begin again. When Amy remarks to Reese that such a story could never really happen and that it is just an urban legend, Amy negates the warnings established in the first film, causing a series of events that leads to her almost-downfall. In the world of *Urban Legend* films, the disbelief cast on the Final Girl both internally and externally leads to the problems of the film. Just as Natalie disbelieved the gang initiation urban legend, which killed Brenda's fiancée, Amy disbelieves the Pendleton story, causing the death of her crew members.

But *Urban Legends: Final Cut* is far more interested in the tropes of filmmaking—particularly those of Alfred Hitchcock. One of Hitchcock's most valued tropes was the MacGuffin, a term he explained in a series of conversations with Francois Truffaut:

> The main thing I've learned over the years is that the MacGuffin is nothing. I'm convinced of this, but I find it very difficult to prove it to others. My best MacGuffin, and by that I mean the emptiest, the most nonexistent, and the most absurd, is the one we used in *North by Northwest*. The picture is about espionage, and the only question that's raised in the story is to find out what the spies are after. Well, during the scene at the Chicago airport, the Central Intelligence man explains the whole situation to Cary Grant, and Grant, referring to the James Mason character, asks, "What does he do?" The counterintelligence man replies, "Let's just say that he's an importer and exporter." "But what does he sell?" "Oh, just government secrets!" is the answer. Here, you see, the MacGuffin has been boiled down to its purest expression: nothing at all![7]

The MacGuffin is essentially nothing but something that some if not all of the characters desire. In *Urban Legends: Final Cut*, the MacGuffin is Travis' film *The Gods of Men*, which sets off the entire series of events. The closest the film gets to exploring its MacGuffin is towards the end when Ottman points the camera at Trevor and Amy after their viewing of Travis' film. Their faces are bored and confused and they are befuddled by how Travis could have done so poorly. This is, of course, revealed to be a fake film. In the nature of teen-driven horrors, the notion of good filmmaking is rarely considered outside of fans of the genre. *Urban Legends: Final Cut* is content to poke fun at what makes a good movie.

Amy is not only Soloman's impediment as a Final Girl, but also a symbol of what was denied to him. Soloman cannot accept the subjectivity of art and film and falls into the trap of his own mind. It is Amy who, throughout the film, grapples with self-doubt, from her perception of events to her own abilities as a filmmaker trying to escape the shadow of her father. In her final and elaborate confrontation with Soloman, Amy regains a sense of control. Not only were her fears and worries founded in something real, she ends the madness while flexing her own knowledge of cinema over the coded pretentiousness of Soloman:

AMY: You filmed Sandra's death.
SOLOMAN: It's called "cinéma vérité." Nice touch, don't you think?
AMY: It was out of focus. But you know what they say; those who can't do, teach.

Urban Legends: Final Cut managed to make a small profit, earning $21 million at the box office on a $14 million production budget.[8] While the film cannot be considered revolutionary within the cycle of 1990s Teen Horror, it did offer a tongue and cheek comment on the nature of filmmaking and criticism. That knowledge of film and access to authority cannot be held by one generation or one perception. Film criticism is an ever-evolving conversation that changes; the only certitude is death for those who cannot accept change.

9

Cutting Class
Disturbing Behavior (1998), *The Faculty* (1998) and *Teaching Mrs. Tingle* (1999)

There is something rotten in the small island town of Cradle Bay. In veteran television director David Nutter's first foray into feature films, 1998's *Disturbing Behavior*, Steve (James Marsden) and his family move to Cradle Bay in hopes of finding a fresh start after the suicide of Steve's older brother Allen. But not everything is as it appears in the beatific town as an insidious clique known as The Blue Ribbons begins to target Steve and his new friends Gavin (Nick Stahl) and Rachel (Katie Holmes).

Disturbing Behavior was produced by MGM, which was looking to move into the teen horror/thriller market by utilizing some of Kevin Williamson's established tropes, popular TV actors (particularly Katie Holmes, who played one of the leads in *Dawson's Creek*) and intertextuality and transparency with film audiences through characters who know what's going to happen. While *Disturbing Behavior* does not focus on the ever-popular pop culture references that were abound in other films, it does call to attention the oppressive castelike system that any high school experience can yield. When Steve and Gavin first meet in the school's cafeteria, Gavin swiftly and easily displays his knowledge of the stakes of this particular high school.

> GAVIN: It's a class system here at C.B. High, Stevie Boy. Check it out. There you got your motorheads, car jocks. All the world's a gasket and a lube job and a pack of Luckys. Music of choice: Posi-traction overdrive, classic rock.... Skynyrd, The Allmans, Bruce. Drug of choice: Beer, Miller Genuine Draft. Keggers can't be choosers.... Over here you have your microgeeks ... nerds, whiz kids and various other bottom feeders. Music of choice: The sound of an Apple PC booting up. Drug of choice: Stephen Hawking's "A Brief History of Time." And a cup of jasmine tea on a Saturday night. Over there you have your skaters. Riffin,' raging kids and their ramp tramps. Baggy pants, Dickie wools, doing 50–50 grinds ... with a gnarly grab finish on a homemade half-

pipe in the woods. Music of choice: The whack of a hacky sack. Drug of choice: Ecstasy, E-tab. Baby, longer lovin' through science.

Disturbing Behavior only made $17 million at the North American box office against its $15 million budget, not including marketing expenses, rendering it as a bizarre cultural artifact. Though it is not lacking in ambition, has an awkward feel to it, as describe by the website *Crave*:

> *Disturbing Behavior* has moments of over the top entertainment, but for the most part it's a plot-hole laden, awkwardly paced film. What it lacks in common sense it tries to make up for with a sincere anti-conformity message, but when the heroes are this drab—or, in the case of Nick Stahl, so ridiculously overwritten—you start to sympathize with the villains a little bit.[1]

The film introduces The Blue Ribbons slowly. After an extended opening credit sequence, which is claustrophobic mixture of sounds and dim lights, the film picks up with Gavin spying on a parked car in the town's Lovers Lane. The couple inside go from making out to fighting, with the young man lamenting, "why would you do that to yourself?" upon catching a glimpse of the young woman's ankle tattoo. Keen to go further, the young woman attempts to perform oral sex on her partner despite his claims of needing his "fluids." After a moment or so of enjoyment, the young man snaps her neck, killing her. The police arrive and cover up the murder. Already this scene sets up a confluence of subversions with a young woman sexually available and willing but dying by the hand of her partner—someone who supposedly loves her. *Disturbing Behavior* does not imply that sex itself is bad but that the expectation or denial of it can be deadly.

On Steve's first day he meets Dr. Caldicot (Bruce Greenwood), whose goal is to slowly transform as many teens as possible into members of the Blue Ribbons—an elite group of students who represent the clean, austere, rarified air of high school popularity. Their aesthetic is coded as decidedly clean cut, 1950s prepsters who favor the yogurt shop and volunteer work over parties. New members are admitted via a microchip inserted into the eye of the transformee and shed whatever previous incarnation and style they favored for that of a true Blue Ribbon. The only problem with the Blue Ribbons is that once sexual arousal enters their minds, they become hostile and violent. While parents have warned of the outside dangers of sex, such as STDs or unwanted pregnancies, rarely have they considered the possibility of violence in sex.

Steve soon bonds with Gavin and Rachel, both of whom are outsiders. While Gavin's parents seem to be cut from the same cloth as Steve's (as seen in their easy admittance into the Blue Ribbons parents' association), Rachel is decidedly "white trash," as Gavin calls her. Gavin's performance as hero is cut short midway through the film, as he is transformed into a Blue Ribbon at his parents' request, and it falls on Steve and Rachel to get to the bottom of Cladicot's scheme.

Rachel is one of a very few characters in 1990s teen horror who are of a decidedly lower class status (the other main examples being Leigh Ann in *Teaching Mrs. Tingle* and Nancy from *The Craft*). Early in the film, via Blue Ribbon vision—a point-of-view shot Nutter uses a handful of times to illustrate a member's sexual arousal—one of the Blue Ribbon members Chug's (A.J. Buckley) sexual arousal upon his catching sight of Rachel is coded as robotic and predatory. While Rachel is viewed as everything the Blue Ribbons are not—lower class, poor, clothed in ripped black outfits, someone who plays by their own rules—Chug's arousal overtakes him. After Rachel rebuffs his invitation to the yogurt shop, he takes his anger out on other teenage delinquents. He eventually corners her in the boiler room of the school, asking her out once again:

CHUG: Will you go out with me?
RACHEL: No.
CHUG: (screaming) WHY NOT?!

He then grabs her, saying, "Come on, Rae-Rae, give up the plate for ol' Chug." It is only after Chug attempts to sexually assault her and she fights him off that the janitor Newberry (William Sadler) comes to her defense by setting off rat traps, which emit a sound that causes the Blue Ribbons' microchips to malfunction. This drives them into a further rage and sets the stage for the final confrontation.

Nutter's portrayal of Rachel's assault is in keeping with some of the tenets that third wave feminism was trying to instill into mainstream culture. Throughout Rachel's introduction, the camera adopts a male gaze through the eyes of Steve, whose attraction to her is almost immediate. The camera slows down as Rachel emerges into the shot, representing not only Steve's attraction, but also the introduction of Katie Holmes as a sexy bad girl—a break from the clean-cut image she was developing on *Dawson's Creek*. The film needs to infer Rachel's sexual viability and, on an intertextual level, to acknowledge the actress' proverbial shedding skin. Despite her sexualization throughout the first half of the film, Rachel is also a verbose character who has opinions and even her own catchphrase, "razor," meaning "cool."

After Rachel flees Chug's assault, Steve goes to her home, determined to get to the bottom of what is going on at the school. When Rachel answers the door, she is wearing a baggy sweater and is far less styled than she was previously, indicating the weight that the assault has already placed on her. Even though Steve and Rachel's relationship becomes romantic shortly after her assault and places her firmly in the normalized "girlfriend" narrative trope, where she out and out supports and helps Steve throughout the rest of the film, her role does highlight the impact and violence of assault, contributing to a mainstream, teen directed conversation about consent.

In tandem with the Rachel and Chug narrative, Steve is dealing with his own would-be Blue Ribbon partner Lorna (Crystal Cass). After Gavin is turned into a Blue Ribbon, Steve attempts to go to his parents for help. He arrives home to discover Lorna waiting for him, claiming that she was tutoring his younger sister. Nutter once again employs the Blue Ribbon vision as Lorna gazes at Steve, sexualizing him. As opposed to Chug's violent reaction toward Rachel, Lorna becomes violent towards herself, slamming her face into a hallway mirror after Steve rebuffs her. While this is the only portrayal of violence from a woman, it is important to note that not only is it against herself but she also tarnishes her most valuable asset as a popular girl—her face.

The discrepancies between Rachel's assault and Steve's rejection of Lorna serve to highlight the vast differences between the acceptance of male and female sexualities, particularly perceived between the lenses of "good" vs. "bad" girl and of "high class" and "trash." While Steve walks away confused but unscathed by his encounter, Rachel becomes withdrawn and ultimately softer—less "razor" than before—and her assault is never spoken of. It is the audience who bears witness to both and sees how little it affects Steve and the increasingly overt effect on Rachel.

The latter half of the film is a cat and mouse game between Caldicot and Steve (with Rachel in tow). Steve and Rachel find documents listing Caldicot's former employer as a mental institution and pay it a visit. There they discover Caldicot not only has a daughter around their age, but that she is interned in the mental institution, a victim of an early Blue Ribbon trial that has left her barely coherent.

Upon their return to Cradle Bay, Steve learns his parents have signed him up to the Blue Ribbon program and he and Rachel are apprehended by the clique. Steve manages to break free and save Rachel before the chip is implanted. As they escape, Chug attacks them and Rachel, through a semi-delirious state, hits Chug in the head, killing him. As they race to the ferry, which is their way off the island, they are thwarted by the Blue Ribbons, who are intent on turning them. Newbury shows up in his pick-up truck, which he has rigged with the sonic rat traps. He sacrifices himself by driving off the side of a cliff, taking the Blue Ribbons with him. As he goes, he screams a line from Pink Floyd's "Another Brick in The Wall (Part II)." Newbury's self-sacrifice is another example of the film's inversion of the lower-status character as a less-than trope. While the Blue Ribbons dismiss Newbury as a "retard," Steve learns that he is far more intelligent and perceptive than anyone thought. It is Newbury who sees through the Blue Ribbons and ultimately destroys them through a simple rat trap device. While the thought process behind the Blue Ribbons is that of creating a purified, rarefied breed of clean-cut students, the foundations of the group are built on classism and elitism, developed from a throwback of America's Greatest Generation. But the Blue Ribbons are unable to cope with rejection, lust, fear or freedom, and when one falls, so do they all.

The film splits into two vastly different endings, both of which are available on the film's DVD. In the theatrical ending, Steve and Calidcot fight and Steve wins by also throwing him off the cliff. Steve then joins Rachel, their friend UV (Chad Donella) and Steve's younger sister on the ferry off the island. The film then cuts to an unruly, inner-city school where a new student teacher is being introduced. It is revealed to be Gavin, who is still under the control of his microchip. The film ends there, setting itself up for a never transpired sequel. In the original/alternate ending, Steve arrives on the ferry and reunites with his friends only to be confronted by Gavin holding a gun. UV shoots Gavin before he can pull the trigger and Gavin dies in the arms of his friends.

Disturbing Behavior's failure to make an impact may not have solely been through faults of the film. MGM was determined to break into the market of upmarket teen films. As Nutter said a year after the film was released:

> I read 300 bad reviews and I agreed with every one of them.... My biggest regret is that I worked with a lot of young actors who had such wonderfully high ideals, and.... I kept telling them that this was going to be something special, this was going to be something different, this one was going to mean something.... [And] then to see them let down that way just makes me sick to my stomach.[2]

According to an article by Patrick Goldstein in the *Los Angeles Times*, *Disturbing Behavior* was part of a trend that many films of this era fell prey to—testing and consumer research.[3] Popularized by the Weinstein brothers at Miramax and Dimension, such films were released not only as entertainment, but also as a consumable product. And part of selling a product to consumers is to refine said product until it fits with the market. After *Disturbing Behavior* wrapped up production, MGM put the film through its paces with the National Research Group (NRG)—essentially the Blue Ribbons of analytical data research. NRG advised MGM to shorten the film's run time, which was originally close to two hours, as their research showed the teen demographic did not like films that were longer than 90 minutes or had too much talking.[4] MGM took this advice and shortened the film from almost two hours to a scant 80 minutes, which renders the film as oddly paced and riddled with plot holes. This turned into a cycle of testing and editing away any element of the film that received negative feedback until MGM was up against the film's release date.

What was released was a film about conformity attempting to consume and overtake any elements of contemporary high school life that were viewed as unclean or unworthy and supplementing it with staid values and morals that were corruptible as long as its victims were able to become sexually aroused. *Disturbing Behavior* may not have had the most subtle hand when dealing out societal critiques, but it did not back away from the notion of forced conformity as lambs being led to the slaughter.

If *Disturbing Behavior* was an attempt by a rival studio to capitalize on the success of the Dimension formula, *The Faculty* (1998) may be the mecca of the said formula. December 1998 was the first Christmas in two years where Dimension did not have a *Scream* film at the ready. Instead Dimension released a script they had purchased and were now fast-tracking after the success of *Scream*.[5] *The Faculty* was originally conceived of by screenwriters David Wechter and Bruce Kimmel, both of whom were primarily known for small TV films, such as *Likely Stories Vol. 2* (1983). In Hollywood's post–*Scream* gold rush, Dimension was optioning and buying scripts and looking to Kevin Williamson to do a polish or update so they felt similar to *Scream* in terms of style, references and characters. If it worked once it could surely work six to seven more times. As Yahoo News reported in October 1997 when the film was announced:

> Dimension Films, the genre film division of Miramax, is hoping to get the film [*The Faculty*] before the cameras in March so it will be available for release in December 1998, which has become the *Scream* slot in the holiday season for the company.[6]

The Weinsteins and Dimension were not shy about marking their territory in the landscape of Hollywood. While older brother Harvey would be immersed in handshaking and special screenings in preparation for Oscar season, which falls over the Holidays, younger brother Bob would be utilizing their prepared marketing scheme in an effort to scare up the biggest box office possible.

Williamson was offered the chance to direct *The Faculty* but turned it down to focus on his pet project, *Teaching Mrs. Tingle* (1999), which had often been resigned to the backburner. Dimension then approached another hot young director, Robert Rodriguez, who was fresh from legitimate indie successes *El Mariachi* (1992) and *Desperado* (1995) and the Miramax/Dimension produced cult-hit *From Dust Till Dawn* (1996). While Rodriguez seemed an odd pick to helm a teen science-fiction alien invasion film, he was part of the beloved stable of auteurs at Miramax and Dimension and knew how to handle the Weinsteins. As Rodriguez said at the time of the film's announcement:

> We're both big fans of the teen horror genre, and I'm really excited to finally work with Kevin [Williamson] after coming close so many times in the last couple of years. Because we both work with Dimension, this becomes a family film.[7]

As far as Dimension was concerned, *The Faculty* was fully an effort by Williamson and Rodriguez, with Wechter and Kimmel relegated to the sidelines and mentioned in name only in the credit of the film, but certainly not in the marketing materials. The press release for the film highlights the collaborative nature of the script with Williamson stating:

> What I attempted to do with Robert's help, is to pay homage to one of my favorite films—*Invasion of the Body Snatchers*. There's something about the theme of conformity versus individuality that rings true in every decade.... It's kind of like *Scream*, you don't have to see all those horror movies as a kid. You count on the screenwriter to have seen them.[8]

The Faculty sees an array of students from different social statuses dubiously befriend each other in an effort to prevent their school, and eventually the world, from being taken over by a parasitic alien race. *The Faculty* is indebted to films like *Invasion of the Body Snatchers* (1956), which is based on Jack Finney's 1954 novel *The Body Snatchers*, as well as John Carpenter's 1982 remake of *The Thing* and makes no attempt to hide or code these influences. It is less overtly indebted to the 1985 John Hughes teen classic *The Breakfast Club*, which sees a group of teens who have nothing in common bond over a forced Saturday in detention.

The Faculty presents a variety of high school archetypes—the jock Stan (Shawn Hatosy), the slacker Zeke (Josh Hartnett), the goth Stokely (Clea DuVall), the popular girl Delilah (Jordana Brewster), the nerd Casey (Elijah Wood) and the new girl Marybeth (Laura Harris). In *The Breakfast Club* Hughes demonstrates the importance of individuality and acceptance (albeit through yet another whitewashed lens) by stripping the characters of the social elements and attributes that confine them to their particular roles and forcing them to interact through boredom. The lesson that each of those characters learns, is that—to paraphrase a line from the film—everyone has the capacity to be a brain, an athlete, a basket case, a princess, and a criminal. Those in *The Faculty* are forced to acknowledge that not only do they care about one another, but their facades of hiding who they are only serve to draw more attention to them as the aliens make greater headway.

It is not an attractive young girl but an adult woman who is at the center of the opening sequence. *The Faculty* begins with the titular faculty operating as normal, offering a view into the mechanics that oppress the teens. The teachers lament to Principal Drake (Bebe Neuwirth) that none of their trips or projects can go forward because all funding and attention has been diverted to the football team. Principal Drake makes the point that they live in a small football town and there is no way around it. Rodriguez takes pains to ensure that the fragility and suffocating nature of this town is shown through these shots as the camera moves slowly in on increasingly tight frames around the teachers, indicating the lack of choice that already exists around them. The teachers leave the school for the night, but Principal Drake goes back because she has forgotten her keys. While retrieving them, she is harassed by Coach Willis (Robert Patrick) who, unbeknownst to Drake, is the first teacher infected. Willis stabs her in the hand coolly, saying, "I always wanted to do that" before she escapes. Drake makes it outside of the school, locking it shut and trapping Willis, only to turn to another teacher, Mrs. Olson (Piper Laurie), who pulls out a pair of scissors and stabs Drake repeatedly, also saying, "I always wanted to do that." From then on, the teachers aren't all right. Suspicions have been raised and the question of who infected Coach Willis will pull the movie forward.

The film then swiftly works to introduce all the main characters with the camera swooping around the high school entrance as Zeke sells drugs, Delilah tells the cheerleaders how to do their hair, Stokely and Stan bump into each other, and Casey gets beat up. Rodriguez utilizes the camera's movement to swiftly infer that while these characters can share the same space, they rarely share anything else. Mary Beth, whose first day at the school is the same day of the aliens' arrival, aids in bringing these misfits together. She is pretty enough so Delilah will take the time to talk to her and Zeke will take an interest in her, and she is intent on befriending the standoffish Stokely.

The only way for the core team to work together is to acknowledge their individual strengths, which Williamson and Rodriguez highlight by having each character bring a piece of knowledge to the table. While eating his lunch alone by the football field, Casey stumbles across a dried-up parasite and not knowing what it is, takes it to his science teacher Mr. Furlong (Jon Stewart). Then, while working with Delilah on an article for the school paper, he witnesses Coach Willis and Mrs. Olson implanting the school nurse (Salma Hayek) with a parasite. Stokley, a science fiction fan, can pull from her knowledge how the aliens function. The drug that Zeke sells on the side is deadly

9. Cutting Class   111

to the aliens. Stan, who has just left the football team to concentrate on his studies, realizes something is wrong in the school. This of course leaves Mary Beth who, at the film's climax, is revealed to be the alien queen. Mary Beth sees her takeover as that of goodness. There is no panic or uncertainty when someone is infected; they merely join the hive mind. In essence, everything that is both wonderful and awful about being a teenager is done away with in favor of blind allegiance. As said in the final battle between Mary Beth and Casey:

> MARY BETH: You know in my world Casey, there were limitless oceans as far as the eye could see. Beautiful, huh? Till it started to dry out. So I escaped, came here, and I met you, all of you, and all of you were different from the others. You were lost and lonely, just like me. And I thought that maybe I could give you a taste of my world. A world without anger, without fear, without attitude.... I can make you a part of something so special Casey, so perfect, so fearless.... Don't you want that, Casey?
> CASEY: I'd rather be afraid!
> MARY BETH: Fine. Alright. Have it your way! 'Cause this is where your land of fiction gets it right: we win. End of story!

While the faculty are not the only villains in the film, or even the main antagonists, their power shows the amount of control and influence teachers or authority figures can yield. When Casey convinces his parents there is something wrong at the school, they arrive with police officers in tow only to see that everything has been covered up. Principal Drake uses this opportunity to infect the police by taking one of them into her office. Drake is also nearly able to get Casey's mother, but Casey quickly agrees to see a therapist to dissuade her from a one-on-one with Drake. As characters ask, "Why us. Why our school?," Casey responds, "If you were going to take over the world, would you blow up the White House *Independence Day* style, or sneak in through the back door?"

When it is revealed that Mary Beth is the Alien Queen, her method of infiltration comes as no surprise. While she is nice, pleasant and attractive, she has no social collateral. She has nothing anyone wants. Not even the loner Stokely wants to be her friend. Mary Beth uses that to gain the trust of the people who might thwart her. She initially infects Coach Willis and leaves him to do the rest while she observes.

While *Disturbing Behavior* may focus on the terror that a single clique can create in a controlled location such as a high school, *The Faculty* focuses on the fear of a crowd. As sociologist Murray Milner describes in his book *American Teenagers, Schools and the Culture of Consumption*:

> Crowds are another example of status groups. Because they are a status group and a subculture they show an enormous concern with lifestyle and acceptance by peers.

Often they engage in behaviors that are highly reminiscent of castes [a dividing system based on social power]. Crowds are often composed of multiple overlapping cliques. In contrast to crowds, cliques are relatively small numbers of individuals who interact with one another regularly. Crowds are a social category, a type of subculture, a reference group, and a status group; cliques are small groups that embody, transmit, and transform such subcultures.[9]

In order to survive, the heroes of *The Faculty* must form a clique in the face of the crowd. Even then it offers little protection as Delilah, Stan and briefly Stokley are turned before Casey kills the alien incarnation of Mary Beth, causing all the parasites to die and their hosts to return to normal.

It is in *The Faculty*'s high-mindedness that most of the complicated thematic problems occur. A voiceover of a newscaster opens the final scene of *The Faculty*, which gives updates on all the characters: Zeke is on the football team living up to his potential and seemingly dating his attractive teacher (Famke Janssen) who he beheaded while she was infected; Stan and Stokley are dating and Stokley is wearing a more traditionally feminine outfit over her preferred black; and Delilah and Casey are dating. The final scene implies that some facets of the press have written off the incidents at this small high school while others are paying close attention. Despite the obvious plot holes (one can assume there is a very nice memorial to Principal Drake after the group, thinking she was the Queen Alien, attacked and disintegrated her body), the more pervasively troubling aspects of *The Faculty* have to do with the individual character resolutions.

The narrative arc of the film rides on a group of teens working together to stop the colonization of their world by an alien species that wants to use the civilians' bodies as hosts. The cost of this is the death of the group members' individuality. The characters ultimately learn that they can and should accept themselves, but that self-acceptance isn't enough for the audience. They are left only with the girlification of Stokley, even though Stan seemed attracted to her throughout the film; the international attention given to Casey, which Delilah delights in; and Zeke's readmission to the all-powerful football team despite his intelligence and ability to learn and create. Stokley's transformation has become particularly problematic, as it implies that her acceptance of herself is one of codified femininity. She goes from a goth nerd loner to a sunny, happy, cardigan-buyer when the right boy notices her. As Timothy Shary writes of this trope:

> Fairy tales like Snow White, and more *Cinderella*, speak to the classic expectation that women need to change to find proper liberation from their gloomy circumstances, and that their makeover must be recognized by men who sweep in to take them away from the troubles around them. Girls' nerd stories operate under virtually identical conditions, with a further emphasis on validation in addition to escape. In the very

visual medium of youth films, this means that boys must realize that nerdy girls are in fact pretty after all. Hence, the adherence to a beauty standard explains the common depiction of female nerds in youth films, as the industry promotes appearance over intelligence, and conformity over individuality.[10]

In *The Faculty*'s final moments, protagonists are given the right to conform. Another film would have shaded this ending with a dark or sinister undertone, but *The Faculty* had products to sell.

Just as these characters have shed the personas they have been saddled with since they began school, their new identities seem linked to even deeper and more ridged identities. Perhaps these are the personas that were always meant for these characters, or perhaps they simply chose another stereotype. Milner writes of stereotypes present throughout high schools everywhere:

> These include norms about beauty, athletic ability, clothes and style, athletic uniforms and letter jackets, speech, body language, collective memories, humor, ritual, popular music, dancing and singing, and space and territory. It is not news to point out that these concerns are often important to adolescents. The important thing to see is how they are all variations on the same theme: seeking status through conformity in order to fit in, that is, to gain a sense of acceptance and belonging. The paradox is that in order to be successful in the "conformity game" students must constantly change, elaborate, and complicate the norms in order to gain a competitive advantage.[11]

The final scene of *The Faculty* presents a return to normality and the characters happily embrace their new roles, achieving to some degree what they were lacking at the beginning of the film. But for a movie about strength in individuality, *The Faculty* comes up short in its last moments with a too-easy ending that still sanctifies socially prescribed roles.

The Faculty would go on to earn just over $40 million at the North American box office against a $15 million production budget—decidedly less than the *Scream* franchise had so far netted Dimension.[12] As film critic Gary Dauphin wrote on the film's release:

> Williamson and Rodriguez don't ruminate on impaled, violent death with much gusto choosing instead to go the half-baked ideological route: the alien's perfectly regimented commercial order squares off against, as what one kid identifies most succinctly, as the freedom to be a D student.[13]

The Faculty's marketing campaign employed many elements that had worked well for *Scream* and *I Know What You Did Last Summer*, the foremost being an attractive cast the target demographic was sure to have at least some passing knowledge of. It featured R&B singer Usher, who has a glorified cameo role as one of Stan's football buddies, and put heartthrob Josh Harnett—fresh off a similar campaign for *Halloween H20* (1998) just months earlier—at the front and center. Marketing also pushed the film's mainstream alternative soundtrack featuring a cover of Pink Floyd's "Another Brick in the Wall, Part II" by alt-rock super group Class of '99, which featured former Rage Against the Machine guitarist Tom Morello. What was unique to *The Faculty*'s campaign was its tie-in with the clothing brand Tommy Hilfiger. Dimension Films partnered with the brand to create an ad campaign featuring the cast of *The Faculty* that ran alongside of the film's ad campaign. The print ads were shot on set and featured in teen magazines and the television commercial was in heavy rotation on the WB network. The commercials are of particular interest as they attempt to make the young stars seem authentic by making them look bored in front of the camera as an off-screen male voice yells that they need more camera, lights etc. The commercial culminates with Clea DuVall asking the camera, "What do you want me to do?" Then Josh Harnett falls over, stands back up and takes off his Tommy shirt. The music changes and all the cast appear informally hanging out in their branded Tommy gear.[14] The implication is clear; while there may be a lot of adults behind the scenes, the Tommy Hilfiger brand is something that even the cool, exasperated kids wear. It was during this period in the mid to late 1990s that the Hilfiger brand tried to dominate the teen market. They did so particularly through their Make a Scene campaign, which featured rap and R&B performers.[15]

The Faculty feels like the beginning of the end for the 90s teen explosion. It was too codified, too commercial and too consumable. While the pedigree for the film both in front of and behind the camera was almost untouchable (particularly at the time), *The Faculty* proved that some formulas have a very brief shelf life.

Teaching Mrs. Tingle is the rare film that sees institutionalized education and pedagogy nearly destroyed by a war between two women. Originally titled *Killing Mrs. Tingle* before the Columbine shootings, *Teaching Mrs. Tingle* is 1990s horror impresario Kevin Williamson's first and only feature film as director and screenwriter. The film had a long gestation process while it was shopped around Hollywood. Its strange black comedy with thriller elements did not sit well with many executives. After *Scream*, Miramax was keen to give Williamson as many opportunities as possible with several caveats along the way. *Teaching Mrs. Tingle* was always going to be made and made by Dimension Films, but they first needed Williamson's completed *Scream 2* script and polishes and producer credits on *The Faculty* and *Halloween H20*. Finally, on August 11, 1999, *Teaching Mrs. Tingle* hit theaters. The film would ultimately be the first major disappointment for Dimension Films of this cycle, grossing only $8.9 million on a $13 million production budget.[16] Critics' opinions of the film were decidedly unfavorable, with *Variety* calling it "a pat, hollow exercise."[17] While the film has faults, it does ambitiously tackle questions of how and why some people are chosen for greatness and others are predetermined to fail.

The film follows three high school seniors, Leigh Ann (Katie Holmes), her best friend Jo (Marisa Coughlan) and the slacker heartthrob Luke (Barry Watson), as they cross the malevolent force in their high school, Mrs. Tingle (Helen Mirren), shortly before graduation. Leigh Ann's sole goal in the final days and weeks of her high school career is to get the top GPA, allowing her to become class valedictorian, which will secure her the scholarship needed to attend college. The film emphasizes Leigh Ann's lower-class status, showing her single mother (Lesley Ann Warren) working at a diner to support them both. Leigh Ann's closest ally is her best friend Jo who dreams of escaping to Los Angeles after graduation to pursue her acting career. Jo's dream is so open-ended that it allows her to focus on helping Leigh Ann however she can. The only thing standing in Leigh Ann's way is the cruel and vindictive history teacher Mrs. Tingle. Mrs. Tingle is clearly established as a threat and nuisance to not only the students but also to the faculty. As Leigh Ann presents her final history project, a leather-bound journal written by Leigh Ann detailing the life of a young woman trying to survive the Salem witch trials, Mrs. Tingle cruelly mocks her and dismisses her project. The only way Leigh Ann can beat the stuck-up, upper-class achiever Trudie (Liz Stauber), who has a slight grade advantage, is to ace the final exam. Luke crashes Leigh Ann and Jo's quality time, informing them that he stole Mrs. Tingle's final history exam, giving Leigh Ann the edge she needs. Mrs. Tingle appears and blames Leigh Ann for the stolen exam and threatens to expose and expel the three of them the following day when the Principal (Michael McKean) returns. Leigh Ann, Jo and Luke attempt to appeal to Mrs. Tingle by going to her house that evening only to have Mrs. Tingle further threaten them. The threats escalate into a physical attack from both sides that sees Mrs. Tingle knocked unconscious. The three teens decide to tie her up and hope that they can make their case to her. The rest of the film details the days that follow, with Mrs. Tingle bound to her bed while Leigh Ann, Jo and Luke attempt to keep their plan afloat while Mrs. Tingle attempts to manipulate and disband the group.

Teaching Mrs. Tingle provides an interesting and unique entry into not only the 1990s Teen Horror Cycle but also into teen films in general, as it details the effects of a bad teacher. Most films about student-teacher relationships tend to focus on the "good" teacher—the kind that inspires students to achieve their personal bests inside and outside of the school system. These teachers appear most notably in films like *Dead Poets Society* (Peter Weir,

1989) and *Dangerous Minds* (John N. Smith, 1995).[18] These films work to show the faults within the system of regimented education that can't possibly work for every student, validating individuality within a system that abhors it. As Mary M. Dalton details in her article in *Mirror Images: Popular Culture and Education*:

> Over the last fifty years, Hollywood films have repeatedly presented codes that constitute schools as sites of limited resistance staged by students and, sometimes, by a progressive teacher or two. Mostly, these good teachers are constructed as counterpoints to callous administrators and "bad" teachers who are either scared of students, bored by them, or eager to control them. Schools are constructed as spaces where the disconnect between what matters to students (and the good teachers who champion them) and what matters to faculty is a profound rupture and is not sutured in any convincing way by the final frames of most of the films.[19]

Teaching Mrs. Tingle subverts this trope and subgenre by aligning every character as threatened by and ultimately against Mrs. Tingle. An early scene shows her striding over to Principal Potter and asking about the status of her request for research materials, which Principal Potter informs her the school will not be able to fill because of budgetary restrictions. Mrs. Tingle asks him to look at the budget once more. Before she leaves for class, they have the following interaction:

> MRS. TINGLE: Oh, by the way, Happy Birthday.
> PRINCIPAL POTTER: It's not my birthday Mrs. Tingle.
> MRS. TINGLE: No, not your natal birthday, the AA one. You've been sober, how long is it now?
> PRINCIPAL POTTER: Four years.
> MRS. TINGLE: There! I knew it was this week. Me and dates, you know, that's the curse of being a history teacher. Well congratulations, that's quite an accomplishment. Just think, not one sip of alcohol in over four years, that's almost unbelievable.

As she leaves, it is not only clear that Principal Potter is shaken by the interaction but that Mrs. Tingle knows everyone's secrets. As several of the students present their oral projects, she gleefully takes them to task as well, as seen in this exchange with Luke:

> LUKE: [Luke rises from his desk, walks up to the front of the classroom and places a rock on Mrs. Tingle's desk] Plymouth Rock.
> MRS. TINGLE: Your work, Mr. Churner, is very reminiscent of a young man who sat in that same chair some 20 years ago. He, too, had the words "No future" printed on his forehead. Do give your father my best.

In many teen movies, the "bad" teacher is presented as one of several narrative obstacles the protagonists must overcome[20] but is rarely the site of horror and tumult. *Teaching Mrs. Tingle*'s narrative centers around one woman's desire to crush another woman. While the film does obliquely hint at reasons for Tingle's motive, it is never explicitly stated. Tingle's apparent central modus operandi stems from the very subject she teaches: history. As she proclaims rhetorically in the film, "Haven't you learned by now that history always repeats itself?" A woman of Tingle's stature and age within this relatively small town has granted her a front seat to the town's goings on and dirty dealings. She is beholden to all the things that have come to pass already and cannot foresee a future that is unfamiliar; she cannot see Leigh Ann advancing beyond her mother's status nor Luke advancing beyond his father's. This generation, for Tingle, is doomed to repeat the histories of their parents. Leigh Ann is the one who is actively trying to break through this barrier through legitimate means by working for the best grades. The film opens in Leigh Ann's bedroom, which is decorated with all her achievements, awards and pictures of her and Jo. While in almost any other case this kind of décor would seem shrine-like, Williamson takes pains to show the impact of Leigh Ann's mother on her. While her mother is a kind woman who wants Leigh Ann to succeed, she also functions as a ghost of Christmas past and present—a constant reminder of what Leigh Ann is up against—and her prizes serve as a reminder of the hard work she has put in to relieve herself of her supposed future.

Williamson set out early on to develop a thematic framework for the film, drawing most notably from Leigh Ann's own history project about the Salem Witch Trials. The witch trials of 1692 and 1693 have provided some of the most fruitful and varied historical and artistic representations. In the winter of 1692, the young girls of the Salem Township began accusing others of being witches, leading to many trials and the deaths of 22 people. The trials were most famously adapted by Arthur Miller in his play *The Crucible* (1953), which he wrote as an allegory to the then-current McCarthy trials (an endeavor to weed communists out of Hollywood). Since Miller's play achieved great acclaim and is still produced to this day, the term "witch hunt" has become synonymous with moral panic that seeks to excluded targeted people from a society or a community.

From the early scene in which Tingle mocks Leigh Ann's journal, the two women trade barbs about the use of the world irony:

LEIGH ANN: It's completely factual; she was burned at the stake.
MRS. TINGLE: Always the victim, aren't we, Ms. Watson?
LEIGH ANN: Well there are certain similarities between society today and seventeenth century Salem. I guess that would be the irony of it all.
MRS. TINGLE: Irony is the opposite of what is or might be expected. For example, if Ms. Watson was expecting an A on her history project, she might find the actual result to be rather ironic.

Leigh Ann's implication in this exchange is that humanity seems incapable of learning from its past, thus repeating multiple cycles of the same narratives over and over again, which is a loose interpretation of the word "irony." Through most of the film, while Tingle is tied to her bed, she takes great delight in chiding and mocking Leigh Ann for being the smartest girl in school but not understanding the definition of irony.

Williamson keeps the Salem Witch Trials and burning as punishment themes present throughout the film, such as when Mrs. Tingle tells the teens that even sometimes the innocent burn and when she cries out that they will "burn" for knocking Mrs. Tingle unconscious. What is perhaps most ironic and odd about the premise of the entire film is that no one accused of witchcraft in Salem or New England was burned. Burning was a central European method of dispatching witches most notably in Germany and France in the 1400s. In the United Kingdom and eventually New England, burning witches was against the law, so they were hanged instead.[21]

When the settlers were colonizing it was a common belief that the Devil walked among and tempted them, and if an individual was in league with the Devil he or she could renounce him and his powers and still save his or her soul and place in the community. As historian and author Stacy Schiff writes in her books *The Witches: Salem, 1692*:

> In isolated settlements, in dim, smoky, firelit homes, New Englanders lived very much in the dark, where one listens more accurately, feels most passionately, imagines more vividly, where the sacred and the occult thrive. Their fears and fancies differed little from ours, even if the early American witch has as much in common with our pointy hatted crone as Somali pirates do with Captain Hook. Their dark, however, was a very different dark. The sky over New England was crow black, pitch-black, Bible black, so black it could be difficult at night to keep to the path.[22]

The accused witches in Salem were hanged because they did not repent because they had done nothing wrong. The community within Salem that allowed these atrocities to occur did so because they were scared of being accused next in the free-for-all madness. *Teaching Mrs. Tingle* attempts to show Leigh Ann as a competent and dedicated student whose dream is to become a journalist. It fails to back that up, though, by allowing this factual error, which historian Mrs. Tingle never corrects, to overtake the narrative.

Ultimately, *Teaching Mrs. Tingle* is about old versus new narratives and history. It shows a new generation attempting to forge its own path while Mrs. Tingle, representing old school values, prevents anyone from climbing above their own station. In essence, it is a form of preventative class warfare. Williamson codes the film by distinctive choices in music. When the film centers around Leigh Ann, Luke and Jo and when they gain ground in the battle against Mrs. Tingle, bright pop songs play, making the film to feel youthful. Whenever Mrs. Tingle dominates the screen, the film is overlain with a more traditional orchestral score similar to that which introduces the Wicked Witch of the West in *The Wizard of Oz* (Victor Fleming, 1939). The most jarring and effective use of the distinction is in a scene showing students arriving to school to then-popular band Eve 6's song *Tongue Tied*. The credits roll on top of the image and as Kevin Williamson's name appears as writer and director, the song cuts and is replaced by the aforementioned intimidating orchestral score as the camera shows fearful students getting out of Mrs. Tingle's way. From there, as elaborated by the history class presentations, Mrs. Tingle is a force that destroys fun and youthfulness. She is the antithesis of the ambition and ambiguity of teenhood. The more the film revolves around Mrs. Tingle, the more the orchestral score is used. The few times the film does integrate pop songs is when Leigh Ann and Luke act on their feelings for each other and at the end, after Mrs. Tingle is fired by Principal Potter and the film reveals Leigh Ann as valedictorian and the three friends happily walk away from high school.

The film complicates itself after the trio takes Mrs. Tingle hostage; a love triangle between the three is established, Mrs. Tingle is revealed to be carrying on a relationship with the school coach (Jeffery Tambour) and Jo preforms an odd one-woman version of *The Exorcist* (William Friedkin, 1973). Every time Leigh Ann reenters Mrs. Tingle's sight, Mrs. Tingle throws a literary or historical reference at her; at one point she calls her Leigh Ann Ophelia. The references for the teens are pop cultural, rather than literary or historically, based. Mrs. Tingle's references, though perhaps highbrow, date her and alienate her from the demographic of the film. While she is and represents everything that is holding the next generation back, she is also hopeless beyond her expiry date.

The film ends with Mrs. Tingle attempting to kill Leigh Ann but instead wounding Leigh Ann's competition, and Mrs. Tingle's preferred student, Trudie. This is the scene that Principal Potter walks in on, allowing him to proclaim, "Mrs. Tingle, I have waited 20 years to tell you this—you're fired."

The resolution to the film is complicated at best; no one mentions Leigh Ann's flawed and completely historically inaccurate final project, the fact that the trio committed several illegal acts or Luke's punishment for instigating all of this by stealing the history exam. The film is all too happy to shut down Mrs. Tingle and her backwards ways without questioning how the events of the film came to be.

Teaching Mrs. Tingle is ultimately an exploration of a past that the adult generation has become stymied in. Their pasts are their present. It is up to the new generation to constantly redefine and examine their potentials without a plan or firm guidance, sometime at the cost of their own morals.

10

Re-Generation
Halloween H20 (1998) and *The Rage: Carrie 2* (1999)

Halloween H20 is about a generational divide, a divide between characters and a divide between film styles. It is a film that is a servant to two masters: John Carpenter's 1978 slasher trope-building *Halloween* and Wes Craven's *Scream*, in which characters reference Carpenter's narrative and the inherent problems within it. As with the majority of the teen slasher films of the late 1990s, Dimension Films played their hand in the film's execution. By the time *Scream* reinvigorated the slasher genre in 1996, the *Halloween* franchise was on its last legs. After the original's success, a sequel was made. It takes place on Halloween and Laurie Strode, the survivor/Final Girl of the first film, is taken to the hospital for care. The mental asylum escapee Michael Myers is hunting her, and a radio report clues him in to Laurie's whereabouts. The rest of the film follows Michael as he tries in vain to kill Laurie, who is revealed to be his sister. Dr. Loomis (Donald Pleasence), who treated Michael and saved Laurie in the first film, is on hand to come to Laurie's aid once again. The film ends with Dr. Loomis blowing up both himself and Michael as Laurie reaches safety; the final images of the film are of Michael falling down, consumed in flames.

While Jamie Lee Curtis went on to have a successful Hollywood career in films like *Trading Places* (John Landis, 1983), *A Fish Called Wanda* (Charles Crichton, 1988) and *True Lies* (James Cameron, 1994), the *Halloween* franchise progressed without her or Laurie Strode. *Halloween 3: Season of the Witch* (Tommy Lee Wallace, 1982) moved away entirely from the scourge of Michael Myers, focusing instead on a small Californian town run by Irish witches plotting to kill children on Halloween. In 1988, after the dismal failure of the third film (though it has gone on to find success as a cult class more recently) and with the rising popularity of Jason Voorhees and Freddy Krueger, producer Moustapha Akkad decided to resurrect Michael. *Halloween 4: The Return of Michael Myers* (Dwight H. Little, 1988) shepherded in a new mythology upheld by two sequels that saw Michael face down the orphaned daughter, Jamie Lloyd (Danielle Harris), of Laurie, who apparently died in a car crash. The franchise landed with Dimension Films in the early 1990s and Bob Weinstein oversaw the utterly bizarre sixth film in the series, *Halloween: The Curse of Michael Myers* (Joe Chappelle, 1995). At this point, the mythology surrounding Michael Myers now involved a Druid cult, a Man in Black, green goo and a very young Paul Rudd. In short, the film was miles, if not oceans, away from the creeping sinister dread that made the first film so effective. After *Scream*'s success, Bob and Dimension Films began to turn their attention to the franchise, which Jamie Lee Curtis expressed interest in returning to.[1]

There had been a plan for *Halloween 7* before *Scream*. Dimension Films had hired Robert Zappia, a young screenwriter whose previous credits included an episode of *Home Improvement* in 1993 and a few episodes of the short-lived television series *Thunder Alley* in 1994 and 1995. Zappia's initial plans for *Halloween 7* had Michael Myers attacking a preppy boarding school. When Curtis expressed an interest in returning to her breakout role, Dimension looked to *Scream* writer Kevin Williamson to do a pass at the script, making Laurie central to the plot. The Writers Guild of America deemed that Williamson's pass had not been enough work to render him sole author of it. Dimension, keen to add the tagline "From the Creator of *Scream*" to anything they could, offered Zappia a hefty amount of money to share a screenwriting credit with Williamson. Zappia declined and Williamson settled for an Executive Producer credit on the film.[2]

In another attempt to capitalize on *Scream*'s success, Dimension used much of composer Marco Beltrami's original *Scream* score (as well as some sections of his score for another Dimension film *Mimic*) in the final cut of the film; this, on top of utilizing John Carpenter's iconic original theme song from the first *Halloween* film over the title credits, led to composer John Ottman's original score being used sparingly throughout the film.[3] Ottman, however, would get the chance to put his own stamp on another film in this cycle in 2000 with *Urban Legends: Final Cut*.

Halloween H20 therefore exists in dialogue with its original film and the new trends and tropes set out in *Scream*. As the title suggests, *Halloween H20* picks up a few days before Halloween in 1998, which is the twentieth anniversary of Laurie's first encounter with Michael. The opening scene follows Nurse Marion Chambers (Nancy Jane Stephens, reprising her role from *Halloween* and *Halloween II*), a former colleague of Dr. Loomis, as she arrives home.

10. Re--Generation

The front door to her house is ajar, so she goes to the neighbor's house to call the police and enlists the teenagers next door, Jimmy (Joseph Gordon-Levitt) and his friend Tony (Branden Williams), for help. The two young men check out the house, notice her office has been ripped apart, steal some beer, and assure Marion that the coast is clear. Marion goes into her office to discover that the file on Laurie Strode is missing. She runs next door for help once again only to find the two boys dead. She returns to her home, only to be killed by Michael as the police arrive.

The film then leaves its initial setting of Illinois and transports to California, where Laurie Strode, now using the name Keri Tate, is the headmaster of a private school. She lives near the campus with her son John (Josh Harnett) who has just turned 17. John is his mother's primary caretaker and it is soon revealed that not only does Laurie suffer from rampant PTSD, but she is also a functioning alcoholic. John begs his mother to let him go on an overnight school trip to Yosemite National Park, but Laurie refuses, as she prefer he stay close to her—especially on Halloween. While John is all too aware of his mother's past, he tells her to let it go, assuring his mother that his uncle is dead.

John meets up with his friends Charlie (Adam Hann-Bryd) and Sarah (Jodi Lynn O'Keefe) who are on the fence about going to Yosemite themselves. John's girlfriend Molly (Michelle Williams) reveals that because her father has not paid her tuition for the semester, the school is preventing her from going, and the friends plan on celebrating Halloween while they have the campus to themselves. Meanwhile Laurie must contend with her nosy but well-intentioned secretary Norma (Janet Leigh) and her supportive boyfriend and school guidance counselor Will (Adam Arkin), both of whom are unaware of Laurie's true identity and the trigger-inducing nature of this holiday for her. After a heated confrontation with John, Laurie accepts that she must let some things in her life go and gives him permission to go on the trip. John and his friends, however, follow through on their plan for an intimate dinner party at the school and Laurie and Will enjoy a quiet evening nearby. Laurie reveals her true identity to Will, who is surprised but ultimately understanding. This conversation handily introduces Michael, who arrives on the almost deserted campus and attacks John and his friends. Charlie, Sarah and Will are killed in the ensuing rampage, while the security guard Ronny (LL Cool J) is accidently wounded by Will right before he is killed by Michael. John, Molly and Laurie have the opportunity to escape, but Laurie sends the two teens to get help while she goes back to the school and confronts her brother. After a raucous battle, Laurie seemingly kills Michael. As the ambulance is about to drive away with his body, Laurie highjacks the vehicle and drives away. She purposefully crashes the car and the wreckage pins Michael to a tree. Laurie, holding an axe, pauses for a moment as Michael silently reaches out his arms to her pleadingly. She brings the axe down on his neck, decapitating him.

The film's debt to *Scream* can be most clearly seen through its treatment of Laurie. Her role in the film is neither a cameo nor an ineffectual adult; she is part of a two-part narrative between herself and Michael. Without Laurie, the story does not function. And *Halloween H20* does not go the way of other popular slasher sequels such as *Friday the 13th Part 2* (Steve Miner, 1981) or *A Nightmare on Elm Street: Dream Warriors* (Chuck Russell, 1987), which sees the franchise's original Final Girls return only to be dispatched by the monster, making way for a new cast to take over the fight. While John and Molly are clearly the central characters in the younger generation narrative, they are ultimately targets for Michael and motivation for Laurie, driving the whole film towards the climactic battle between the siblings.

Laurie in *Halloween H20* shares many of the character traits that are held by Sidney Prescott at the beginning of *Scream*. Laurie is not a carefree teenager, nor a carefree adult woman. She is in a position of authority but is barely holding it together. Sidney in the same way is trying to act the part of a normal teen while dealing with the pain of her mother's violent death. The 1990s Teen Horror Cycle particularly situates trauma as existing inside the narratives of the film, impacting the characters as they move through the preordained role. In doing so, the creators of the films (Kevin Williamson in particular) acknowledge the omnipresent role that trauma can play in one's life. The portrayal of trauma in these films is not a deeply mystifying trait but rather a tangible one that feels accessible to the audience. These films deal with the consequences of violence, the lasting impact traumatic events can have on survivors, and the idea that sometimes survival is not enough.

As *Halloween H20* introduces Laurie and her narrative after the opening kill, a camera roams through a deserted building, eventually revealed to be the school where Laurie now works, Hillcrest Academy. The camera adopts the roaming gaze that Carpenter used so expertly in the original film as a young Michael brutally murders his older sister. In *H20* the gaze of the camera breaks when Laurie wakes up screaming and the earlier sequence is revealed to be a dream. In this sequence, it is established that Laurie's trauma has in part adopted her brother's gaze, indelibly linking them and offering her no escape. *Halloween H20* does not explore Michael's psychosis as a familial symptom (as Rob Zombie would explore in his *Halloween* reboots) but rather something that Laurie can access, coding her trauma as filmic.

Halloween H20 is also beholden to its brethren not only through iconography and some of the mythology of Michael Myers, but also through the tropes laid out in other popular slashers that came after the original. *Halloween H20* provides a set of characters—particularly John, Molly, Sarah and Charlie—as potential knife-fodder for the silent and seemingly unkillable Michael Myers. The film ensures Michael can get access to his signature weapon, a kitchen knife, and that the climactic battle and previous kills can happen in a secluded, lowly populated environment. There is also a strong tie to past through the character of Norma, played by Jamie Lee Curtis' mother, Janet Leigh, who played one of cinema's most enduring and iconic characters in *Psycho* (Alfred Hitchcock, 1960), Marion Crane. Marion was Norman Bates' first victim in the film: a young woman who stopped in the wrong motel after stealing a large sum of money. The audience never finds out what happens to the money, as Marion is killed in the shower by the motel owner's mother. *Halloween H20* gleefully trots out Leigh for several early scenes in which she drives the car Marion drove in *Psycho*, talking about her maternal instincts to Laurie and lamenting that the water in the girls shower room is blocked up. The film even hands Norma one of the iconic lines from *Halloween* when Laurie bumps into the town sheriff before Michael Myers descends on her and her friends and the sheriff laughs the incident off saying, "It's Halloween, everyone's entitled to one good scare." Norma rattles off the same line to Laurie before she leaves the campus for the night, wishing her boss a Happy Halloween.

While *Halloween H20* does not explicitly allow the characters to engage with a horror film by flexing their film knowledge, it heavily alludes to such knowledge. In a brief scene in Sarah and Molly's dorm room, the two watch *Scream 2* as Will arrives to check on them. For Laurie, it is implied she has not seen horror films, nor is she even aware of them, because she has lived one. While Michael still menaces in the same fashion he did 20 years ago and has had 20 years to stew on whatever drives his violent tendencies, Laurie has had 20 years to repeatedly relive that night and wonder what she might have done differently.

Halloween H20 develops its parallels of existing in the shadow of *Scream* and *Halloween* by harkening back to specific scenes from the original. Early in the film, Laurie is teaching an English class where Mary Shelley's *Frankenstein* is being discussed. Molly finds her attention waning as she gazes out the window. There she catches a glimpse of Michael standing outside the school gates. It is only when Laurie, the teacher, calls on Molly to share her thoughts on *Frankenstein* that Molly's focus returns to the classroom. This scene is almost identical to one of the original film in which teenage Laurie is distracted by Michael appearing outside her classroom, the spell only broken when the teacher calls on her. In *Halloween H20* Molly expresses that Victor Frankenstein should have done something about the monster sooner, before it killed those closest to Victor. Molly elaborates that Victor acted because he "had nothing left to lose" after the monster killed everyone Victor loved. In *Halloween*, Laurie's teacher asks her about the differences in the philosophy of fate; Laurie replies that destiny or fate can been seen as a force or an element. In the original franchise of the film, Michael was a force of destiny and of nature; he could never be stopped and Laurie's fate was tied to his. In *Halloween H20*, Laurie is allowed to change her fate, saving those she loves before the monster can kill them. These ties to her son, friends and colleagues keep her from turning into a monstrous force of destruction and hubristic recklessness like Dr. Frankenstein.

The mitigating factor in Laurie's life is her son John. While well-intentioned, John grows increasingly frustrated at his mother who he tends to and protects but who ultimately prevents him from achieving any kind of selfhood beyond her. Laurie is traumatized by the events that occurred decades earlier but John only knows of them second hand. He cannot truly empathize with Laurie's pain, though his sympathy allows him to function as yet another coping mechanism for her. Ironically, it is the independence that John longs for that puts him in harm's way. While John attempts to drive the narrative of the film forward, he is ultimately thwarted by the return of his uncle and is forced to experience the same trauma Laurie deals with. John rhetorically asks Laurie what Michael Myers is waiting for to return, trying to prove to his mother that Michael is long dead. Laurie realizes later in the film, on some level, that Michael was waiting for the next generation to turn 17—the same age Laurie was in the first two films. John's narrative is what ultimately pushes Laurie to confront her brother. After sending John and Molly away to get help, she closes the gates to the school and destroys the security box to prevent the gate from reopening, forcing the siblings to face each other one on one. As John Kenneth Muir describes this transition:

> She must stop Michael before he kills her seventeen-year-old boy, as he killed her best friends back in 1978 and as he killed her boyfriend Will in 1998. This is important because the innocent teenager who believed that fate had selected one destiny for her makes an opposite conclusion in adulthood. Laurie finally moves past the crisis of her youth and takes fate (and an axe) into her own hands.[4]

Ultimately, *Halloween H20* is Laurie's story, filled out by extra characters who act as her mirror in confronting what she has lost in the 20 years since the original film. *Halloween H20* is also the first and only film of a previously developed major franchise to refocus and reorient on the story of the Final Girl, offering her a conclusion as well as closure to her narrative. The other major horror franchises such as *Friday the 13th*, *A Nightmare on Elm Street*, *Texas Chainsaw Massacre* and even *Halloween* itself would re-emerge in the new millennium in the glut of horror remakes that became omnipresent for a brief period of time. *Halloween H20*'s success is heightened by the inclusion of the series' original Final Girl who found legitimacy through Hollywood's interest in what happens when a woman confronts the very thing that has refused to let her rest. In *Halloween H20* Laurie Strode finds peace and no longer views her fate as preordained force.

The Rage: Carrie 2 (1999) is a rather bold entry into the Teen Horror Cycle of the 1990s. It borrows some of the blueprints from its beloved originals—the Stephen King book *Carrie* and the 1976 film adaptation by Brian De Palma—but reorients it to reflect the circumstances of its own decade. *The Rage: Carrie 2* had problems from the get-go. After two years in development, the film went into production in early 1998. After just two weeks, its original director Robert Mendel quit over creative differences and was replaced by Katt Shea,[5] best known for films like *Streets* (1990) and *Poison Ivy* (1992). *The Rage: Carrie 2* begins with a heavy nod to the original. A young girl sits in the middle of a room asking her mother to play with her while the mother paints the room red, muttering, "You can't have her," repeatedly. Soon the police arrive and take the mother away to an asylum. Before authorities take the daughter to foster care, she runs back into the house, slamming all the doors with the power of her mind.

The film catches up with the girl, now a teenager, Rachel (Emily Bergl). She has one close friend, Lisa (Mena Suvari), who reveals that she lost her virginity that weekend and while she doesn't want to say to whom, Lisa seems pleased. It is revealed that Lisa slept with Eric (Zachery Ty Bryan), one of the football players at their school who plays a game with the rest of the team in which points are amassed for sleeping with different girls; the prettier and cooler they are, the more points are received. When Eric rejects Lisa, she kills herself, and the only evidence of her tryst with Eric lies in a roll of film that Rachel was going to develop for Lisa. While developing the film, Rachel deduces that Lisa and Eric were involved and informs the school guidance counsellor Sue Snell (Amy Irving, reprising her role from the original). The police intend to bring statutory rape charges against Eric, as Lisa was a minor. Rachel soon connects with one of the football players Jesse (Jason London) who wants no part in his friends' game and feels an attraction to Rachel. In the midst of this, Sue, who has seen glimmers of Rachel's power, takes Rachel to the ruin of the high school that was destroyed in the first film and begs Rachel to seek help from the scientific community to control her powers. Rachel refuses to be a "guinea pig" for the science community and leaves.

Sue visits Rachel's mother, who reveals to Sue that Carrie White and Rachel share the same father.

The popular high school cheerleader Tracy (Charlotte Ayanna), who intended to date Jesse, targets Rachel. While Jesse and Rachel continue to see each other and fall in love, Tracy and some of the other jocks hatch a plan to bring Rachel down. After Jesse helps the team to a big victory on the football field, both Rachel and Jesse are taken to the after party separately. While the group initially seems happy to have Rachel there, they quickly turn on her, broadcasting to the whole party a video of Jesse and Rachel having sex. This triggers Rachel's powers and she kills everyone, including Sue Snell who arrived at the party in an attempt to help Rachel. Jesse arrives on the scene after most of the carnage has been completed and tries to convince Rachel that he loves her. She spares him, throwing him from the now burning house. The final scene shows Jesse—a year out from the incident and at college—still haunted by Rachel.

The original *Carrie* deals explicitly with female power and how it is used in a high school setting. As the original author Stephen King elaborates:

> *Carrie* is largely about how women find their own channels of power, and what men fear about women and women's sexuality ... which is only to say that, writing the book in 1973 and only out of college three years, I was fully aware of what Women's Liberation implied for me and the others of my sex. The book is, in its more adult implications, an uneasy masculine shrinking from a future of female equality. For me, Carrie White is a sadly misused teenager, an example of the sort of person whose spirit is so often broken for good in that pit of man and woman eaters that is your normal suburban high school. But she's also Woman, feeling her powers for the first time and, like Samson, pulling down the temple on everyone in sight at the end of the book.[6]

If *Carrie* is about the corruption of female power from the bullies to Carrie herself, then *The Rage: Carrie 2* is about misogyny. The pack of boys who establish their elitism through their prowess on the football field continue to shepherd the herd through their proliferation of female sexuality. While the boys in the group continually repeat that the sex is consensual (though under false pretenses, as the young women are merely points to them) they shame those same women for engaging in it. While social status was at the core of *Carrie*, sexuality is the root of *The Rage: Carrie 2*. The film explores the constant negotiation between young adults for physical and emotional intimacy that paints a haunting portrait of the abuse running rampant and unfettered through the school.

The points based game the film captures was not developed out of thin air but was taken from a very real scandal that took place in Lakewood, California in 1993. As the *New York Times* reported:

The tale of the Spur Posse in some ways sounds like an old story about bad boys and fast girls, about athletes who can do no wrong and the people who fawn over them. But it comes as codes of sexual conduct are colliding with boys-will-be-boys mores and as unemployment and broken marriages are troubling the still waters of this piece of suburbia southeast of Los Angeles.[7]

The statistics concerning rape and sexual assault in high schools is terrifying to say the least. According to the Center for Disease Control 30 percent of female rape victims are between 11 and 17. The findings of the Justice Department reveal that 20 percent of young women between 14 and 17 have faced sexual assault or attempted sexual assault.[8] And that is simply the data that has been reported; due to the stigma of sexual assaults and violence, many cases go unreported. While *The Rage: Carrie 2* deals with the bizarre, ritualistic game that only some of the football players participate in, it is enough to cause the death of Lisa, sending Rachel right into their fold. It becomes clear to the members of this group that their participation not only yields social status, but also power over young women, keeping them subservient and in line. The most telling moment of this is when they use the sex tape of Rachel and Jesse, which neither of them had knowledge of, to shame and mock Rachel. Similarly to Carrie, Rachel is teased with the possibility of inclusion and acceptance for who she is and who she dates only to be laughed at in the end. Shea uses kinetic camera movements to mimic Rachel's confusion and eventual rage. Earlier, the film highlights Rachel's tattoo, which she shares with Lisa, of a heart surrounded by thorns. This is an easy metaphor for Rachel's own prickly exterior, shown in the classroom when she says, "I don't believe in love," to which the teacher responds, "Then you've got bigger problems than passing this class." When Rachel channels her powers to get revenge on everyone at the party, the heart tattoo begins to throb and the thorns animate and spread all over her body creating warrior-like markings.

When Timothy Shary talks about *The Rage: Carrie 2* in his book *Generation Multiplex* he describes it as a "tough girl film":

> A distinct and interesting category of the youth delinquent subgenre is the tough girl film, in which one or more girls stake out their identity through rebellious acts. Because most youth delinquency films dwell on male delinquency, films about female usually take on a motivated activist aspect. In some cases, the protagonists are reacting directly to mistreatment by men, but in all cases these characters appear to knowingly question and defy patriarchy through a wide-range of means.... The tough girl films before the mid-'90s never found a specific identity, let alone a niche in the movie market. By the turn of the century, as Bernard Weintraub pointed out, teenage girls had gained potency at the box off as well as on screen.... [These late-90s tough girl movies] present revisions of the tough girl image through their protagonists, suggesting that the impetus

for young female authority began manifesting itself long before the current generation.[9]

Rachel has one direct link to the past in the film: Sue Snell. In the original film, Sue attempted to be a secret ally to Carrie White, allowing her to have a happy high school experience, which all went horribly wrong. In the intervening 23 years, Sue, the only survivor of that night, sees an opportunity to once again help Carrie through Rachel. The difference between Carrie and Rachel is that Rachel is nowhere near as naïve as Carrie. Rachel knows the school and knows her place in it; she hopes to see through her time there and get out. Not unlike the coven in *The Craft*, it is not until a misogynist sexual misdeed or rumor occurs that Rachel is forced to take action, and that action is to bring it to the attention of the authorities. Rachel attempts to play by the rules and get some kind of justice for her friend, but the pervasive power of the jocks circumvents that and ultimately pushes Rachel to use her supernatural powers to protect herself. As director Katt Shea remarked in an interview about the film in 2016:

> I hoped to bring the pain and triumph of being a social pariah to life. To be blunt and honest it's a movie about revenge and bullies getting what they deserve. We can't do that in life, we get to do that in our fantasies and movies and it's satisfying until we grow beyond that and don't need to feel revenge at all. You realize everybody's got his or her own pain and compassion and love is the only answer. In the meantime, watching a revenge movie seems satisfying.[10]

The Rage: Carrie 2 offers a retread of the same themes and powers present in Stephen King's 1974 book and De Palma's 1976 adaptation while adapting itself to the present concerns of the time. Yes, Tracy and her equally mean-spirited friends can be seen as contemporary, but the power of this film lies in its willingness to take on the exploitation of young women and damaging breeding grounds for young men to feel powerful in. It is an examination of some of the worst fears of high school, which renders the horror of *The Rage: Carrie 2* not in Rachel or her powers but in the cruelty of the other students. And perhaps most depressingly, these kinds of games and tactics have not gone away, but become more prevalent as social media platforms allow for constant bullying and trolling. While the film attempts to show the romantic, consensual part of sex that is part of a healthy relationship, it also shows how that experience can be coopted and turned against the participants. The film remains a rather brave bastion in the midst of the 1990s Teen Horror Cycle for asking what is to be done when young men insist on being boys.

11

Lust for Life
Wicked (1998) and *Idle Hands* (1999)

Though technically released in 1998 when it premiered at the Sundance Film Festival, *Wicked* (Michael Steinberg) was all but forgotten until it was quietly dumped on DVD in 2001.[1] Between *Wicked*'s premiere and its subsequent release on DVD its star Julia Stiles had ascended to pop culture teen royalty known for playing awkward but fiercely intelligent outsiders in films like *10 Things I Hate About You* (Gil Junger, 1999), *Down to You* (Kris Isacsson, 2000), and *Save the Last Dance* (Thomas Carter, 2001) before finding a more regular role as a reoccurring supporting character in the amnesia-action Jason Bourne franchise. If Stiles' star power was enough to see the film released in 2001, it certainly was not enough to overcome the oddness of the film, which sees its star as Ellie, a young teenager in a new suburban development, discovering her sexuality and latching on to her father (William R. Moses) as the object of her desire. This obsession leads Ellie down a path of destruction. *Wicked*'s sexualization of a young girl mirrors those events from Kubrick's *Lolita* (1962). It also reflects the early 1990s fad of the deadly, sexual ingénue as seen in Katt Shea's *Poison Ivy* (1992) or *The Amy Fisher Story* (Andy Tennant, 1993), which portray Drew Barrymore as a highly sexualized and deadly young woman. While *Wicked*—not intended to parallel real life events—premiered at Sundance, the Bill Clinton and Monica Lewinsky scandal broke out.

It now seems nearly impossible to comprehend the extent to which the Lewinsky scandal dominated the still relatively new 24-hour news cycle; it was all anyone could talk about. As Gil Troy writes in his book, *The Age of Clinton*:

> Like the double helix of the DNA—a popular 1990s metaphor—two mutually reinforcing moral panics ensued. The Republicans cast Bill Clinton as the Folk devil, threatening the republic's soul, not just its judicial system, with adultery, lies, and cover ups that became perjury and obstruction of justice. To Democrats, [lead prosecutor against

Clinton] Kenneth Starr was the Folk Devil, threatening the republic's Constitution, not just its elected leader, with overzealousness, leaks and abuse of power. That both the president and the prosecutor were supposed to be role models not Folk Devils intensified the mass distress.[2]

This scandal opened up a dialogue about the rampant sexual politics that the conservative right so deeply opposed. Was it the smooth-talking, charming Clinton who seduced a young and naïve intern into becoming yet another of his extramarital sexual conquests or was it Lewinsky, an attractive and ambitious young woman who saw an opportunity to seduce the most powerful man in the world, who should be the center of the suspicion? While arguments and talking heads raged, *Wicked*, which took an emphatic stance on a young woman's sexuality and her need for fulfillment at any cost, premiered.

By 1990, nearly half the U.S. population was living in a suburb.[3] The intensified migration of well-to-do families moving of out of urban centers led to the rise of the middle class and politicians' obsession with that middle class. *The Atlantic* reported on this trend following the release of the 1990 census in 1992:

> Americans have been getting out of the cities as soon as they can afford to buy a house and a car. They want to escape the crowding and dangers of urban life.... As Kenneth T. Jackson argues in Crabgrass Frontier, a history of suburbanization in the United States, the pull factors (cheap housing and the ideal of a suburban "dream house") have been as important as the push factors (population growth and racial prejudice).[4]

While the millennium would see an increased resentment towards these suburban landscapes with the children who grew up in them fleeing as quickly as possible, the suffocating nature of these selective communities was palpable and suspect as early as the 1970s and 80s with films like *The Stepford Wives* (Bryan Forbes, 1975) and *Blue Velvet* (David Lynch, 1986) playing out elaborate, violent fantasies and secrets that were supposedly held within these communities. *Wicked* wastes no time setting up a network of infidelities Ellie's parents both engage in—her father Ben with the Swedish au pair Lena (Louise Myrback) and her mother Karen (Chelsea Field) with their beefcake neighbor Lawson (Patrick Muldoon). These affairs are introduced briefly and set the stage for both the unfolding conflict and also the confining tone of the film. As American urbanist Lewis Mumford wrote of suburbs in 1961:

> a multitude of uniform, unidentifiable houses, lined up inflexibly, at uniform distances, on uniform roads, in a treeless communal waste, inhabited by people of the same class, the same income, the same age group, witnessing the same television performances, eating the same tasteless prefabricated foods, from the same freezers, conforming in every outward and inward respect to a common mold.[5]

By removing citizens from the hustle and bustle of urban life, it left them with time on their hands. Maybe too much time. And as the communities were centered around the same housing designs, the suffocating sameness of it all weighed heavily on the characters in the film. Early in *Wicked*, Karen and Ellie are shown to be at an impasse with Ellie constantly threatening to run away to Los Angeles and Karen, knowing that Ellie will never get that far, not chasing after her. Their tension becomes increasingly palpable as Ben returns home from a business trip and gives his youngest daughter a stuffed animal while giving Ellie a makeup set. Here director Michael Steinberg and writer Eric Weiss are careful to insert several instances of Ellie gazing at her father and elaborating that she could never actually leave home because her father would be lost without her. She takes to wearing the makeup religiously and severely, almost daring her mother to call her out while her father finds it charming, even telling Ellie late one night that she is his favorite daughter.

Karen and Ellie get into a physical fight one morning before Ellie leaves for school with a full face of makeup. After Ellie and Inger leave for school, an unseen person stalks and bludgeons Karen to death using the hefty tragedy mask from the family's comedy and tragedy mask statues. After a brief period of mourning Ellie asserts herself as the woman of the house, wearing her mother's dresses, cooking dinner for the family and still applying makeup. Ben allows Lena to return to the fold as his girlfriend and they eventually marry, driving Ellie's mental state into further decline. The night of Ben and Lena's wedding, Ellie winds up in Lawson's house and Lawson falls for the 16-year-old Ellie, begging her to run away with him. When Ellie returns home, Ben is incensed, but Ellie counters him by threatening to tell Lena that Ben sexually assaulted her. Ben relents and ends things with Lena. Ellie begins to seize control of the house and tells her father she is no longer going to school. Now that she can control her father, she rejects Lawson. Ellie is soon murdered in the same manner as her mother with the remaining comedy mask. The coda reveals that Inger has taken to Ellie's ways of manipulation and that Lena is her next target.

Rarely do teen-marketed thrillers and contemplation of incest go together, but for all its faults, *Wicked* attempts to merge the two themes, taking from the traditions of Greek theater and the psychology of Carl Jung. The Greek mythological figure of Electra is one of the most famous of all classical characters. She is the daughter of King Agamemnon and Queen Clytemnestra. With the aid of her brother, she plots the death of her mother after the Queen murders Agamemnon. The story of Electra has been adapted into multiple plays, operas and films but it is perhaps most synonymous with Freud's analysis of the Oedipal complex. The Electra complex sees young women competing with their mothers for their fathers' attention. *Wicked* employs a series of events that point to such a complex. Ellie desires her father, kills her mother who is oppressing both of them, takes on the role of her mother and is once again almost-thwarted by the same nanny Lena in her quest for her father's fidelity. *Wicked* presents the role of women as consumptive and consuming. The only way Ellie knows how to be a woman is by playing out a stereotypical role—dressing attractively and ensuring dinner is ready when her father gets home from work. Never does she recognize that Ben desires the strong-willed, casual and ostensibly make-up-free Lena. Inger taking on the mantle of Ellie in the conclusion of the film offers the anti-feminist notion that women are inherently volatile, particularly when it comes to competing for men and their attention. Professor Kathleen Rowe Karlyn lays out the problematic filmic terms that incestuous depictions often display:

> The topic of incest has come out of the closet and entered popular culture in recent years. It is an unspoken presence in the tragic and still-unsolved case of JonBenet Ramsey, the five-year-old beauty queen who was murdered in her home in 1996. In addition to its very real existence in the social world, incest has emerged as the subject of popular discourse on talk shows and in tabloids, teen films, art films, and blockbusters, suggesting a powerful resonance between the cinematic and the political, the symbolic and the real.[6]

Wicked offers an anti-feminist (particularly anti–Third Wave) lens through which to view the 1990s horror thrillers. If Third Wave feminism was about enabling women to own and reclaim their sexuality from the male gaze that insidiously overrides media, *Wicked* is about the paranoid fantasies that can destroy even the most banal cul-de-sac.

Slackers, burnouts, and losers are a part of almost every teen film but, occasionally they get to be the hero rather than the comic relief or secondary character who affirms the choices of the main character. Writer Andrew Kopkind writes of the term slackers:

> It is increasingly used to describe the generation of the nineties, the early twentysomethings who seem to constitute a youth culture more coherent than any seen since the sixties. But even a cursory tour of the new media will turn up enough slacker references to suggest that a kind of consciousness—less than a movement but more than a mood—is slouching along to be born.[7]

The word "slacker" was popularized in 1991 with the release of American director Richard Linklater's film of the same name. As Linklater himself describes the origin of the slacker archetype:

> A modern notion [of the slacker] would be people who are ultimately being responsible to themselves and not wasting their time in a realm of activity that has nothing to do with who they are or what they might ultimately be striving for.[8]

11. Lust for Life

Rodman Flender's *Idle Hands* (1999) explores teens stunted by a relatively affluent suburban lifestyle whose drug consumption numbs them to the very real dangers of life. It is not until Anton (Devon Sawa) is possessed by a demon and begins killing people in the small town that the characters are able to break out of their complacency. Anton only realizes this when he discovers his parents' bodies and shows his friends Mick (Seth Green) and Pnub (Elden Henson), both of whom Anton inadvertently murders. The possession becomes localized in Anton's hand and the hand eventually drags him to his neighbor Molly's (Jessica Alba) house, forcing him to interact with the girl he has had a crush on for years. When Molly shows interest in him and asks him to the Halloween dance, Anton takes the drastic measure of severing his hand with a meat cleaver to prevent it from inadvertently hurting Molly. The hand escapes and Debi LeCure (Vivica A. Fox) arrives in the small town ready to do battle with the ancient evil. Anton with Mick and Pnub arrive at the dance to find Molly, worried that the hand is already after her. The hand does indeed attack, scalping the lead singer of The Offspring who are playing the dance. Chaos breaks out and the hand captures Molly. Anton, Mick and Pnub manage to save Molly in time for Debi to throw her ritualistic knife at the hand, defeating it. Mick and Pnub ascend to heaven but return to be Anton's guardian angels while he and Molly become a serious item.

The film operates as a supernatural slasher with the antagonist as, literally, part of the hero. As Debi says, the demonic force is looking for the laziest person—in essence the last person anyone would suspect of masterminding multiple murders in a small community—to do its bidding. But *Idle Hands* focuses on a male hero or Final Boy, a rare but not totally uncommon trope. Anton is the quintessential slacker, waiting for life to come to him as he is sheltered by the protectiveness and leniency of his parents, who ensure him a steady supply of snacks and cable television. While Anton is seemingly content to live out his time at home glued to the television, he cannot work up the nerve to talk to Molly. It is not until he finds the lyrics book she drops, giving him a chance to return it, that he can articulate his feelings about her to Mick and Pnub. Anton cites her insightful lyrics and apparently artistic inclinations as the base for his crush. This is not just sexual attraction; it is deeper than that and is therefore inherently more problematic to his way of life.

Idle Hands was released by Columbia Pictures just ten days after the April 20, 1999 Columbine shootings. As CNN reported of the studio's decision to maintain the release date after talks of delay:

> Despite a national debate now raging on the subject of Hollywood's depictions of violence, drug use and sexual activity, the studio officials decided against changing the release date. They released a statement in which they say the picture "bears no resem-

blance to that tragedy (at Littleton) and is a comedy based on a totally different subject.[9]

The film floundered upon its release grossing only $4 million against its $25 million production budget.[10] The film's poster read "The comedy that gives horror films the backhand," already anticipating backlash against the prestige genre films that Dimension Films was intent on producing. Though the film's aesthetic embraces the sleekness of others like *Scream* and *I Know What You Did Last Summer*, with adept camera work and a cool, young, recognizable cast, *Idle Hands* is intent on shifting focus to the slackers who cannot seem to make anything go their way. The film opens with the bloody murders of Anton's parents after they see "I'm Under the Bed" painted on their bedroom ceiling. After Anton's father (Fred Willard) goes to investigate and does not return, his mother follows suit and meets an equally grisly fate. This scene parallels *Scream*'s opening but with the parents succumbing to the force the main characters will soon face.

As the film gets underway, Anton eventually notices his parents' absence, but he seems less concerned than one would perhaps normally be. Anton is far more concerned with scoring pot from Mick and Pnub and watching for Molly. Mick and Pnub initially act as the Greek chorus, deriding Anton for not even speaking to Molly. When Anton figures out that he killed his parents, he calls his friends who are initially more excited by the sexy music video on the television than the dead bodies before them—yet another symptom of a generation raised and taught by MTV. When Mick chides Anton for not knowing about the spate of killings that have been happening, asking, "Don't you watch the news?" to which Anton replies, "No, I hate that show." Removed from the world and sheltered by their parents, these teens do not have to act unless they choose to. Their inaction at the beginning of the film is what brings the demonic force to their doorstep.

Though *Idle Hands* is happy to parody this notion of the media obsessed generation, it often falls prey to it with an inundation of jokes at the expense of pace and narrative. The film insinuates an embedded knowledge of the genre and as a parody of said genre, contentedly spends time on satire of a rather complicated coming-of-age story. Once Anton's parents are dead, it is up to him to be the adult. As lead actor Sawa said at the time of film's release:

> They recorded the movie with crowd reactions, and it's funny to hear the crowd just go up in an uproar when I start smoking pot. Like the whole place just goes, "Yeah." And it's like, wow! Society is just nuts, you know? Here I am smoking pot, and everybody is just cheering in the audience[11]

After the trio figure out that Anton is not only behind the murder of his parents but also the other murders which have been on the rise in their small slice of Americana, Anton's hand takes over, attacking and killing both Mick and Pnub. Anton buries his friends and his parents only to have his friends return from the dead to berate him:

ANTON: Hey, I didn't kill anyone on purpose, okay?
MICK: Yeah, well, we weren't in hell! I mean, there was this bright white light at the end of a long tunnel, right, and there was these chicks' voices, and that music…
ANTON: Music?
PNUB: Yeah, kinda uncool music, like, Enya. And these chicks' voices, they were saying, "come to us, come towards the light."
ANTON: So what happened?
MICK: We figured, fuck it, I mean, it was really far!

For these characters, the promise of their parents' heaven with adult contemporary music is not nearly as much fun as teasing Anton, eating junk food and watching television. While Mick and Pnub serve as a literal reminder for Anton of his potentially dead-end ways, his hand pulls him towards Molly. With Anton severing his hand and making a conscious choice to get off the couch next to his dead friends and save the day, *Idle Hands* presents less of a hero's journey and more of a self-actualizing narrative. Flender says of this mixture of immaturity in the face of maturity, "I think every healthy person at one point in their life has been the kid at the table who sticks peas up their nose. I know it's something I used to like to do … that's the attraction of this film."[12]

The tone of *Idle Hands* draws from two disparate sources: *Cinderella* and *Evil Dead II* (Sam Rami, 1987). *Cinderella* sees a young woman desperate to attend a dance in hopes of meeting her true love, which in turn helps her social status. In this fairy tale, Anton would be the aforementioned Cinderella, Mick and Pnub would be the evil stepsisters who are happy to oppress the hero (in this case with pot and mockery rather than outright housework), Debi would be the Fairy Godmother who can aid the solution to the problem and Molly, of course, would be the prince. In *Idle Hands* it is up to Anton to overcome the demonic supernatural forces to make it through the bloodbath of the ball and step up to claim his rightful place. Bruno Bettelheim relates this movement in *Cinderella* to childhood in his book *The Uses of Enchantment*:

> Every child believes at some period in his life—and this is not only at rare moments—that because of his secret wishes, if not also his clandestine actions, he deserves to be degraded, banned from the presence of others, relegated to a world of smut. He fears this may be so, irrespective of how fortunate his situation may be in reality. He hates

and fears those others—such as his siblings—whom he believes to be entirely free of similar evilness, and he fears that they or his parents will discover what he's really like, and then demean him as Cinderella was demanded by her family. Because he wants others ... to believe in his innocence, he is delighted that "everybody" believes in Cinderella's. This is one of the greatest attractions to this fairy tale. Since people give credence to Cinderella's goodness, they will also believe in his, so the child hopes.[13]

As many teen films are, *Idle Hands* is, at its core, about the attempt at transformation—the movement from childhood to adulthood. Flender codes the film as a comedy in hopes of rendering the story more palatable to a larger and potentially untapped male teen market. In the film Anton, though played by teen heartthrob Devon Sawa, wears an unflattering outfit, has bad skin and has not been to school in months. Where most the films in the 1990s teen cycle focus on female characters, *Idle Hands* wants examines the trajectory of those teen boys who were thought to have been left behind by the ambition of women in the wake of Third Wave feminism and Girl Power.

Idle Hands mirrors *Evil Dead II* most overtly through depictions of a young man's psychosis tested by his own sentient hand, which he willingly severs. Within the world of *Evil Dead II*, Ash (Bruce Campbell) is fending off demonic forces, which have already killed his girlfriend, in a cabin in the woods. The forces almost manage to overtake him and possess his hand, but Ash severs his hand, which then returns to constantly taunt and attack him. *Evil Dead II* situates male horror and mania in the remote homestead, where a man can be most tormented by a part of himself he thought he had control over. In a similar way, *Idle Hands* lifts its title from the saying, "Idle Hands are the tools of the Devil," which is believed to have been adapted from Bible and various forms of classical literature and, like Ash, links the horror in the film to some part of Anton which can be manipulated by a malevolent force. *Idle Hands* speaks to Anton's penchant for smoking pot, masturbating and generally not doing too much, which makes him susceptible the Devil. Like Ash, Anton must face his weaknesses and overcome them before he can save anyone else.

The mythology within *Idle Hands*, based on supernatural forces, varies quite significantly from the other films of this cycle, which are based on scenarios perceived as having the potential to take place in real life because they involve "real" people as the killers. But what the other films miss that *Idle Hands* does is ruminate on the force of self both as a protagonist and antagonist. Scholar Jessica Balanzategui writes of this move from realistic to supernatural slasher:

> Through the conceit that the killer is or has access to the supernatural, the focus tends not to be on the gory nature of the murders—the traditional slasher's central semantic

spectacle—but on the syntactic tensions which underlie the killer's complex relationship with the protagonist. The supernatural is employed to engage the viewer in an overtly disorientating oscillation between the perspective of the hero/ine and the villain. This interplay of perspectives obscures the viewer's access to the "true" narrative fabula—as is structurally heralded by a collapse into the whodunit quest—and complicates the binary between good (hero/ine) and evil (killer). In so doing, these films embellish the flux of identification which often functioned as a deeply engrained syntactic element of the classic slasher yet was rarely or explicitly explored in the narrative.[14]

Idle Hands locates the horror in a teenage boy's hand—a hand used for pot smoking, masturbation, and murder. This localized horror identifies itself as all the things teens are supposed to grow out of, not give into. Anton's journey directs him towards responsibility and a relationship—two things that seem very adult and not very cool. By elevating the evil hand as the part of Anton that wishes to cause harm and act on impulse, *Idle Hands* shifts perceptions of masculinity. Anton's adulthood may still involve some slacking but, most importantly, it involves significant relationships with other people who are not just meal tickets.

12

The Millennium Approaches
Cherry Falls (2000), *Final Destination* (2000) and *Scary Movie* (2000)

Geoffrey Wright's *Cherry Falls* (2000) was the first true victim of the slasher revival. From a troubled production to a troubled back-and-forth with the MPAA, *Cherry Falls* was not set up for success. Caving to MPAA pressure, the film's theatrical release was shelved by USA Films and Rogue Pictures in favor of a heavily edited version screened on the USA Channel once on July 29, 2000.[1] With *Cherry Falls*' 14 million dollar budget, the film has the backhanded honor of being the most expensive television film ever made.[2]

Word about *Cherry Falls* spread after its brief appearance on American television (and it did receive some limited theatrical releases in Europe) due to the film's rather clever inversion of the slasher trope of sex not equating death.

In the small town of *Cherry Falls*, a serial killer begins picking off virgins, causing a mass panic in the town. These events lead to the climax, which features a house party orgy with students desperate to pop their cherry lest they lose their lives. The simple conceit makes for a fascinating viewing and has led many horror and slasher fans to seek out the film in recent years. There has also been much speculation about its problematic production and release. In 2016, Shout Factory—a distribution company that specializes in reissuing films that have been hard to find with updated extras—released a Blu-Ray edition of the film with audio commentaries by Wright and interviews with Producer Marshall Persinger and writer Ken Selden. The insights of the creative team offer more in-depth summaries of what went on during the production and the reviews with the MPAA, which the site Bloody Disgusting described in their review of the Blu-Ray:

> In a post–Columbine world, the media eye was on violence in cinema. The late 90s and early 00s saw many horror films trimmed of much of their violence…. Wright informs his listeners that all of these shots were filmed, but unfortunately had to be removed … to appease the Senate, the MPAA and USA Films.[3]

12. The Millennium Approaches

While *Cherry Falls'* intrigue comes from its titillating premise, it is ultimately about the sins of parents—specifically those of the Final Girl Jody's (Brittany Murphy) parents. The film shows the killer in shadow and it is clear the silhouette is that of a woman. The opening scene shows two teens killed at the local Lovers Lane. When the police and Jody's father Sherriff Marken (Michael Biehn) arrive on the scene, they discover the word "virgin" carved into the victims' thighs. The next evening, another teen is killed in the same fashion with the same carvings on her thigh. The sheriff's department decides that it is in the town's best interest to share this information in a meeting with the parents, which Jody and her friend Timmy (Keram Malicki-Sanchez) sneak into. The killer then murders Timmy and attacks Jody who gets away. Sherriff Marken comes to his daughter's aid and takes her to the station to give a report. Jody describes the woman who attacked her as having long black hair with a white streak in the front. Sheriff Marken calls his old friend and current principal of the high school Tom Sisler (Joe Inscoe) and tells Sisler that the woman Jody describes sounds like Lora Lee Sherman, which makes both men nervous. Jody overhears the call and begins to investigate who Lora Lee Sherman is or was. Throughout all of this, the school descends into chaos with an open season on sex.

At the beginning of the film, Jody is dumped by her boyfriend Kenny (Gabriel Mann) for not having sex with him. Kenny attempts to reconcile with Jody after her near-death experience, but she is less interested in him and more interested in her sensitive and thoughtful English teacher Mr. Marliston (Jay Mohr). Jody confronts her mother (Candy Clark) about Lora Lee Sherman and her mother reveals that they all went to high school together and that one night the four most popular boys in school, including Jody's father, raped Lora Lee. The community defended the boys and Lora Lee left town, never to be heard of again. As the high school students plan an orgy so they can lose their virginities, the killer attacks and kills Principal Sisler and kidnaps Sheriff Marken. Jody, who happens to be biking by Mr. Marliston's house, catches sight of Mr. Marliston lifting a heavy object into his house and offers to help him. Jody discovers that the heavy object in question is her father and Mr. Marliston knocks her unconscious. When Sheriff Marken and Jody awake, Mr. Marliston tells them that he is Lora Lee and Marken's son—the byproduct of the rape—and he dons a wig and women's clothes to enact the revenge that Lora Lee never had. Mr. Marliston believes that by punishing virgins in the town, all the children of the community who protected the rapists would be shamed:

> MARLISTON: It's a stinking hypocritical world isn't it Brent? Where rapists become pillars of the community, with stinking hypocritical people in it who wouldn't

miss their own befouled lives much so … so … so what better way than to take away the only innocence they have left … their precious virginal children.

Kenny arrives at the house looking for Jody and Sheriff Marken uses this opportunity to attack Marliston. This act allows Jody and Kenny to escape, but Sheriff Marken is killed in the process.

Jody and Kenny make a run for it, leading Marliston to the orgy party where he causes chaos and wounds a number of students. Marliston wounds Kenny and fights with Jody who manages to push him out a window; he is impaled on a fence post. The film ends as the police question Jody as to her father and Mr. Marliston's involvement with the killings, to which Jody feigns ignorance. As Jody leaves the police station, she catches a glimpse of a figure that might be the real Lora Lee Sherman, but it disappears. The film concludes with a shot of the water from the waterfalls on the edge of town turning red.

Cherry Falls continues to deviate from the traditional Reagan-era politics, which seemingly equated sex to death, that influenced slashers in their 1980s heyday. The film invites its young characters to engage willingly and consentingly in sexual intercourse. This conceit flies in the face of the fear that sex can lead to disease or unwanted pregnancies and is therefore best avoided. At the beginning of the film, Jody believes she's doing what is right for her by not having sex with her pushy boyfriend. As the pattern of victims becomes clear after the second killing, Sheriff Marken questions Jody about her sexual activity:

MARKEN: I need to ask you a personal question.
JODY: About what?
MARKEN: It's about you and Kenny, about how far you've gone.
JODY: Gone?
MARKEN: Gone. You know, base wise. Are you two kissing?
JODY: Of course. I'm not a child anymore, Dad. That's normal.
MARKEN: I'm not criticizing. Have you gone further than that? Listen, I wouldn't ask you this unless it was absolutely necessary. Can you go further than you have?
JODY: Yes. But you don't have to worry about that, okay. We just broke up the other day.
MARKEN: Yup.
JODY: [shocked] Are you disappointed? Are you disappointed that I'm still a virgin?
MARKEN: No, not at all.
JODY: Okay.
MARKEN: I'm very, very, very proud of you. You're still my little girl.

Jody's virginity and proximity to one of the men who raped Lora Lee puts her at the greatest risk. Her closeness with her father and Mr. Marliston

12. The Millennium Approaches

(before he is revealed to be the killer) makes Jody's sexuality palpable. Jody and her father share several emotionally intimate moments and when he teaches her a few self-defense tactics, the camera lingers on their bodies after she flips him over, intentionally or unintentionally implying some kind of attraction between them. Mr. Marliston on the other hand is portrayed as the correct choice for Jody; he is not as flippant or as movable as Kenny and he seems to respect Jody and her classmates for their intelligence. Interestingly, the film *Never Been Kissed* (Raja Gosnell, 1999) released the year before *Cherry Falls* sees a similar dynamic play-out but through a romantic comedy lens with the student as an undercover of-age reporter and the teacher attracted to her but keeping his distance. Of course, *Never Been Kissed* offers the best possible outcome while *Cherry Falls* represents the teacher-student dynamic at its most nightmarish.

Pat Gills' paper "The Monsterous Years: Teens, Slasher Films and the Family" explores the notion of the embedded monster within a family that the hero of the film must overcome:

> The family structure that interests me in horror films, however, is an absent one. Teen slasher films both resolutely mock and yearn for the middleclass American dream, the promised comfort and contentment of a loving, supportive bourgeois family.[4]

The Marken/Marliston/Sherman family is a blended one with Jody and Marliston as half-siblings—one an ideal and one a subversion of the promise of the American middle-class family. *Cherry Falls* breaks away from some of the familial promises set forth in films like *A Nightmare on Elm Street* (Wes Craven, 1984) where the parents played a part in the horror but have no means to support their children who must face down the monster. The young men who raped Lora Lee Sherman are the monsters who bred another monster in the form of Mr. Marliston, but that same DNA also bred Jody who must stop him in order to save her life and the lives of her friends. The binding ties in *Cherry Falls* run deeper and more sinisterly than in many other slasher films.

When Marliston is revealed to be the killer, *Cherry Falls* embraces some of the more problematic tropes of horror films that have come before it—namely that of a cross-dressing sexualized killer most prominently seen in Alfred Hitchcock's *Psycho* (1960) and Brian De Palma's *Dressed to Kill* (1980). With these films released two decades apart, one would hope there would be a better understanding of the political implications of situating the horror within a killer struggling with complex identity issues. Instead, these films are complicit in coding these kinds of narratives as horrific and other. Carol Clover elaborated on the fluctuating gender roles of the killer as an extension of his or her desire in her book *Men, Women and Chainsaws*:

> The killer's phallic purpose, as he thrusts his drill of knife into the trembling bodies of young women, is unmistakable. At the same time, however, his masculinity is is severely qualified: he ranges from the virginal to the sexually inert to the transvestite or transsexual, and is spiritually divided.... In this respect, slasher killers have much in common with the monsters of classic horror—monsters who, in Linda Williams's formulation, represent not just "an eruption of the normally repressed sexual energy of the "civilized male" but also the "power and potency of a non-phallic sexuality." To the extent that the monster is constructed as feminine, the horror film thus expresses female desire only to show how monstrous it is.[5]

While this is a leading theory throughout slasher films, *Cherry Falls* takes pains to show that the horror and the monstrosity visited upon this town is the product of a secret the community upheld. When the town of Cherry Falls thought they were protecting their best and brightest, they set in motion a series of events that would bring violence not necessarily upon themselves, but upon their children. Mr. Marliston's role in the film is thus doubly troubling to the town. Not only is he the byproduct of a horrific event, he is also a trusted person within the community. He is not an outsider everyone is suspicious of; he is the person they leave in charge of their children. Marliston's revenge in *Cherry Falls* comes from within the system. Though the film never explicitly states it, it is probable that Marliston was able to target certain students as virgins because of his proximity to them. He exudes the confidence of a teacher that students want to be liked by, and throughout the film Jody finds ways to gain his affection, relating to him that his lessons are making an impact on her. But this, of course, is not an innocent student-teacher relationship. Clover comments on the incest that makes this relationship different from other such tropes:

> The patently erotic threat is easily seen as the materialized projection of the viewer's own incestuous fears and desires. It is this disabling cathexis to one's parents that must be killed and re-killed in the service of sexual autonomy. When the Final Girl stands in the light of day with the knife in her hand, she has delivered herself into the adult world.[6]

In *Men, Women and Chainsaws*, Clover writes extensively on the killer's weapon embodying a phallic-like status, and *Cherry Falls* emphasizes that theory. The killer's knife is wielded in front of the victims and cuts into the flesh on their thigh as a means to mark them and their lack of sexual experience. In the final showdown between Marliston and Jody, Marliston is able to overtake Jody. He climbs on top of her, grunting and attempting to stab her. The clarity of the killer's knife as a phallic symbol may have never been so fully realized on screen before or since. Clover's text, written in 1992, deals with films from the previous two decades, and it is clear that the film industry has never known how to truly handle teen sexuality. They cannot reveal

12. The Millennium Approaches

themselves to be fearful of it, nor too condoning, which leaves them in an uneasy situation. The sexuality that is depicted when teens are consenting and enjoying the experience is one that looks to romance, viewing sex as the final barrier between star-crossed lovers. As Timothy Shary writes of this phenomenon:

> Yet while many youth films from 1983 to 2013 featured teens in a quest to have sex, the majority are decidedly negative in their portrayals, demonstrating the complications of sex, as well as the aggravations and confusions, and potential dangers. Youth find themselves involved in sexual activities in one form or another, whether intercourse, foreplay, or the basic negotiation of sexual preferences, and the majority of the narratives in this erosphere could be characterized, even when they tend to take seriously the stakes of sex.[7]

Cherry Falls removes those perceived notions that if sex does not bring about pregnancy or disease, it can at least ruin a teen's social capital. In some of the most inventive scenes in the film, the student who is earlier admonished for being a "slut" is giving sex tips to a group of rapturous girls hours before the orgy party. For a brief period Marliston gets part of what he wanted in ruining the purity of the next generation, but he also destigmatizes sex, creating a free and open dialogue about how to use condoms and the best methods for taking bras off. However, this reprieve is brief. As shown in the final scenes of the film, Jody has fallen in line with the town's silence and will not publicly condemn the men who started the madness in the first place. Jody's complacency is on one hand understandable, as she wants to preserve her father's memory and reputation, but on the other, much bigger hand, it further silences the town and community of Cherry Falls and leaves the unspoken crimes to fester. Jody has, as Clover wrote, "delivered herself into the adult world."[8] However, the adult world in *Cherry Falls* is a monstrous place that Jody continues the traditions of.

Premonitions have always inspired fear in the hearts of man. Humans able to see into the future and possibly alter its outcome have historically been met with skepticism, punishment and, in some cases, even death. James Wong's *Final Destination* (2000) sets the idea of premonitions, the future, youth and horror within one young man, Alex (Devon Sawa). As Alex and his classmates embark on a class fieldtrip to Paris, Alex briefly falls asleep before the plane takes off and, in his premonition, sees a fiery explosion erupt on the plane shortly after take-off. Alex wakes up in a panic and as his friends and classmates say the same things and the same faulty table breaks on the plane, he begins yelling for everyone to get off. This outburst leads to a fight between the hot-headed Carter (Kerr Smith), Alex, and some of their other classmates who are also rushed off the plane in the ensuing chaos. One of the teachers Ms. Lewton (Kristen Cloke) offers to stay behind with the trouble-making group and catch the next plane to Paris. As the group hurls accusations and tensions rise in the terminal, the plane takes off and, just as Alex predicted, erupts in flames, claiming all the lives aboard. The FBI arrive on the scene and interview the survivors who also include Clear (Ali Larter), Hitchcock (Seann William Scott), Alex's best friend Tod (Chad Donella) and Carter's girlfriend Terry (Amanda Detmer). While the group is rattled, they are wary of Alex whose premonition saved them. They also begin dealing with survivor's guilt.

Shortly after the accident, an unseen force attacks Tod in his bathroom, killing him. Alex receives a premonition that Tod may be in danger and rushes to the scene where Tod's death has been ruled a suicide. Soon the other survivors begin to die, each in an elaborate scenario caused by an unseen force, which makes them look like accidents. Alex realizes that they cheated death by getting off the plane and that death is coming for them in the order they would have been killed on the plane. If one of them manages to evade death in one instance, it will move on to the next person. After Carter cheats death, the force moves on to Clear and Alex saves her. The three remaining survivors believe they have cheated death for the final time and a while later in Paris, they make a toast to life and friends who cannot be there. In that moment, Alex has another premonition and realizes that death has just been waiting. It strikes again, circling back to kill them all.

Final Destination began its life as a spec script for the television show *The X Files*, written by Jeffrey Reddick who says of his inspiration for the story:

> I was actually flying home to Kentucky and I read this story about a woman who was on vacation in Hawaii and her mom called her and said "Don't take the flight tomorrow, I have a really bad feeling about it." She switched flights and the plane that she would have been on crashed. I thought, that's creepy—what if she was supposed to die on that flight?[9]

After all the success of the slasher revitalization, New Line Cinema was looking for a piece of the action. Having been the studio behind *Nightmare on Elm Street*, the studio was struggling to break back into the teen market after milquetoast attempts like *Campfire Tales* (Martin Kunert, 1997), which went straight to video with little fanfare. As *Final Destination* producer Craig Perry said of developing the film at New Line:

> It was fresh and original. We were given the latitude to explore the ideas. [*Final Destination*] was the perfect synthesis of what New Line wanted. It was different. It was unique in how it treated its audience. It treated you with respect. And ultimately, it was a way for audiences to explore the things we can't define, the things that frighten us ... and get away with it.[10]

12. The Millennium Approaches

The creative team of James Wong, whose previous directing credit consisted of episodes of *The X Files*, and writer Glen Morgan, who also wrote for *The X Files* among other television series, altered the ages of the characters who were initially conceived to be adults forced together after they escaped death. Ageing them down allowed for entry into the tantalizing teen market.

Final Destination carries the torch from other films of this cycle, such as *Idle Hands*, that employ a supernatural element as the antagonist. Rather than a demonic force as in *Idle Hands*, a shadowy figure, unwilling to draw attention to itself but unrelenting in its endeavors, is the killer in *Final Destination*.

Early in the film as they board the plane Alex, Tod and George (Brendan Fehr) pass a baby in First Class and George says, "No God would take this plane down." Then they pass a mentally handicapped man in their section and George continues his thought with, "Only a really fucked up God would take this plane down." This simple and brief exchange plants but then dismisses the notion of God in this world. Death becomes an omnipresent figure in the survivors' lives but God does not. Usually God is evoked in times of mass tragedy as a comfort blanket for the nation with newscasters repeating the oft-said cliché, "our thoughts and prayers are with the victims and their families." George's glib remarks on the plane recall that our society is still ready and willing to call upon God when needed. Part of the nihilism of *Final Destination* is that of course the baby and handicapped man die, implying that God does not exist and something more powerful does.

After Tod dies, Alex and Clear break into the mortuary where his body is being held for its autopsy. They notice scratches on Tod's body, implying that he struggled as he died and therefore his death may not have been a suicide. At that moment, the sinisterly helpful mortician Bludworth (Tony Todd) appears and tells them about Death's Design.

> BLUDWORTH: You have to realize is that we're just a mouse that a cat has by the tail, every single move we make from the mundane to the monumental, the red light that we stop at or run, the people we have sex with or want with us, the airplanes that we ride or walk out of, it's all part of death's sadistic design. Leading to the grave.... In death there are no accidents, no coincidences, no mishaps, and no escapes.

In Bludworth's words is the thematic core of *Final Destination* (as well as its sequels): the notion of control and self-determination in the face of expectations.

When the film begins, Alex and his classmates are seemingly regular teens in their final year of high school—some clinging to it and the status it has provided them and some desperate to get out and live without restrictions.

These characteristics—high school success versus high school rejection—are the norm of any teen film. *Final Destination* offers another look at this dichotomy with death, not just social status or ambition, hanging over the characters' heads. Death is a certainty for everyone, but for most, being a teenager is when one feels the most invincible. Teens are often at a physical peak, they have developed interests and identities outside of the homestead, and they are beginning to daydream about the possibilities of life. As Tod says in his speech at the memorial for the plane accident:

> TOD: We say that the hour of death cannot be forecast. But when we say this, we imagine that the hour is placed in an obscure and distant future. It never occurs to us that it has any connection with the day already begun, or that death could arrive this same afternoon—this afternoon which is so certain, and which has every hour filled in advance.

Final Destination takes those dreams away, forcing the survivors to think only about death and how to avoid it. The deaths within the film are mostly tied to the private rooms of homes rather than to spectacular events such as the explosion of the plane. The accidents the teens succumb to reflect society's concerns and worries over teens. Tod's seeming suicide is chalked up to guilt over getting off the plane when his brother stayed on, Hitchcock's decapitation by the train tracks suggests risky and unsupervised behavior, and Clear's trap in her home where electrical wires and gasoline begin flooding her studio delve into the fear of an outsider who has no one to monitor or protect them. Even the initial accident and final twist implicated the dangers of straying too far from the homestead. Travel and independence go hand and hand, even on a school trip. It is a signifier of a child maturing ever steadily towards adulthood. The fears and danger of *Final Destination* are designed to trap the characters within their homes, where death will quietly strike.

The film deftly sets up a world that does not believe Alex or is fearful of him. Carter notably and brashly tells Alex at the memorial after the accident that he will "never die"—a true sign of hubris and youth. Others like Hitchcock want to know if they should ask a girl out, while Clear, who becomes attracted to Alex even though they never spoke before the accident, is grateful for the second chance he gave her. Out of all the survivors Clear was the one person who chose to get off the plane of her own freewill; she was not late getting to the plane or tangled up in the fight between Carter and Alex. She made a choice because she believed Alex's fear and panic. She is Alex's sole ally who believes him without reproach or the assumption of something more dubious. She believes in Alex's intuition as a survival tool.

Thomas Hine wrote of the nature of imaginative and nonlinear thinking in his book *The Rise and Fall of the American Teenager*:

12. The Millennium Approaches

Yes, dreams and fantasy are important in a society where your ability to create a salable self-influences your fate more strongly than does your family or class. But ultimately, the society does not support overactive imaginations; it suppresses them. Yes, no one can help being young, and our society has dug a chasm between adolescence and true adulthood. But for the healthy individual, a sense of self that continues from childhood into adulthood manages to overcome such barriers.[11]

The dreams and desires of teenagers are often not believed or are tarnished by belief in the realities of the real world by older generations who have seen it all before. In *Final Destination*, Alex and his friends work to evade and cheat death in hopes of having any kind of chance at a life in which they are allowed to make decisions for themselves. But they soon learn that the other adults, even the FBI agents who track Alex, are wary of him and the constant monitoring of them takes away their rights to travel and access the world around them. The teens' attempts to cheat death are in order to have a chance at life, but they are riddled with fear and uncertainty.

In one scene later on in the film, Alex has retreated to a cabin in the woods, fortifying it in hopes of stopping death in its tracks by being inactive. While he is unbelieved by most of the outside world, he realizes that he has not been able to save everyone. He only returns to his town when he realizes he switched seats on the plane and that he is not the next in line for death's clutches; Clear is.

In Alex's abilities to intuit death's plans to some degree, he functions as both hero and his own harbinger of doom or, as John Kenneth Muir delineates, a Cassandra figure. Cassandra was the daughter of King Priam of Troy in Greek mythology and while she can see into the future, she is cursed, no one will believe what she says.

> In the slasher-movie paradigm, the Cassandra complex is an important thematic factor. Sometimes I call this trope "Just Ignore the Old Crazy Person," because the Cassandra figure is often a drunk or elderly person [such as Ralph in the *Friday the 13th* series or even Dr. Loomis in *Halloween*] .... What's the point of including such characters, dramatically speaking, in a slasher narrative? In large part, Cassandra figures serve as explicit reminders that man proposes, and God disposes, or that fate will have its way. Even when people are directly warned about looming dangers, they don't necessarily pay attention or find themselves able to escape the fate the universe has set out for them. The Cassandra figure is the canary in the coal mine, the one who learns of danger ahead but whose message just can't be heard in time to change fate.[12]

In this repurposing of the Cassandra figure, *Final Destination* is coded as a darkly comedic tragedy with Alex at its center haplessly trying to effect change but succeeding only a few times.

In this way, *Final Destination* does begin to bridge the gap between the slashers that came before it and looks towards a trend of the new millennium:

Torture Porn. While some audience members visibly cringe when the term is mentioned and some critics stick their noses in the air when they encounter it, Torture Porn also offer a catharsis to the slick-polish of many contemporary films. On one hand, they can be made purely for a release of ratcheted up tension such as in the making of *Cabin Fever* (Eli Roth, 2002) or they can employ a more political stance such as in *Hostel* (Eli Roth, 2005). In either case, Torture Porn loves to linger on violent scenarios often at the price of narrative and pacing. In *Final Destination*, the mythology and structure is set up relatively quickly with the teens catching on. Then the film delves into individual scenarios and set ups, with Wong using his camera to highlight innocuous objects such as a fan or kitchen scissors or a small fan to infer danger. Of course, the objects focused on rarely yield the death blow, as Wong and Morgan prefer a surprise emerging from the scene to do such.

In his piece on the nature of puzzles and elaborate deaths in slasher films, scholar Ian Conrich terms films like *Final Destination* and the *Saw* franchise as "grand slashers."

> In the grand slasher, death appears all-pervasive and generally cannot be escaped or defeated. The victims are part of a scheme or preordained plan, and the deaths are often hyper-elaborate. These are essentially survival horrors and puzzle films, in which death itself can be manipulating a situation and in which victims have to second-guess a system in which the horror that awaits can be protracted and torturous.[13]

These grand slashers often mimic the style of the Grand Guignol, a theater in Paris at the turn of the 20th Century that specialized in highly violent theatrical spectacle based events. *Final Destination* embraces this Mouse Trap–like aesthetic, building the audience up towards one expectation of violence but then offering a further reward with an even more gruesome outcome. As Conrich writes:

> [Whilst] the attraction of the slasher was who would be the next victim and the method in which they would die, and whilst the neo-slasher offered the additional attraction of guessing the killer's identity, the appeal of the *Final Destination* films has little to do with knowing which victim is next or what the killer looks like. The *Final Destination* films instead foreground attempts to prolong life, with the screen at times structured around the futile creation of "death-free" zones, but with the knowledge that the individual cannot escape his or her grisly fate.[14]

The fate of the characters in *Final Destination* is that of learned dependency. As the 1990s drew to a close and the new millennium dawned, society was just beginning to embrace the internet. The concern over teens withdrawing from "normal" social activities was growing exponentially after the Columbine shootings and moral certitudes were hard to find. Parents and children alike were struggling to define new roles for themselves in the face of an ever-changing society. *Final Destination* implies that even if these families could see into the future, they would not want to. Premonitions invoke a sense of evil and something dubious at play rather than a beatific entity showing the way. Even though Alex can save some of his friends, he is still a suspect of parents and the authorities; he is, potentially, someone to be feared because he can not explain his abilities. *Final Destination* illustrates the need for teens to take those final steps from childhood to adulthood even though it may, in the end, be a rather brief journey.

For every major franchise or movement within popular culture, there have been parodies of the tropes and themes within them. Whether they appeared as short sketches in *In Living Color* or *Saturday Night Live* or as full length films such as *Young Frankenstein* (Mel Brooks, 1974) or *Airplane* (David Zucker, Jim Abrahams, Jerry Zucker, 1980), parody and satire seek to undermine the prevailing attitudes that the originals profess as gospel. One of the earliest and most powerful examples of this transference of message and power is Charlie Chaplin's *The Great Dictator*, released in 1940 at the start of Hitler's attempt at world domination. Chaplin's skewing of Hitler's own propaganda film (*The Triumph of the Will*, Leni Riefenstahl, 1935) allowed for mass populations to begin outright questioning the Führer—his power and his outlook—if they were not already. Writer Robert Potter wrote of parody that it can make the terrifying and malevolent forces at work appear "abnormal and inappropriate"[15] rather than as the new normal.

As the 1990s came to a close, the audiences for meta-horror films directed at teens dwindled. Though *Scream 3* was still successful by the box office numbers, many felt it was a rushed production that lacked the cohesion of the first two films. Other franchises such as *I Know What You Did Last Summer* and *Urban Legend* were not being pushed through with the same fervor they had been only a few years prior. With the rise of films like *Final Destination*, which would be the bridge for a new type of horror, the time seemed right to parody the movement that had taken hold in popular culture only a few short years before. However, this idea was shared by a few different sources, including Shawn and Marlon Wayans as well as Jason Friedberg and Aaron Seltzer. Dimension preferred the Wayans' take on the would-be film and to ensure no competition, the company bought Friedberg and Seltzer's script, maintaining ownership of the parody with no immediate imitators in sight. However, due to a decision made by the Writers Guild of America, Seltzer and Friedberg are still credited as writers on *Scary Movie* (2000).[16]

The Wayans Brothers have been comedy icons for over three decades. The oldest brother in the family, Keenen Ivory Wayans, began his career as a successful stand-up comedian. He gained notoriety for the 1990s variety sketch show *In Living Color*, formatted similarly to *Saturday Night Live* but with a critical eye to race relations in sketches like "Homey D. Clown" and "The Homeboy Shopping Network." During this time, more of Wayans' brothers entered the entertainment industry and with them, the family went on to keep *In Living Color* going for four seasons and shortly thereafter branched out into films that Keenen was already producing and directing such as *I'm Gonna Git You Sucka* (1988), *Low Down Dirty Shame* (1994) and *Don't Be A Menace to South Central While Drinking Your Juice in the Hood* (1996).

The plot of *Scary Movie* closely resembles the first *Scream* film with Cindy Campbell (Anna Faris) stalked and repeatedly attacked by Ghostface as her friends die around her. The film even includes Gale Weathers and Dewey Riley substitutes: Gail Hailstorm (Cheri Oteri) and Special Officer Doofy (David Sheridan), respectively. The main deviation from *Scream*'s plot is that Cindy and her friends are all in an accidental hit-and-run that occurred the previous Halloween, implicating them in the crime. This element is, obviously, pulled from *I Know What You Did Last Summer*. While *Scary Movie* reaches the same climax as the first with Cindy's boyfriend and her friend threatening to kill her and her father, the two manage to stab each other while the real Ghostface shows up and dispatches with them both. The final scene reveals the mastermind killer to be Doofy, who had been faking his disability, and he rides off into the sunset with Gail.

The notable additions to the plot of *Scary Movie* are Shorty Meeks (Marlon Wayans), a pot-smoking, over the top comic relief, and Brenda Meeks (Regina Hall), the tough black friend of the central group of white friends. Both characters are trope personified to the level of absurdity. The awkwardness of their forced inclusion in other more mainstream white-dominated films is highlighted as a critique of the tokenism that Hollywood is so often fond of patting themselves on the back for. These characters are also the highlight of the film, giving the two strongest performances. Wayans and Hall reach the comedic heights required of them while also grounding their scenes in social commentary. Writer Vanessa Willoughby wrote of the tokenism of the black friend:

> I consumed [teen] movies with equal parts greedy delight and hope, pushing down the unsettling feeling that these films were made not for me, but for my white friends. Like my white friends, I learned how to be a proper teenager through these movies—except most of the films I watched didn't have many black characters. When they did, it was most often the "token black friend," a girl who existed to support the white characters and to act as representative of an entire race.[17]

While *Scary Movie* may appear to be a silly comedy relying on overt parodies of everything from *Scream* to *The Blair Witch Project* (Eduardo

12. The Millennium Approaches

Sanchez and Daniel Myrick, 1999) to *The Matrix* (Lana and Lilly Watchowski, 1999), it is also a commentary about the overwhelming lack of inclusive diversity within this horror cycle. Horror in the 1990s offered up some classic films that sought to include people of color at the center of its stories. Films such as *Tales from the Hood* (Rusty Cundieff, 1995), *A Vampire in Brooklyn* (Wes Craven, 1995), *The People Under the Stairs* (Wes Craven, 1991) and *Candyman* (Bernard Rose, 1992) among others created some space for the black experience within the mainstream genre film. The 1990s Teen Horror Cycle often forgot about these notions of inclusivity, preferring a nearly all-white, if not a completely all-white, cast. While there are exceptions such Rochelle in *The Craft* and Karla in *I Still Know What You Did Last Summer*, their inclusion can feel like a byproduct of tokenism. Ashlee Blackwell on her site *Graveyard Shift Sister* refers to this phenomenon as "pod people," where black characters seem to exist completely isolated from their own communities in service of a white character as a friend or savior.[18] Blackwell elaborates on this theme:

> This particular market had a mass appeal and visually spoke volumes about the diversity conversation in the 90s. Subjectively, diversity when I was coming of age was in fact about quotas: one was enough. Maybe two to be really radical. Even in horror movies.[19]

Scary Movie works as commentary on the very feelings Blackwell describes. While the film is indebted to its own ridiculous gross-out humor, it is also often and frequently a commentary about the exclusion of black culture within the realm of general white pop culture, which all too frequently dominates the market while appropriating black culture. Scholar Robin R. Means Coleman writes in her book *Horror Noire: Blacks in American Horror Films from the 1890s to Present*:

> In the past, Blacks have been the source of "the funny" in comedy-horror, putting on full-display their incredible talents for being simultaneously petrified and hilarious. Unfortunately, the performances were at the expense of Blacks' humanity. Today, "Black horror" says that Blacks no longer need to be assigned "saint-like goodness to counteract the racism ... automatically direct[ed] towards a Black character on screen." The loyal, saintly, or hilariously harmless Black need not to be equivalent of a "normal" White character. The Wayans' *Scary Movie*, which has grossed an incredible $157,019,771 domestically and $278,019,771 worldwide, turned the joke back on horror. The movie, and its sequels, includes spoofs of horror's clichéd treatment of Blacks, thus exposing such practices. By turning the lens back on itself, Blacks have worked to subvert such treatments through their own comedy.[20]

The Wayans provide this expose-quality by requiring the characters to embrace their own tropes and ineptitudes. The female victims are tortured through their adherence to and reliance on their cosmetic beauty, as seen when Ghostface rips out Drew Decker's (Carmen Electra) breast implants right before she is hit by her parents' passing car. As Shorty laments of the passing of Drew:

> GAIL: What can you tell us about the victim?
> SHORTY: Well, she had a phat ass! It was like BANG!

Other victims, such as Shannon Elizabeth's Buffy, also have their bodies repeatedly commented upon. Buffy's physical assets become her defining characteristic as she embodies the Helen Shivers beauty queen character from I *Know What You Did Last Summer*:

> BEAUTY PAGEANT MC: [singing] Here she is. Miss Teen, she's so fine. Such lovely tits…
> [Buffy rips the crown and flowers out of the previous winner's hands]
> BUFFY: Give me my crown, bitch.
> BEAUTY PAGEANT MC: [singing] … and a great behind. There she is, doggy style anytime. And I'll do her behind and behind. Oh, there she is. She loves 69…

The white female victims represent the tropes of those slasher victims of the 1980s; few had any real personality and if they did, they were some combination of vapid and/or sex-crazed. In *Scary Movie*, Drew's death is inevitable, as was Casey's in *Scream*. Drew is vapid and dumb, seemingly deserving of death and Buffy is cruel and narcissistic, a bad person whose demise is cheered for by the audience.

In one of the most telling sequences of the film, Brenda goes to the cinema to watch *Shakespeare in Love* (John Madden, 1998), one of Miramax's iconic Oscar winners, and proceeds to talk on her cellphone much to the chagrin of the white audience all around her. The scene culminates as Ghostface is about to stab Brenda, but he is thwarted when the audience does the deed for him. The scene evokes laughs but also confronts the audience with the black stereotypes in popular culture and in popular spaces.

> BRENDA: Hey baby, you back just in tiiiime! She's about to get in on with Shake-a-speare! He found out she's a girl.
> YOUNG MAN: Shut UP!
> BRENDA: [turns around with the camera pointing at the young man behind her] Yeah I got you! I got you on camera! You on candid camera now! You ain't know 'dat!
> BRENDA: [her cell phones rings and everyone groans as they know what is going to happen] Hello? Hey girl! Ah, I'm in the movies! Uh-huh, yeah Shake-a-speare in love! Ohh-ohh! You lying! You lying!
> YOUNG MAN: For Christ's sake, will you just shut your trap!
> LADY: Shut up!
> BRENDA: [to her friend on the phone] Hold on…
> [to the audience of the movie theater]

12. The Millennium Approaches

BRENDA: I don't know why ya'll is acting like this! My girlfriend already saw the movie and she says they don't even stay together in the end!

Scary Movie's challenge was to parody and satirize the films that came before it, distilling their essence into something both fun and tangible. But it had the double challenge of parodying a film cycle that took pride commenting on what came before it. The 1990s Teen Horror Cycle is notable because of how it commented on the formulaic elements of slashers of the 1970s and 1980s and imbued them with a sense of righteousness and vocalization of the (white) female voice. In *Scary Movie*, the Wayans brothers not only comment on the still problematic elements of the horror film (i.e. sexualization of victims and over-the-top violence inflicted on the female body for entertainment), but they also reframe the narrative to include black characters who are allowed to comment on the proceedings rather than just serve a white character.

Scary Movie's massive success meant a sequel was in order. *Scary Movie 2* was released in 2001 with Cindy, Brenda (having miraculously survived her multiple stabbings) and Shorty as the only returning characters. With an increased budget of $45 million, *Scary Movie 2* made just over $140 million worldwide, still a success but not at the level of the first film. The Wayans left the franchise after the second film with Marlon Wayans saying:

> [We] read in the trades one day they were doing "Scary Movie 3" with somebody else... Dimension owned the movie. They had the right to pick whatever creative staff they wanted and failed at it. We had talks with the Weinsteins but couldn't come to terms. They thought we were worth X, and we thought we were worth Y. They felt they could do the franchise and re-create those results without us.[21]

All told, the *Scary Movie* franchise has had four sequels, each evolving with the times to include J-Horror and found footage parodies among others. With the whiff of diminishing returns in the air, the Wayans were significantly better off leaving the franchise early before it became infested with the biggest name it could get: Charlie Sheen (star of *Scary Movie 4* and *Scary Movie 5*). What the Wayans accomplished in the first film in particular was highlighting the disparity between reality, tropes and stereotypes, offering a view into the morbid absurdity of Hollywood's cultural whitewashing.

13

It's All Coming Back to Me Now

Urban Legends: Bloody Mary (2005), *I'll Always Know What You Did Last Summer* (2006) and *Scream 4* (2011)

The game Bloody Mary may be well known but the third *Urban Legends* film seeks to unravel the mystery behind the titular Mary. Like many contemporary American horror films, *Urban Legends: Bloody Mary* uses its running time to delve into the secrets of a small town, which many thought had been buried with the past until a new generation discovers there is something festering in their hometown.

Beginning in 1969, *Urban Legends: Bloody Mary* follows Mary (Lilith Fields) as she and her friends attend prom with the local heroes of the football team. The boys drug the girls' drinks and while Mary's two friends succumb to the drug, Mary realizes what is about to befall her and makes a run for it. Her date, the captain of the football team, catches up with her in a storage room. When he tries to grab Mary, she bites his hand and he knocks her unconscious. The football captain believes her to be dead and places her body in a nearby trunk. The film then flashes forward to 2004 where Samantha (Kate Mara) is telling the story to her friends at a sleepover since the three high school seniors could not get dates to the prom after Samantha wrote an expose stating that the football players are automatically given good grades for being on the team. The girls decide to say "Bloody Mary" out loud and the next morning all three of them are missing. A few days later they return dirty and bruised but are ultimately fine. While it was the football players Samantha wrote the expose on who drugged them and locked them up in a factory on the outskirts of town, Samantha begins to see the ghostly apparition of Mary all around her. The students in on the prank begin dying horrible, elaborate deaths based on urban legends. One of the would-be victims passes Samantha a letter she received with news articles from 1969 about Mary's disappearance. Samantha begins to investigate and comes across the names of the other two victims from the 1969 incident, one of whom killed herself and the other, Grace (Tina Lifford), who still lives in town. Samantha and her brother David (Robert Vito) go to speak to Grace who is hesitant to get involved, but David sneaks around her house and finds scrapbooks and drawings indicating Grace's obsession with urban legends, including multiple clippings about the murders at Pendleton University and Alpine College from the previous *Urban Legends* films.

With the eventual help of Grace, Samantha and Robert discover that the fathers of the football players who played the prank on Samantha were behind the assault and manslaughter of Mary in 1969; it is also revealed that Samantha and David's stepfather Bill (Ed Marinaro) was the former captain of the football team and Mary's killer. Further flashbacks reveal that Mary was not dead when he placed her in the trunk, but because she was trapped, she died a slow, painful and lonely death. Bill kills David and pursues Samantha in the town's graveyard where she is trying to bury Mary's remains to put her spirit at rest. Mary's ghost appears once again and pulls Bill into Hell with her.

Directed by Mary Lambert—well-known in the horror community for her direction of *Pet Sematary* (1989) and *Pet Sematary 2* (1992)—*Urban Legends: Bloody Mary* is an aggressively told story, taking its inspiration from the then current J-Horror ghost story trend to the grisly and gruesome deaths that awaited characters in films like *Saw* (James Wan, 2004) and *Final Destination* all wrapped up in a whodunit thriller. Part of the appeal this film is the sheer energy that careens between narratives, styles and storytelling devices, marking it as an un-unified mess but also a rather pleasingly hectic attempt at committing the story of Bloody Mary to screen. The reviews, as one might imagine, were less than kind, with Dread Central labeling it as "nothing remarkable" and the website HellHole calling it an "average experience"; *Urban Legends: Bloody Mary* was not reviewed by larger outlets. Aiming to retain its rights to the franchise, Sony shot the film quickly and cheaply and released it on DVD with little to no fanfare. The film was originally just about the Bloody Mary story, but Sony insisted other urban legends as well as the colleges where the first two films took place be mentioned.[1] *Urban Legends: Bloody Mary* functions as a fascinating attempt at merging two radically different styles of filmmaking—the post-modern whodunit of the 1990s and the glossy gore of the new millennium. While the film ultimately fails as anything more than an oddball entry into the *Urban Legends* franchise, it does boldly attempt to mesh styles while grappling with the secretive codes of toxic masculinity that breed within a small town.

The game Bloody Mary has several iterations but most commonly the players must stand in a darkened room or area and say, "Bloody Mary" three times—usually in front of a mirror, inciting Bloody Mary herself to appear. Some versions say she will scare the player to death, turn their hair white or claw at their face. While the game is thought to have several origins, one of the most common is based on a witch named Mary Worth who lived in Chicago during the Civil War. It is said that Mary used to capture slaves who were fleeing to the North for freedom and keep them chained in her cellar for punishment and experimentation. Eventually the locals grew wary of Worth and killed her. After her death, strange and malevolent events plagued anyone who would set foot in her home.

However, differing version of the legend and game ascribe the moniker of Bloody Mary to multiple women, including Mary I of England, whose mission as a monarch was to bring Catholicism back to England. The truer invocation of Bloody Mary within the context of urban legends falls more in line with the previously mentioned Mary Worth or any number of other women bearing the name Mary and the moniker of witch.

The most important aspect of this urban legend, which comes to bear in the film, is that of the mirror. Many generations have grown wary of mirrors' supposed magic; though the reflection is accurate, it is reversed, causing many to believe there is some element of dimensional interaction between the known world and another. As the website *Diabolical Confusions* elaborates:

> Most dominantly, mirrors have been used by witches, warlocks, and the practitioners of magick for many, many centuries... From the advent of mirrors in general, practitioners or magick have used in a technique called "scrying," which is a practice which enables the individual to physically see things in a medium, in this case, the mirror.[2]

Scholar Elizabeth Tucker went on to further apply this history to the uses of contemporary adolescents suggesting that:

> college students' stories of apparitions in mirrors reflect a search for affirmation of a complex, sometimes contradictory self. These apparitions differ radically from what the viewer expects; instead of seeing her own face, a female student may see the face of a young man. Instead of seeing his own full-length reflection, a male student may see the image of a grim young man wearing black clothes. Seeing the opposite of what one expects is startling and frightening; the stimulus for telling stories makes it possible to understand perceived experience.[3]

Urban Legends: Bloody Mary situates this historical and contemporary fear and wariness of mirrors as something to dispel a current truth. Through

Mary's reappearance through a game based on mirrors, the characters find out the local histories told to them and believed by them are false and that they must seek their own truths. The film goes on to employ the vengeful female spirit, which was making a rather large cultural comeback in North America with films like *The Ring* (Gore Verbinski, 2002) and *The Grudge* (Takashi Shimizu, 2004). Author David Kalat refers to this spirit in his book *J-Horror: The Definitive Guide to The Ring, The Grudge and Beyond* as the "Dead Wet Girl,"[4] a figure marked by its black hair covering its face and clothed in a white tattered night gown. The use of ghosts and the supernatural in *Urban Legends* is particularly interesting, as the ghost is meant to right a past wrong and, in doing so, recasts an entire generation. Author Bill Ellis writes of this transgression between generations and the natural and supernatural world:

> The legend-trip is more than an initiation into the supernatural; it functions as a ritual of rebellion, the trip is the significant thing to the adolescent, and the legend serves mainly as an excuse to escape adult supervision.... Hence the ritual curses spoken on Bloody Mary's grave are directed not so much at a witch—a person who embodies an ideology counter to conventional society—but as a representation of adult morality. Legend-trips create a play-like situation that gives participants an excuse to indulge in deviant behavior that explicitly "gives the finger" to Bloody Mary and other bogies, but the actions [rebellion] in fact defy adult figures and adult authority.[5]

The would-be antagonists of *Urban Legends: Bloody Mary* have already set their sights on Samantha and her friends as a targets of a prank. Samantha's expose on the football team is less tawdry school gossip and more questioning of inherent privilege bestowed on a select few. The jocks need and want to keep their semi-secret advantage, so they aim to scare Samantha and her friends into keeping quiet about it—which, at first, they do. Samantha, though unhurt, is shaken by the events of that night and wants to put them behind, but the ghost of Mary will not let her. Mary's ghost and Grace lead Samantha down a path to discover what happened the night of the prom in 1969, which has become a town ghost story since Mary's body was never found. That path for Samantha is one of sinful fathers. The boys who drugged and raped two girls and killed another preached a similar story to their sons, giving them the idea for the prank exacted on Samantha. The misogynistic leanings of one generation can pass on to another. In the film's climax, Samantha and David's stepfather Bill is willing to kill his own stepchildren in favor of keeping the secret. The initial set up of Bill is that of a candidate for mayor in their small town. Bill's lack of punishment has allowed him to rise through the ranks of the establishment but it has not cured his hatred.

Cinematic ghosts, even before the J-Horror trend, often had a message for the living. Sometimes what was wrong or untrue had to be corrected, hence the need for them to come back to impart their message. As John Kenneth Muir writes:

> The fear of death is at the heart of all horror films, on a basic level. But the ghost story concerns a fear beyond even that one. In the cinematic ghost story lurks our fear that there is survival after death, but it is not a survival we hope or seek.[6]

In *Urban Legends: Bloody Mary* the unjust nature of the patriarchal world order extends beyond death and beyond generations. Samantha must rely on Grace to constantly explain to her what is going on and how the horror might be stopped. Though awkward, this relationship between a woman of past trauma and one of new trauma shows the camaraderie between women the film aims to illustrate.

Sylvain White's *I'll Always Know What You Did Last Summer* (2006) exists somewhere between a remake, reboot and sequel. Most interestingly, it functions as a belated sequel, attempting to recreate the function of the slasher heyday of the 1980s that once again centers around the killer. *I'll Always Know What You Did Last Summer* does try to keep its audience guessing by functioning like a neo-slasher, only revealing its supernatural mythology at the very end.

In a small Colorado town, Amber (Brooke Nevin) and her boyfriend Colby (David Paetkau) and friends Zoe (Torrey DeVitto) and Roger (Seth Packard) decide to play a Fourth of July prank on their small town. While visiting the town's annual amusement park, the group is careful to spread the word of the Fisherman—an urban legend who stalks and kills teens around the Fourth of July if they have somehow trespassed. They pull a prank with their friend PJ (Clay Taylor), who is seemingly attacked by the Fisherman (who is Roger in disguise), which goes horribly wrong. PJ ends up impaled on a pipe after attempting a skateboarding trick designed to escape the Fisherman. The friends make an ill-advised pact to burn the evidence of their involvement and go about their lives as if it never happened. A year passes and things start to go wrong, though. Amber and Colby break up after Colby is taken aback by the responsibilities of real life and Amber is determined to get out of their small town and has drifted away from Zoe who is intent on getting her music career on track. Roger has taken a job fixing ski gondolas in the off-season and is wracked by guilt over the events. Amber begins receiving text messages that read, "I know what you did last summer." She attempts to regroup with her friends who disbelieve her. Later that night Roger contemplates suicide and produces the hook they used in the prank, which he salvaged and kept. The Fisherman appears and kills him. Amber's friend Lance (Ben Easter) has also become a target as he and Amber have grown closer. The Fisherman continues picking them off one by one and the friends begin to suspect one other and other members of the community as the person behind the killings. Finally, when Lance and Amber are the only remaining survivors, the Fisherman is revealed to be Ben Willis as a zombified, undead killer who has apparently been travelling the country punishing teenagers. Amber realizes that the best way to hurt him is to wound him with the hook that they used in the prank. Amber stabs Ben Willis in the head with the hook and pushes him into a wood-chipper. Lance and Amber survive and maintain that they have no idea why someone would attack them. In the final scene, Amber is driving to LA to meet up with Lance when her car breaks down and she loses cell phone reception, allowing the Fisherman to strike once more.

I'll Always Know What You Did Last Summer was originally intended to be produced and released in 2000, continuing the story of Julie, Ray and Karla from the franchise's first sequel.[7] However, the project remained dormant after the low box office of *I Still Know What You Did Last Summer* and was eventually picked up and brought to life by two smaller film companies, Original Film and Destination Films. The rushed production with its original director, who dropped out and was replaced by Sylvain White, meant that preproduction on the film was completed in two weeks, though it was meant to take several months.[8] The film apes on more successful horror films that came out in the years prior, such as Verbinski's *The Ring*, which created a disturbing nightmarish mise-en-scene using almost entirely blue filters. White's embracement of this style creates a haphazard pace to the film that involves multiple bright flashes and quick cuts in scenes meant to depict great tension, and its sedate color palette highlights the blandness of the interactions between characters and scenes. Films like *I'll Always Know What You Did Last Summer*, which attempt to parlay some successful elements of their predecessors into an increasingly edgy and intense aesthetic, lose what worked in the first films. While flawed, *I Know What You Did Last Summer* and *I Still Know What You Did Last Summer* set the horror against beatific landscapes shot to increase to the dichotomy between an Americana-filled backdrop and the dark secrets of the characters.

The main thrust of the film is indebted to the narrative arc of *I Know What You Did Last Summer* and *Scream*. It functions as a whodunit with multiple characters given motivation for attacking these teens who truly do have something to hide. Their paranoia is part of their unraveling, so, when they finally come to face The Fisherman, they are wounded and weak emotionally and physically. In an interview with IGN actress Brooke Nevin elaborated on her role in the film and its place in cinema.

I'll Always Know What You Did Last Summer follows a similar formula to the first two films, but it was a blank slate in terms of the cast so I didn't really feel any pressure to mimic any of the previous characters.... It is always the debaucherous teens that get their innards pulled outwards first, isn't it? There's something to be said for horror films having an undertone of some moral parable.[9]

I'll Always Know What You Did Last Summer plays even more with the implications and themes of responsibility and guilt. The inciting event in the film is no accident; it was a heavily choreographed prank in which the main characters are responsible for what befalls them. By continuing to spread the legend of Ben Willis, the friends—in a similar way to saying Candyman five times—cause the Fisherman to appear.

> AMBER: So you've all heard the story right? About what happens on July 4th?
> COLBY: Whoa, Amber, you wanna freak everyone out?
> AMBER: No! I just like hearing you tell it.
> FRIEND: What are you guys talking about?
> COLBY: The Fisherman. Every Fourth of July he gets out his hat and slicker, he sharpens up his hook and runs wild.
> AMBER: But only after teenagers.
> COLBY: That's right, but only the ones with dirty little secrets. What about you Zoe? I bet you got some dirty little secrets.
> ZOE: Yeah, I heard you suck in bed.
> COLBY: Hey, seriously. A guy on my ski team knows this girl who went camping last summer and they saw the Fisherman. Two days later, two kids didn't make it out of the woods.
> ZOE: So he's like Santa Claus? But in reverse, he only goes after the kids that are naughty.
> COLBY: No! He's more like Jack the Ripper, except the guy never got caught.

I'll Always Know What You Did Last Summer fuses different elements of the 1990s Teen Horror Cycle—particularly its preponderance on the whodunit narrative and its bend towards urban legends as source material—but attempts to call back to the slasher heyday with the return of the original monster antagonist. Jessica Balanzategui wrote of this device:

> Usually the answer to the "whodunit" question delivered at the climax of these films reveals a seemingly harmless person who has been hinging in the community unscrutinised: his (or less often her) monstrosity lurking beneath a mask of normality.... These self-aware slashers achieve a sense of play through renewing and updating the whodunit quest typical of slashers of the early 1980s. The mystery plot quite literally becomes a game in the postmodern slasher.... Thus, the postmodern slashers place the whodunit game at the center of their ludic and self-reflexive deconstruction of the subgenre, as viewers are tasked with deploying their intertextual knowledge of the slasher formula in order to resolve the mystery of the killer's identity.[10]

The film situates Ben Willis in the lineage of Freddy Krueger, Jason Voorhees and Michael Myers by having him return to the narrative after seemingly

13. It's All Coming Back to Me Now 163

having been active in the eight or so years in-between films, which negates the cat and mouse game the late 1990s neo-slasher preferred. It does, however, fit neatly into the 1990s aesthetic through its inclusion of a real flesh and blood killer. In their depiction of the supernatural, the final minutes of the film become consumed in hashing out some kind of mythology that the film never quite gets a handle on. As Balazategui notes of the supernatural elements in slasher films:

> Supernatural slashers draw to the surface the anxieties that ere a latent feature of early slashers and render them central conceits. Through drawing these disorienting contradictions to the foreground, supernatural slashers thus render the underlying foundations of the classic form overt before subverting and renewing them.... This transition from implicit to overt supernatural elements functions as a concomitant aggrandizement of the killer's unrelenting powers, reinforcing classic slasher elements rather than representing a meaningful shift in thematic preoccupations.[11]

The initial films set up the franchise to deal with the trauma of responsibility and causality. They dealt with the ties that the best and brightest have to a small town and how trauma can forever tie them to a place and time negating their own ambitions and dreams. The two original films situated the trauma in Julie James's guilt over her involvement in the initial accident and the subsequent deaths of her friends. In this way, Ben Willis and The Fisherman came to represent a personified version of Julie's guilt and heavily hinted at PTSD. In *I'll Always Know What You Did Last Summer*, the hubris of the internal group is what sets the actions into motion. The original film posited a murkier modus operandi for Ben Willis, but in the second sequel he has become a Robin Hood–esque figure, dealing out punishment to teens who get away with crimes. Amber's rather brutal murder of The Fisherman (hook to the head and consumption by wood chipper) plays more into the new millennium tropes and dismemberments dispatched by films like *Saw* and *Cabin Fever*. The ethically complicated and flawed characters play into the demands of an audience that values gore and brutality over morality.

In the 11 years since *Scream 3*'s release, Harvey and Bob Weinstein had left Miramax and started The Weinstein Company, which would now house the *Scream* franchise, as they still retained ownership of Dimension Films.[12] Under The Weinstein Company they continued to produce prestige pictures with some element of European flare, such as the Oscar-nominated *The Reader* (Stephen Daldry, 2008) and *Inglourious Basterds* (Quentin Tarantino, 2009). In 2007, three direct-to-video labels were created. One of these, Dimension Extreme, took on many of the gory, over-the-top European films—such as *Inside* (Julien Maury and Alexandre Bustillo, 2007) and *Eden Lake* (James Watkins, 2008)—that were marking a mark on the festival circuit scene. It also continued the practice of producing low-budget films, which were key to Weinstein retaining the rights to certain horror properties such as *Hellraiser: Revelations* (Victor Garcia, 2011) and *Children of the Corn: Genesis* (Joel Soisson, 2011). *Scream 4*, however, was meant to be a return to the prestige genre form, if all went according to plan.

Since *Scream 3*'s release in 2000, horror films had worked their way through several permutations including Torture Porn and the North American J-Horror movement. In many ways, horror was coming down from a too-wild party—gutting and flesh removal and creepy girls with straggly black hair who were developing stronghold within nightmares—but the iconic horror villains were still keeping the party going. *Scream 4* attempts to claw back on the guts, blood and supernatural elements that were beginning to spin out of control for most mainstream audiences. The question faced by Wes Craven once more was, what would drive someone to kill in 2011? As Craven said at the time of the film's Blu Ray release:

> That's the whole reason I'm still doing this at my age. It's not just about screams and sex, but matters that are serious to us as adults. I like to think I'm making films in the film business, where movies are making enough numbers for the studios to let me keep working, but you also want those films to have content that makes you proud you made the film. That's not easy, but it's a fun puzzle to figure out.[13]

Scream 4 was on the table as early as July 2008[14] with Craven on board to direct. He worked on an outline with original screenwriter Kevin Williamson who, after producing a draft of the script, left the production while still maintaining sole writing credit on the film. From there Ehren Kruger, writer of *Scream 3*, was brought on for rewrites with additional rewrites by Paul Harris Boardman, whose previous screenwriting credits include *Dracula 2000* (Patrick Lussier, 2000), *Hellraiser: Inferno* (Scott Derrickson, 2000) and *The Exorcism of Emily Rose* (Scott Derrickson, 2005). In an interview with *Cinemablend*, Craven elaborated on the development process:

> [Bob Weinstein] told us, there was not going to be a *Scream 4* for a long period mostly because of *Scary Movie* and because he didn't want us just making it because we could, so I think it was smart of him to wait until we could comment on an entire decade and a decade that was the 21st century; that's a significant landscape to set your picture on.[15]

Scream 4 begins with a film within a film in a film. The first of two false openings is for *Stab 6*, the fictional franchise within the film that has carried on in the *Scream* cinematic universe. In it, two teens receive threatening phone calls and Facebook messages. After their bloody deaths, the film hard cuts to two young women, Rachel and Chloe (Anna Paquin and Kristen Bell), who are about to watch *Stab 6*, but Rachel quickly begins lamenting the state of horror.

13. It's All Coming Back to Me Now

RACHEL: That was so fucking stupid. Pure horseshit, the death of horror right in front of us.
CHLOE: I jumped, it scared me.
RACHEL: A fucking Facebook killer? You're kidding me.
CHLOE: I guess now it would be Twitter, that would make more sense.
RACHEL: A bunch of articulate teens sit around and deconstruct horror movies, until Ghostface kills them one by one it's been done to death, the whole self-aware, post-modern meta shit.
CHLOE: I like the *Stab* movies. They're scarier. It's not aliens or zombies or little Asian ghost-girls, there's something real about a guy with a knife who just snaps. It could really happen.
RACHEL: I can't do it. These sequels don't know when to stop. They just keep recycling the same shit. Even the opening scene, there's some random girl who gets a call which undoubtedly gets her killed. There's no element of surprise, you can see everything coming.
[Chloe stabs Rachel in the stomach with a kitchen knife]
CHLOE: Did that surprise you?

This scene is then revealed to be a trick opening to *Stab 7*. The two fake openings to *Scream 4* serve to highlight and address audience expectations in the years since Casey Becker (Drew Barrymore) picked up her phone of doom one night. Craven also goes on to explain that these fake openings were intentionally playing with time by having characters use a Sidekick phone, which was outdated by a few years when *Scream 4* premiered. To subvert expectations, production took the time to create openings that would not be entirely outside of *Scream*'s realms but that did not include quite as much style or realistic violence.[16]

Scream 4's true beginning centers on two Woodsboro teens—Marnie (Britt Robertson) and Jenny (Aimee Teegarden)—who are watching *Stab 7* and lamenting the state of horror. Jenny disappears upstairs to prank Marnie with a Ghostface phone app. The real Ghostface shows up and kills Marnie, then begins tormenting Jenny until he kills her with a garage door. Her death is reminiscent of the death of Tatum (Rose McGowan) in the first film.

Before the real Ghostface arrived on the scene, Jenny and Marnie discussed the state of the *Stab* franchise.

MARNIE: It begs the question that if the beginning of *Stab 7* is *Stab 6* then is the beginning of *Stab 6*, *Stab 5*? And if so, then what is *Stab 4* about?
JENNY: You're overthinking it.
MARNIE: Am I? Or did whoever made it just under-think it. There's a reason I don't watch these movies.
JENNY: I can't believe you haven't seen them, we live in Woodsboro.
MARNIE: That has nothing to do with Woodsboro. I thought you said *Stab* was based on true story.
JENNY: The first three, the original trilogy is based off of Sidney Prescott but

then she threatened to sue them if they used her story so then they just started making stuff up. *Stab 5* has time travel, which is by far the worst.

In the three openings, the final of which introduces *Scream 4*, Jenny and Marnie set up the world in which the fictionalized versions of the first *Scream* films have run amok and taken on a life of their own. For *Scream 4*, the opening is a rational way of explaining why there were no endless sequels despite each film generating a healthy box office return. In *Scream 4*, the violence must come from somewhere and as the film continues, we see that it comes from the void the films have filled in the lives of all the characters. Craven explains of those openings:

> *Stab* is up to ... number seven and the kids talk a great deal about that because we established that the first three *Stabs* basically were based on the life of Sidney Prescott. So then she sued them for using her story and for ... making the one sequel after another. So that's kind of our poking fun at people who just make endless sequels.... Within the context there is the evil version of people ... that are aware of original them ... a certain copying of them in a way to get at Sid's arriving in town. She thinks having dealt with all the ghosts and perhaps even living in a town in a peaceful way that could put the stuff behind her. So that's part of what those traces are doing; they're saying it's not over.[17]

Scream 4's plot follows Sidney's teenage cousin Jill (Emma Roberts) and her friends, horror movie fan Kirby (Hayden Panettiere) and Olivia (Marielle Jaffe), who are helping Jill through her breakup with Trevor (Nico Tortorella). Soon they learn that Jenny and Marnie have been killed and that Ghostface may be behind it once again. Sidney has returned home for the final stop on her book tour for her book *Out of Darkness: A True Story of Survival* and Jill and her friends deem Sidney the Angel of Death, as murder seems to follow her wherever she goes. Once Jenny and Marnie's bodies are discovered, Dewey (who is now Sheriff of Woodsboro) asks that Sidney stay in town while they figure things out. Sidney agrees, staying with her Aunt Kate (Mary McDonnell) and Jill.

Gale appears on the scene warmly greeting Sidney but struggling with jealousy over the accolades that Sidney's book is getting as Gale struggles to write her next book. More murders occur and Gale is wounded by Ghostface at a *Stab*-A-Thon screening organized by the high school film club. Jill, Kirby, Trevor, Charlie (Rory Culkin) and Robbie (Erik Knudsen) reconvene after the *Stab*-A-Thon madness at Kirby's house. Sidney arrives, too, and Ghostface kills Robbie, Trevor and Kirby. In the style of Billy and Stu, Jill and Charlie reveal themselves to be the killers. Jill goes to give a flesh wound to Charlie but kills him. When Sidney questions Jill, she responds:

> JILL: What world are you living in? I don't need friends. I need fans. Don't you get it? This has never been about killing you? It's about becoming you. I mean,

for fuck's sake, my own mother had to die, no great loss there, so I could stay true to the original. That's sick, right? Well, sick is the new sane. You had your 15 minutes, now I want mine! I mean, what am I supposed to do? Go to college? Grad school? Work? Look around. We all live in public now, we're all on the Internet. How do you think people become famous anymore? You don't have to achieve anything. You just gotta have fucked up-shit happen to you. So you have to die, Sid. Those are the rules. New movie, new franchise. There's only room for one lead, and let's face it, your ingénue days, they're over.

Jill's motivation for the murders stems from living in Sidney's shadow her whole life—a burden the other characters must bear as well. Gale deals with it most explicitly as Sidney rewrites her narrative from that of victim to survivor in her own book, surpassing Gale's book *The Woodsboro Murders*, which the *Stab* movies were based on. When the murders start again, Gale sees an opportunity to reprise her former role of tabloid, shock journalist, which almost gets her killed. The rest of the town seems stunted by the events—events that once shook a community to its core and never truly went away.

Scream 4 pits Sidney and Gale against each other through Sidney's determination to be a survivor rather than a victim and Gale's desire to reach her 1990s glory once again through the stories of victims. When Gale is seriously wounded by Ghostface at the *Stab*-A-Thon, she can no longer further her narrative, as she herself must decide to be a survivor rather than a victim. As Gale tells Dewey in the hospital:

GALE: Promise me something?
DEWEY: Anything.
GALE: Catch that motherfucker.

Jill's obsession with becoming Sidney is that of becoming the Final Girl, a hero who survives to the end and, in Jill's mind, reaps the rewards. What Jill lacks is true trauma; her orchestration of the events prevents her from reaching that final echelon of heroics. Sidney survives a stab wound inflicted by Jill, who Sidney, Gale and Dewey later stop at the hospital. Jill attacks all of them and they are forced to kill her. *Scream 4*, like its commentary on the *Stab* films, illustrates that the initial trauma can never be supplanted, duplicated or evolved.

Scream 4 ultimately plays off the ending of the first. After Billy and Stu are killed, Randy warns Sidney that killers can come back for one final scare, to which she responds with a final bullet to Billy's head and the declaration, "not in my movie." The final moments in *Scream* show Gale reporting from the scene of the crime, which she so narrowly escaped alive. Thus, it is Gale that spreads the knowledge of what has happened, once again creating a media circus as she did after Sidney's mother's death. The story would go on to inspire others to follow in Billy and Stu's footsteps either for notoriety (as with Mickey in *Scream 2*) or for vengeance (as with Debbie in *Scream 2* and Roman in *Scream 3*). Jill, however, sees the true goal not as being a murderer but as being a survivor. She brings death to Woodsboro in hopes of getting the same attention she has seen lavished on Sidney. In the final chilling moments of *Scream 4*, news crews are lined up outside the hospital breathlessly reporting on the heroics of Jill who, unbeknownst to them, lies above them dead. Jill is another victim of a media obsessed culture—one that sought to control a narrative in hopes of attaining fame and fortune at the cost of other people's lives. When Sidney tells Jill not to fuck with the original, she is, in essence, not only standing up for herself and her story, but also once again claiming the narrative as hers. While *Scream 4* offers up a new generation of characters to carry on the torch of the franchise, it kills them off, because all roads lead back to Sidney and the night of Stu's party. Western culture is content to relive tragedy after tragedy in hopes of creating fear, uncertainty and ratings. In *Scream 4*, Sidney acts as a reminder that trauma is rooted in the real and can never be manufactured.

Conclusion

In viewing the teen horror films of the 1990s together as a single film cycle, links, both big and small, to the feminist movement become evident. These films sought to portray young men and women not as victims of a malevolent force but as survivors. Those who survive these films (and there are a great deal more survivors within this horror cycle than in many others) are tasked with the weight of what that survival means. The extension of these characters' narratives forces them to explore trauma, guilt and responsibility (particularly in the case of Sidney from the *Scream* films and Julie from *I Know What You Did Last Summer*). The implementation of an intertextual relationship between the characters and the audience made the potential victims, rather than the killers whose motivations were often borne out of a previous event linked to the protagonist, more relatable to the audience.

The 1990s were rife with intertextual or post-modern references, meaning that characters would and could often cite other cultural texts, such as movies and television shows, to make sense of the filmic world around them. This is not something the 1990s Teen Horror Cycle invented but was rather a general conversation beginning to develop out of North America as seen in everything from *The Simpsons* to *Clueless* to *Beavis and Butthead*. Characters unaware of the culture around them would have been unidentifiable to the target audience. With the rapid spread of the internet and the rise of the 24 hour news cycle, the generation who came of age as these films were released had a lens through which to view the world outside of their immediate families. They were able to disseminate current events through their own developing lens rather than depending on the opinions of adults around them.

The rampant success of these films meant that studios were keen to mine the formula and once one script—that of *Scream*—was solidified with Kevin Williamson, others followed in quick succession. They deviated from the beloved horror franchises of the 1980s, which were reliant on villains, practical effects and home video rentals to stimulate the revenue. These new 1990s teen slashers could often feel too easy or inclusive for many who preferred their horror films exclusive and hard to find. These new teen horror movies felt too brazenly mainstream to capture the supposed uniqueness of horror franchises that depended on preordained formulas to keep them going. However, the 1990s Teen Horror Cycle illustrated the importance of reorienting iconic tropes in order to make the slasher formula feel fresh and viable once again. The 1990s were also radically different, as the 1980s were dominated by Reagan-era conservatism and the 1990s by the left-leaning central politics of Bill Clinton, who faced his own scandals throughout his eight years as president. The rise of the 24-hour news cycle and the constant stream of national tragedies, which called into question the very nature of the American identity—especially that of its youth—required that films speak directly to young people through characters who questioned the world around them. The youth in the 1990s were dismayed and disenfranchised by the promises of their parents' generation who were perhaps just as unhappy as them. The American Dream was a mirage, and its broken promises seeped into the music and film of the 1990s.

These horror films sought to humanize everyone even if they were not always worthy of it. Few other major franchises would have allowed Gale Weathers to survive time and again, but *Scream* did because Courteney Cox was a major television star and because Gale added an implicit critique of the media savvy world the characters lived in. This was part of the intersection of media critique and business savvy that these films embraced. The teen horror films of the 1990s did not deny the culture or react against it; they embraced it and the litany of complexities that came with it. In the 1990s, the violence and terror did not end when the murders did but when the media moved on to the next national tragedy.

For all that 1990s Teen Horror did for some young women, it failed on numerous levels to include those who were not white cis hetero middle class female (and occasional male) heroes. The inclusion of black characters such as Rochelle in *The Craft*, Hallie in *Scream 2* and Karla in *I Still Know What You Did Last Summer* feel at best under developed and at worst tokenized. This massive discrepancy was similar to the complaints levied against Riot Grrrl and Third Wave feminism of being centered on white women who consistently ignored the systemic problems other women faced. The feminism of the 1990s was deeply imperfect. Feminism today is still imperfect because it still struggles to be fully intersectional. In this regard, the 1990s Teen Horror Cycle was a small step forward—one that began to acknowledge the discrepancies that existed before it. It was part of the mainstream Hollywood discourse on youth and young women, which, on occasion, would allow them to step outside of and overcome the rigid gender roles that had been imposed on them for decades before.

For so long horror films and film in general separated characters into good and bad, with the occasional anti-hero rising above the fray. The films in this book attempted to confuse the two, implicating heroes directly in the events that led to trauma and horror, and examining how horror arises from the death of the American family and the American Dream. In so doing, these films offer a transgressive look at the lives of young people—who seemingly have all the advantages—and complicates them by casting the characters into darkness and forcing them to fight for their survival. It is their privilege that disguises them and allows them to wallow in the narratives created for them. When they are ultimately forced to confront that privilege, they do not undo it but often feel the weight of it. The youths in these films are confronted with the ambiguous notions of good and evil that were prevalent in the 1990s through various sectors all claiming ownership over perceived goodness. While leaders could do good things for many people, it would not excuse the skeletons in their proverbial closets. The 1990s Teen Horror Cycle focuses on the victims because they are what the culture was most interested in. From JonBenét Ramsay to Monica Lewinsky to the students at Columbine High School, victims were the new media's bread and butter.

The films of the 1990s Teen Horror Cycle made teen audiences question what the true nature of violence was and who, if anyone, was to blame. These films' style of self-referential, consumer driven storytelling spread beyond a film cycle and spoke to an entire generation of media, as seen through Kevin Williamson's *Dawson's Creek*, which went on to develop mainstream appeal the year after *Scream*'s release. The 1990s Teen Horror Cycle was an important if brief moment in popular culture when major film studios tapped into the desires of youth culture, creating a zeitgeist which few anticipated. The films in this cycle were commercial, but they also offered some reprieve from the American Dream, which was disintegrating on round-the-clock 24-hour news channels. The characters in these films questioned the world around them and refused to let the killers control their hard fought narratives.

Chapter Notes

Introduction

1. Alan Jones, *The Rough Guide to Horror Movies* (London: Rough Guides, 2005), 47.
2. Ben Bussey, "20 Films That Prove the 1990s was the Worst Decade for Horror," *What Culture* (May 6, 2016), http://whatculture.com/film/20-films-that-prove-the-1990s-was-the-worst-decade-for-horror.
3. *Ibid.*
4. Scott Kessinger, *Scream Deconstructed: An Unauthorized Analysis* (Las Vegas: Stinger Books, 2011), 49.
5. John Kenneth Muir, *Horror Films of the 1980s* (Jefferson, NC: McFarland, 2012), 11.
6. Carol Clover, *Men, Women and Chainsaws: Gender in the Modern Horror Film* (Princeton, NJ: Princeton University Press, 1992), 56.
7. Mikal Gilmore "Welcome to his Nightmare: How Freddy Krueger Became a Pop Icon," *Rolling Stone* (October 6, 1988), http://www.rollingstone.com/movies/features/nightmare-on-elm-street-freddy-krueger-pop-icon-19881006.
8. Jonathan Rhodes, *Watching The Simpsons: Television, Parody, and Intertextuality* (New York: Routledge, 2011), 19–21.
9. Christine Spines, "Chicks Dig Scary Movies," *Entertainment Weekly* (July 24, 2009), http://ew.com/article/2009/07/24/chicks-dig-scary-movies/.
10. Carol Clover, *Men, Women and Chainsaws: Gender in the Modern Horror Film* (Princeton, NJ: Princeton University Press, 1992), 33.
11. Stephen Neale, *Genre and Hollywood* (New York: Psychology Press, 2000), 1.
12. Richard Nowell, *Blood Money: A History of the First Teen Slasher Film Cycle* (London: Continuum Press, 2011), 18.
13. Carol Clover, *Men, Women and Chainsaws: Gender in the Modern Horror Film* (Princeton, NJ: Princeton University Press, 1992), 30.
14. John Kenneth Muir, *Horror Films of the 1990s* (Jefferson, NC: McFarland, 2011), 500.
15. Peter Howell, "The Rise of Girl Power and Geek Culture in '90s Teen Flicks," *The Toronto Star* (October 9, 2014), https://www.thestar.com/entertainment/movies/2014/10/09/the_rise_of_girl_power_and_geek_culture_in_90s_teen_flicks_column.html.
16. Stephen Neale, *Genre and Hollywood* (New York: Psychology Press, 2000), 31.
17. Timothy Shary, *Generation Multiplex: The Image of Youth in American Cinema Since 1980* (Austin, TX: University of Austin Press, 2013), 29.
18. Brian J. Robb, *Screams and Nightmares: The Films of Wes Craven* (Woodstock, NY: The Overlook Press, 1998), 178.

Chapter 1

1. Kurt Andersen, "The Best Decade Ever? The 1990s, Obviously," *The New York Times* (February 6, 2015), https://www.nytimes.com/2015/02/08/opinion/sunday/the-best-decade-ever-the-1990s-obviously.html.
2. Alexis de Tocqueville, "Democracy in America," *Marxists* (April 2017), https://www.marxists.org/reference/archive/de-tocqueville/democracy-america/ch39.htm.
3. William H. Chafe, *The Rise and Fall of the American Century: The United States from 1890–2010* (Oxford, England: Oxford University Press, 2009), 261.
4. Anita Hill, "Testimony to Senate Judiciary Committee," *Speech Vault* (March 2017), http://www.speeches-usa.com/Transcripts/anita_hill-testimony.html.
5. Susan Faludi, *Blacklash: The Undeclared War Against American Women* (New York: Broadway Books, 2006), xi.
6. Rebecca Walker, "Becoming the Third

Wave," *The Essential Feminist Reader*, ed. Estelle B. Freedman (New York: Modern Library, 2007), 401.

7. Andi Zeisler, *Feminism and Pop Culture* (New York: Seal Press, 2008), 89.

8. Marisa Meltzer, *Girl Power: The Nineties Revolution in Music* (New York: Farrar, Straus and Giroux, 2010), 11.

9. Kim Taylor Bennett, "Kathleen Hanna on Tokenism, Therapy and Where Riot Grrrl Went Wrong," *Noisey* (October 21, 2016), https://noisey.vice.com/en_us/article/kathleen-hanna-on-tokenism-therapy-and-where-riot-grrrl-went-wrong.

10. "Winners of 1991," *Time Magazine* (January 6, 1992), 45.

11. Marisa Meltzer, *Girl Power: The Nineties Revolution in Music* (New York: Farrar, Straus and Giroux, 2010), 74.

12. Susan J. Douglas, *Enlightened Sexism* (New York: Times Books, 2010), 19.

13. Gil Troy, *The Age of Clinton: America in the 1990s* (New York: Thomas Dunne Books, 2005), 34.

14. Ibid.

15. James Fallows, "A Triumph of Misinformation," *The Atlantic* (January 1995), https://www.theatlantic.com/magazine/archive/1995/01/a-triumph-of-misinformation/306231/.

16. Gregory Krieg, "Hilary Clinton Shows Her Remarkable Defiance," *Mic* (April 22, 2015), https://mic.com/articles/116152/12-quotes-from-hillary-clinton-show-her-remarkable-defiance#.r8l49zlSL.

17. Ibid.

18. Ibid.

19. Gil Troy, *The Age of Clinton: America in the 1990s* (New York: Thomas Dunne Books, 2005), 225.

20. Kent Babb, "How the O.J. Simpson Murder Trial 20 Years Ago Changed the Media Landscape," *The Washington Post* (June 9, 2014), https://www.washingtonpost.com/sports/redskins/how-the-oj-simpson-murder-trial-20-years-ago-changed-the-media-landscape/2014/06/09/a6e21df8-eccf-11e3-93d2-edd4be1f5d9e_story.html?utm_term=.1c662913eee8.

21. Ibid.

22. OWN, "Watch Oprah's Audience React to the OJ Simpson Verdict in Real Time" (June 13, 2014), https://www.youtube.com/watch?v=1Pevb9LdIy8.

23. Dave Cullen, *Columbine* (New York: Twelve, 2010), 149.

24. William H. Chafe, *The Rise and Fall of the American Century: The United States from 1890–2010* (Oxford: Oxford University Press, 2009), 284–285.

Chapter 2

1. Dr. Carol K. Sigelman and Dr. Elizabeth A. Rider, *Cengage Advantage Books: Life-Span Human Development* (London, England: Wadsworth Publishing, 2014), 373.

2. Ibid.

3. Ben Cosgrove, "The Invention of Teenagers: LIFE and the Triumph of Youth Culture" *Time Magazine* (September 28, 2013) http://time.com/3639041/the-invention-of-teenagers-life-and-the-triumph-of-youth-culture/.

4. Allan Metcalf, *From Skedaddle to Selfie: Words of the Generations* (Oxford: Oxford University Press, 2015), 102.

5. Thomas Hine, *The Rise and Fall of the American Teenager* (Moosic, PA: HarperCollins Publishing, 2000), 19.

6. Colin McGinn, *The Power of Movies: How Screen and Mind Interact* (New York: Vintage, 2007), 193.

7. Timothy Shary, *Generation Multiplex: The Image of Youth in American Cinema Since 1980* (Austin, TX: University of Austin Press, 2013), 7.

8. Carol Clover, *Men, Women and Chainsaws: Gender in the Modern Horror Film* (Princeton, NJ: Princeton University Press, 1992), 35.

9. Robin Wood, *Hollywood From Vietnam to Reagan... And Beyond* (New York: Columbia University Press, 2003), 195.

10. Timothy Shary, *Generation Multiplex: The Image of Youth in American Cinema Since 1980* (Austin, TX: University of Austin Press, 2013), 165.

11. Laura Mulvey, "Visual Pleasure and Narrative Cinema," *Film Theory and Criticism: Introductory Readings*, eds. Leo Braudy and Marshall Cohen (New York: Oxford University Press, 1999), 845.

12. Ibid., 846.

13. Ibid., 840.

14. Robin Wood, *Hollywood From Vietnam to Reagan... And Beyond* (New York: Columbia University Press, 2003), 196.

15. Laura Mattoon D'Amore, *Smart Chicks on Screen* (New York: Rowman & Littlefield Publishers, 2016), 1.

16. Anita Harris, "Not Waving or Drowning: Young Women, Feminism, and the Limits of the Next Wave Debate" *Outskirts Online Film Journal* (May 2001), http://www.

outskirts.arts.uwa.edu.au/volumes/volume-8/harris.

17. Laura Cohen, "Why Clueless is Important for Women" *Marie Claire* (July 17, 2014) http://www.marieclaire.com/culture/a10141/clueless-important-for-women/.

18. Tom Doherty, "Clueless Kids" *Cinéaste*, 21:4 (Fall 1995).

Chapter 3

1. Tasha Robinson, "Interview: Joss Whedon," *The AV Club* (September 5, 2001) http://www.avclub.com/article/joss-whedon-13730.

2. "*Buffy the Vampire Slayer*," Rotten Tomatoes (May 20, 2003) https://www.rottentomatoes.com/m/buffy_the_vampire_slayer/.

3. "*Buffy the Vampire Slayer*," Box Office Mojo http://www.boxofficemojo.com/movies/?id=buffythevampireslayer.htm.

4. Dr. Janina Scarlet, "The Psychology of Inspirational Women: *Buffy the Vampire Slayer*," *The Mary Sue* (March 5 2015) https://www.themarysue.com/the-psychology-of-inspirational-women-buffy-the-vampire-slayer/.

5. Beth Ditto, "Introduction," *Riot Grrrl: Revolution Grrrl Style Now*, ed. Nadine Monem (London: Black Dog Publishing, 2007), 9.

6. Timothy Shary, *Teen Movies: American Youth on Screen* (London: Wallflower Press, 2005), 54.

7. Adam B. Vary, "Bob Balaban Has No Idea How He Became a Brilliant Hollywood Character Actor," *Buzzfeed* (March 4 2014) https://www.buzzfeed.com/adambvary/bob-balaban-how-he-became-a-brilliant-character-actor?utm_term=.reEjOowV2#.pxJlP37vy.

8. James J. Dowd and Nicole R. Pallotta, "The End of Romance: The Demystification of Love in the Postmodern Age," *Sociological Perspectives* 43:4 (2000).

Chapter 4

1. "The Crush," IMDB, http://www.imdb.com/title/tt0106627/trivia?ref_=tt_trv_trv.

2. Steve Newton, "Horror in Vancouver: 16-year-old Alicia Silverstone Talks About *The Crush!*," *The Georgia Straight* (March 7, 2014) http://www.straight.com/blogra/17751/horror-vancouver-16-year-old-alicia-silverstone-talks-crush.

3. Mary Pipher, *Reviving Ophelia: Saving the Selves of Adolescent Girls* (New York: Riverhead Books, 1994), 11–12.

4. *Ibid.*, 88.

5. John Kenneth Muir, *Horror Films of the 1990s* (Jefferson, NC: McFarland, 2011), 273.

6. "The Crush," Box Office Mojo http://www.boxofficemojo.com/movies/?id=crushthe.htm.

7. Jon Savage, *Teenage: The Creation of Youth Culture*, (London: Viking, 2007), 18.

8. Thomas Hine, *The Rise and Fall of the American Teenager* (Moosic, PA: HarperCollins Publishing, 2000), 222.

9. John Kenneth Muir, *Horror Films of the 1990s* (Jefferson, NC: McFarland, 2011), 460.

10. Susan Faludi, *Blacklash: The Undeclared War Against American Women* (New York: Broadway Books, 2006), 133.

11. Mary Pipher, *Reviving Ophelia: Saving the Selves of Adolescent Girls* (New York: Riverhead Books, 1994), 82.

12. *Ibid.*, 103.

13. Sady Doyle, *Trainwreck: The Women We Love to Hate, Mock and Fear... And Why* (New York: Penguin Books, 2014), 212.

14. Mary Pipher, *Reviving Ophelia: Saving the Selves of Adolescent Girls* (New York: Riverhead Books, 1994), 205.

Chapter 5

1. Jack Holland, *A Brief History of Misogyny: The World's Oldest Prejudice* (London: Robinson, 2006), 113.

2. Walter Stephens, *Demon Lovers: Witchcraft, Sex and the Crisis of Belief* (Chicago: University of Chicago Press, 2002), 341.

3. Jack Holland, *A Brief History of Misogyny: The World's Oldest Prejudice* (London: Robinson, 2006), 116.

4. Leo Braudy, *Haunted: On Ghosts, Witches, Vampires, Zombies and Other Monsters of the Natural and Supernatural World* (New Haven: Yale University Press, 2016), 43–44.

5. Sinead Stubbins, "'We are the weirdos, mister': *The Craft* and the Year of the Teen Witch," *The AV Club* (May 3, 2016) http://www.avclub.com/article/we-are-weirdos-mister-craft-and-year-teen-witch-234597.

6. Murray Milner, *Freaks, Geeks and Cool Kids* (New York, Routledge, 2006), 142.

7. Columbia Pictures, *The Craft*. 1996. Print.

8. *Ibid.*

9. *Ibid.*

10. Dianca Potts, "The Lenny Interview: Rachel True" *Lenny* (January 27, 2017) http://www.lennyletter.com/culture/interviews/a707/the-lenny-interview-rachel-true/.

11. Ashlee Blackwell, "20 Years of *The Craft*: Why We Needed More of Rochelle," *Graveyard Shift Sisters* (November 16, 2016) http://www.graveyardshiftsisters.com/2016/11/20-years-of-craft-why-we-needed-more-of.html.
12. "*The Craft*," *Box Office Mojo*, http://www.boxofficemojo.com/movies/?id=craft.htm.
13. Carole Corbeil, "Thumbs Down on *Craft*, One Fist Up For *Carrie*," *The Toronto Star* (June 1, 1996), H4.
14. Emanuel Levy, "Review: *The Craft*" *Variety* (May 1, 1996) http://variety.com/1996/film/reviews/the-craft-2-1200445935/.
15. Chris Eggertsen, "Exclusive: *The Craft* Remake Isn't a Remake—It's a 20 Years Later," *Uproxx* (May 3, 2016) http://uproxx.com/hitfix/exclusive-the-craft-remake-isnt-a-remake-its-a-20-years-later/.

Chapter 6

1. Alisa Perren, *Indie, Inc.: Miramax and the Transformation of Hollywood in the 1990s* (Austin: University of Texas Press, 2013), 126–127.
2. Peter Biskind, *Down and Dirty Pictures: Miramax, Sundance and the Rise of Independent Film* (New York: Simon & Schuster, 2005), 247.
3. Brian J. Robb, *Screams and Nightmares: The Films of Wes Craven* (Woodstock: Overlook Press, 1998), 176.
4. Peter Biskind, *Down and Dirty Pictures: Miramax, Sundance and the Rise of Independent Film* (New York: Simon & Schuster, 2005), 249.
5. Brian J. Robb, *Screams and Nightmares: The Films of Wes Craven* (Woodstock: Overlook Press, 1998), 177.
6. Peter Biskind, *Down and Dirty Pictures: Miramax, Sundance and the Rise of Independent Film* (New York: Simon & Schuster, 2005), 248.
7. Ibid., 152.
8. Brian J. Robb, *Screams and Nightmares: The Films of Wes Craven* (Woodstock: Overlook Press, 1998), 180.
9. Peter Biskind, *Down and Dirty Pictures: Miramax, Sundance and the Rise of Independent Film* (New York: Simon & Schuster, 2005), 255.
10. Ibid., 253.
11. "*Scream*," *Box Office Mojo*, http://www.boxofficemojo.com/movies/?id=scream.htm.
12. Bernard Weinraub, "What a *Scream*" *The New York Times* (June 20 1997), E3.
13. Owen Gleiberman, "Hack to Basics," *Entertainment Weekly* (December 1997), 21.
14. Stephen Neale, *Genre and Hollywood* (New York: Psychology Press, 2000), 40.
15. Carol Clover, *Men, Women and Chainsaws: Gender in the Modern Horror Film* (Princeton, NJ: Princeton University Press, 1992), 35.
16. Ibid., 30.
17. Ibid., 32.
18. Ibid., 33.
19. Ibid., 30.
20. Ibid., 35.
21. Ibid., 37.
22. Sady Doyle, *Trainwreck: The Women We Love to Hate, Mock and Fear... And Why* (New York: Penguin Books, 2014), x–xii.
23. "*Scream 2*: Entertainment Weekly Cover Story," *Scream-Thrillogy* (November 1997) http://www.scream-thrillogy.com/2016/12/scream-2-entertainment-weekly-cover.html.
24. "*A Nightmare on Elm Street 5: The Dream Child*" IMDB (http://www.imdb.com/title/tt0097981/trivia?ref_=tt_trv_trv.)
25. Benson-Allott, Caetlin. "Old Tropes in New Dimensions: Stereoscopy and Franchise Spectatorship." *Film Criticism* 3:38 (2013).
26. Brian J. Robb, *Screams and Nightmares: The Films of Wes Craven* (Woodstock: Overlook Press, 1998), 183–185.
27. Ibid., 184.
28. Carol Clover, *Men, Women and Chainsaws: Gender in the Modern Horror Film* (Princeton, NJ: Princeton University Press, 1992), 35.
29. Lutfiana Hermawati, "Greek Mythological Prophet, Cassandra Was a Woman Cursed with the Gift of Fortelling the Future," *MindProject* (April 28 2016) http://lfianamind.blogspot.ca/2012/04/tree-of-life.html.
30. Evan Dickson, "Kevin Williamson Reveals the Original Plot of *Scream 3*" *Bloody Disgusting* (January 22, 2013) http://bloody-disgusting.com/news/3214615/kevin-williamson-reveals-the-original-plot-of-scream-3.
31. "*Scream 3*," IMDB http://www.imdb.com/title/tt0134084/trivia?ref_=tt_trv_trv.
32. Laura Mulvey, "Visual Pleasure and Narrative Cinema," *Film Theory and Criticism: Introductory Readings*, eds. Leo Braudy and Marshall Cohen (New York: Oxford University Press, 1999), 840.
33. "*Scream 3*," *Box Office Mojo* http://www.boxofficemojo.com/movies/?id=scream3.htm.
34. "Matthew Lillard—Stu *Scream 3* Original Killer," (October 25, 2010) https://www.youtube.com/watch?v=3HaYYh-aIz0.

Chapter 7

1. Randy Palmer, "The *Scream* of Summer," *Fangoria* (November 1997), 15.

2. "Kevin Williamson Enjoying Reign as King of Horror Flicks," *CNN* (August 7, 1998), http://edition.cnn.com/SHOWBIZ/Movies/9808/07/kevin.williamson/.
3. Randy Palmer, "The *Scream* of Summer" *Fangoria* (November 1997), 14.
4. Lois Duncan, *I Know What You Did Last Summer* (New York: Little Brown, 2010), 201–202.
5. Randy Palmer, "The *Scream* of Summer!," *Fangoria* (November 1997), 16–17.
6. John Kenneth Muir, *Horror Films of the 1990s* (Jefferson, NC: McFarland, 2011), 500.
7. Randy Palmer, "The *Scream* of Summer," *Fangoria* (November 1997), 16.
8. "PTSD in Children and Teens," *U.S. Department of Veteran Affairs* https://www.ptsd.va.gov/public/family/ptsd-children-adolescents.asp.
9. "Post Traumatic Stress Disorder," *Anxiety BC* https://www.anxietybc.com/parenting/post-traumatic-stress-disorder.

Chapter 8

1. Jan Harold Brunvand, *The Vanishing Hitchhiker: American Urban Legends & Their Meanings* (New York: W.W. Norton and Company, 1981), xi–xii.
2. Ibid., 52.
3. Ibid., 53.
4. John Kenneth Muir, *Horror Films of the 1990s* (Jefferson, NC: McFarland, 2011), 589.
5. Beverly Crane, "The Structure of Value in *The Roommate's Death*: A Methodology for Interpretive Analysis of Folk Legends," *Journal of the Folklore Institute* 14:3 (1977).
6. Geof Smith, "Final Cuts: The History of Snuff Films," *Digital Destruction* http://www.fringeunderground.com/snuff.html.
7. "Alfred Hitchcock Explains the Plot Device He Called the 'MacGuffin,'" *Open Culture* (July 9, 2013), http://www.openculture.com/2013/07/alfred-hitchcock-explains-the-plot-device-he-called-the-macguffin.html.
8. "*Urban Legends: Final Cut*," *Box Office Mojo* http://www.boxofficemojo.com/movies/?id=urbanlegendsfinalcut.htm.

Chapter 9

1. William Bibbiani, "The Test of Time #6: *Disturbing Behavior*," *Crave* (April 10, 2013), http://www.craveonline.com/site/478393-the-test-of-time-6-disturbing-behavior#4mpuyem0GtMRuVJH.99.
2. Alex Strachan, "For Nutter, a Failed Film Inspires Not Real Regrets," *The Vancouver Sun* (August 18, 1999), C5.
3. Patrick Goldstein, "When Buzz and Test Scores Aren't Good," *Los Angeles Times* (September 18, 1998), F1.
4. Ibid.
5. "*The Faculty*," *IMDB*, http://www.imdb.com/title/tt0133751/trivia?ref_=tt_trv_trv.
6. Chris Petrikin, "*Scream* Scribe, *Dusk* Director Team on Horror Film," *Yahoo News* (October 29 1997), 1.
7. Ibid.
8. *The Faculty* (Hollywood: Dimension Films, 1998) Print.
9. Murray Milner, *Freaks, Geeks and Cool Kids* (New York: Routledge, 2006), 22–23.
10. Timothy Shary, *Generation Multiplex: The Image of Youth in American Cinema Since 1980* (Austin, TX: University of Austin Press, 2013), 46.
11. Murray Milner, *Freaks, Geeks and Cool Kids* (New York: Routledge, 2006), 44.
12. "*The Faculty*," *Box Office Mojo* http://www.boxofficemojo.com/movies/?id=faculty.htm.
13. Gary Dauphin, "Film Review: *The Faculty*," *Village Voice* (January 5, 1999), 94.
14. 20thcenturymase, "Tommy Hilfiger Jeans *The Faculty*," *YouTube* (December 16, 2010), https://www.youtube.com/watch?v=5TxeVgKY-V5Y.
15. "Usher Explains Where the Hilfiger Deal Went Wrong," *MTV News* (July 1, 1999), http://www.mtv.com/news/1435082/usher-explains-where-hilfiger-deal-went-wrong/.
16. "*Teaching Mrs. Tingle*," *Box Office Mojo* http://www.boxofficemojo.com/movies/?id=teachingmrstingle.htm.
17. Dennis Harvey, "Review: *Teaching Mrs. Tingle*," *Variety* (August 23, 1999), http://variety.com/1999/film/reviews/teaching-mrs-tingle-1200458625/.
18. Mary M. Dalton, *The Hollywood Curriculum: Teachers in the Movies* (Newark: Peter Lang Inc., 2010), 5.
19. Mary M. Dalton, "The Hollywood View: Protecting the Status," *Mirror Images: Popular Culture and Education*, ed Diana Silberman-Keller (Newark: Peter Lang Inc, 2008), 19.
20. Ibid.
21. Rebecca Beatrice Brooks, "The Salem Witch Trials Victims," *History of Massachusetts* (August 19, 2015), http://historyofmassachusetts.org/salem-witch-trials-victims/.
22. Stacy Schiff, *The Witches: Salem 1692* (New York: Little, Brown and Company, 2015) 7–8.

Chapter 10

1. Andrew Patrick Nelson, "Franchise Legacy and Neo-slasher Conventions in *Halloween H20*," *Style and Form in the Hollywood Slasher Film*, ed. Wickham Clayton (London: Palgrave MacMillan, 2015) 81.
2. "Halloween H20," *IMDB* http://www.imdb.com/title/tt0120694/.
3. *Ibid.*
4. John Kenneth Muir, *Horror Films of the 1990s* (Jefferson, NC: McFarland, 2011), 558.
5. "The Rage: Carrie 2," *IMDB* http://www.imdb.com/title/tt0144814/trivia?ref_=tt_trv_trv.
6. Stephen King, *Danse Macabre* (New York: Gallery Books, 2010), 180–181.
7. Jane Gross, "Where 'Boys Will Be Boys,' and Adults are Befuddled," *The New York Times* (March 29, 1993), http://www.nytimes.com/1993/03/29/us/where-boys-will-be-boys-and-adults-are-befuddled.html?pagewanted=all.
8. Tierney Sneed, "High Schools and Middle Schools are Failing Victims of Sexual Assault," *U.S. News* (March 5, 2015), https://www.usnews.com/news/articles/2015/03/05/high-schools-and-middle-schools-are-failing-victims-of-sexual-assault.
9. Timothy Shary, *Generation Multiplex: The Image of Youth in American Cinema Since 1980* (Austin, TX: University of Austin Press, 2013), 129.
10. Adrian Roe, *Second Scream: The Definitive Guide to '90s Horror* (Lulu.com: 2016) 259.

Chapter 11

1. "*Wicked*," *Wikipedia* https://en.wikipedia.org/wiki/Wicked_(1998_film).
2. Gil Troy, The *Age of Clinton: America in the 1990s* (New York: Thomas Dunne Books, 2005), 219.
3. William Schneider, "The Suburban Century Begins," *The Atlantic Online* (July 1992), https://www.theatlantic.com/past/docs/politics/ecbig/schnsub.htm.
4. *Ibid.*
5. Lewis Mumford, "Critiques of Post-War Suburbia," *The Suburb Reader*, eds Becky M. Nicolaides and Andrew Wiese (New York: Routledge, 2006), 291.
6. Kathleen Rowe Karlyn, "Too Close for Comfort: *American Beauty* and the Incest Motif," *Cinema Journal*, 44:1 (Autumn, 2004), 70.
7. Andrew Kopkind, "Slacking toward Bethlehem," *Grand Street* (1993).
8. *Ibid.*
9. Andy Culpepper, "*Idle Hands*—A Post-Columbine Test of the Movie Market," *CNN* (April 30, 1999), http://www.cnn.com/SHOWBIZ/Movies/9904/30/idle.hands/.
10. "*Idle Hands*," *Box Office Mojo* http://www.boxofficemojo.com/movies/?id=idlehands.htm.
11. Andy Culpepper, "*Idle Hands*—A Post-Columbine Test of the Movie Market," *CNN* (April 30, 1999) http://www.cnn.com/SHOWBIZ/Movies/9904/30/idle.hands/.
12. *Ibid.*
13. Bruno Bettleheim, *The Uses of Enchantment: The Meaning and Importance of Fairy Tales* (New York: Vintage Books, 2010) 240.
14. Jessica Balanzategui, "Crisis of Identification in the Supernatural Slasher: The Resurrection of the Supernatural Slasher Villain," *Style and Form in the Hollywood Slasher Film* (New York: Palgrave MacMillain, 2015), 162.

Chapter 12

1. Marshall Persinger and Ken Seldes, "Lose It Or Die: The Untold Story Of *Cherry Falls*," *Cherry Falls* (Blu-ray). Shout! Factory.
2. *Ibid.*
3. Trace Thurman, "The Real Story Behind *Cherry Falls*," *Bloody Disgusting* (July 29 2016) http://bloody-disgusting.com/editorials/3400027/story-behind-cherry-falls/.
4. Pat Gill, "The Monstrous Years: Teens, Slasher Films, and the Family," *Journal of Film and Video*, 54:4 (2002).
5. Carol Clover, *Men, Women and Chainsaws: Gender in the Modern Horror Film* (Princeton, NJ: Princeton UP, 1992), 47.
6. *Ibid.*, 49.
7. Timothy Shary, *Generation Multiplex: The Image of Youth in American Cinema Since 1980* (Austin, TX: University of Austin Press, 2013), 251.
8. Carol Clover, *Men, Women and Chainsaws: Gender in the Modern Horror Film* (Princeton, NJ: Princeton UP, 1992), 47.
9. Andrea Albin, "*Final Destination*: Not So Final After All," *Bloody Disgusting* (August 12, 2011), http://bloody-disgusting.com/editorials/25828/special-feature-final-destination-not-so-final-after-all/.
10. *Ibid.*
11. Thomas Hine, *The Rise and Fall of the American Teenager* (Moosic, PA: Harper Collins Publishing, 2000), 28.
12. John Kenneth Muir, *Horror Films FAQ* (New York: Applause Books, 2013), 246.

13. Ian Conrich, "Puzzles, Contraptions and the Highly Elaborate Moment: The Inevitability of Death in the Grand Slasher Narratives of the *Final Destination* and *Saw* Series of Films," *Style and Form in the Hollywood Slasher Film*, ed Wickham Clayton (New York: Palgrave Macmillain, 2015), 106.

14. *Ibid.*, 114–115.

15. Robert Potter, "*The Interview*: The Importance of Parody," *The Diplomat* (December 21, 2014), http://thediplomat.com/2014/12/the-interview-the-importance-of-parody/.

16. Betsy Pickle, "The Wayans Brothers Talk About Horror-Parody *Scary Movie*," *The Cabin* (July 7, 2000), http://thecabin.net/stories/070700/sty_0707000055.html#.WQYnPcm1vVp.

17. Vanessa Willoughby, "What I Learned From Token Black Characters in Teen Movies," *VICE* (September 21, 2015), https://www.vice.com/en_us/article/what-i-learned-from-the-token-black-characters-in-teen-movies-921.

18. Ashlee Blackwell, "Horror in the 90s: Wait! There's a Black Girl?!," *Graveyard Shift Sisters* (January 31, 2014) http://www.graveyardshiftsisters.com/2014/01/horror-in-90s-wait-theres-black-girl.html.

19. *Ibid.*

20. Robin R. Means Coleman, *Horror Noire: Blacks in American Horror Films from the 1890s to Present* (New York: Routledge. 2011) 214.

21. Luis Gomez, "Interview: Marlon Wayans Talks *A Haunted House*, Explains *Scary Movie* Exit," *Chicago Tribune* (January 11, 2013), http://articles.chicagotribune.com/2013-01-11/entertainment/ct-mov-0111-marlon-wayans-20130110_1_marlon-wayans-luis-marmaduke.

Chapter 13

1. "*Urban Legends: Bloody Mary*," IMDB, http://www.imdb.com/title/tt0451957/trivia?ref_=tt_trv_trv.

2. "'Mirror, Mirror, on the Wall...'—The Fear of Mirrors (Eisoptrophobia) and Their Role in Superstition and Magic," *Diabolical Confusions* (February 25, 2011) https://diabolicalconfusions.wordpress.com/2011/02/25/mirror-mirror-on-the-wall-the-fear-of-mirrors-eisoptrophobia-and-their-role-in-superstition-and-magic/.

3. Elizabeth Tucker, "Ghosts in Mirrors: Reflections of the Self," *The Journal of American Folklore*, 118: 468 (2005).

4. David Kalat, *J-Horror: The Definitive Guide to The Ring, The Grudge and Beyond* (New York: Vertical, 2007), 1.

5. Bill Ellis, *Lucifer Ascending: The Occult in Folklore and Popular Culture* (Lexington: University Press of Kentucky, 2004), 124.

6. John Kenneth Muir, *Horror Films FAQ* (New York: Applause Books, 2013), 129.

7. "*I'll Always Know What You Did Last Summer*," IMDB http://www.imdb.com/title/tt0469111/trivia?ref_=tt_trv_trv.

8. *Ibid.*

9. "Interview: Brooke Nevin," *IGN* (August 14, 2006), http://ca.ign.com/articles/2006/08/14/interview-brooke-nevin.

10. Jessica Balanzategui, "Crisis of Identification in the Supernatural Slasher: The Resurrection of the Supernatural Slasher Villain," *Style and Form in the Hollywood Slasher Film* (New York: Palgrave MacMillain, 2015), 170.

11. *Ibid.*, 163.

12. "Dimension Films," *Wikipedia*, https://en.wikipedia.org/wiki/Dimension_Films.

13. Jack Giroux, "Interview: Wes Craven talks *Scream 4* Challenges and Learning of Failures," *Film School Rejects* (October 6, 2011), https://filmschoolrejects.com/interview-wes-craven-talks-scream-4-challenges-and-learning-from-failures-43f6b7e14cf3.

14. "*Scream 4*," *Wikipedia* https://en.wikipedia.org/wiki/Scream_4.

15. Perri Nemiroff, "Interview: *Scream 4* Director Wes Craven On Keep the Franchise Alive," *CinemaBlend*, http://www.cinemablend.com/new/Interview-Scream-4-Director-Wes-Craven-Keeping-Franchise-Alive-24086.html.

16. Wes Craven, Audio Commentary, *Scream 4*, Dir. Wes Craven, Perf. Neve Campbell, Courtney Cox. Dimension Films, 2011. DVD

17. Perri Nemiroff, "Interview: *Scream 4* Director Wes Craven On Keep the Franchise Alive," *CinemaBlend*, http://www.cinemablend.com/new/Interview-Scream-4-Director-Wes-Craven-Keeping-Franchise-Alive-24086.html.

Bibliography

Biskind, Peter. *Down and Dirty Pictures: Miramax, Sundance and the Rise of Independent Film*. New York: Simon & Schuster, 2005.

Braudy, Leo. *Haunted: On Ghosts, Witches, Vampires, Zombies and Other Monsters of the Natural and Supernatural Worlds*. New Haven: Yale University Press, 2016.

Brunvand, Jan Harold. *The Vanishing Hitchhiker: American Urban Legends and Their Meanings*. New York: Norton, 1981.

Christensen, Kyle. *The Final Girl Versus Wes Craven's A Nightmare on Elm Street: Proposing a Stronger Model of Feminism in Slasher Horror Cinema*. Studies in Popular Culture, 34:1 (Fall 2011).

Clayton, Wickham. *Style and Form in the Hollywood Slasher*. London: Palgrave MacMillan, 2015.

Clover, Carol J. *Men, Women, and Chainsaws: Gender in the Modern Horror Film*. Princeton: Princeton University Press, 1992.

Crawford, Anwen. *33 1/3: Live Through This*. New York: Bloomsbury, 2015.

Cullen, Dave. *Columbine*. New York: Twelve Books, 2010.

Dicker, Rory. *A History of US Feminisms*. New York: Seal Press, 2008.

Faludi, Susan. *Backlash: The Undeclared War Against American Women*. New York: Three Rivers Press, 2006.

Grant, Barry Keith. *The Dread of Difference: Gender and the Modern Horror Film*. Austin: University of Texas Press, 1999.

Hine, Thomas. *The Rise and Fall of the American Teenager: A New History of the American Adolescent Experience*. New York: HarperCollins, 1999.

Holland, Jack. *A Brief History of Misogyny: The World's Oldest Prejudice*. London: Robinson, 2006.

Kessinger, Scott. *Scream Deconstructed: An Unauthorized Analysis*. Las Vegas: Stinger Books, 2011.

Milner, Murray. *Freaks, Geeks and Cool Kids: American Teenagers, Schools and the Culture of Consumption*. New York: Routledge, 2006.

Monem, Nadine. *Riot Grrrl: Revolution Girl Style Now!* New York: Black Dog Publishing, 2007.

Muir, John Kenneth. *Horror Films FAQ: All That's Left to Know About Slashers, Vampires, Zombies, Aliens, and More*. Montclair, NJ: Applause Books, 2013.

_____. *Horror Films of the 1980s*. Jefferson, NC: McFarland, 2012.

_____. *Horror Films of the 1990s*. Jefferson, NC: McFarland, 2011.

Nowell, Richard. *Blood Money: A History of the First Teen Slasher Film Cycle*. London: Continuum Publishing, 2011.

_____. *There's More Than One Way to Lose Your Heart: The American Film Industry, Early Teen Slasher Films and Female Youth*. Cinema Journal 51:1 (Fall 2011)

Perren, Alisa. *Indie, Inc. Miramax and the Transformation of Hollywood in the 1990s*. Austin: University of Texas Press, 2012.

Pipher, Mary. *Reviving Ophelia: Saving the Selves of Adolescent Girls*. New York: Riverhead Books, 1994.

Robb, Brian J. *Screams & Nightmares: The Films of Wes Craven*. Woodstock, NY: The Overlook Press, 1998.

Roe, Adrian. *Second Scream: The Definitive Guide to '90s Horror The Decade that Horror Forgot*. London: Publish Nation, 2016.

Shary, Timothy. *Generation Multiplex: The Image of Youth in American Cinema since*

1980. Austin: University of Texas Press, 2002.

_____. *Short Cuts: Teen Movies: American Youth on Screen*. London: Wallflower Press, 2005.

Thompson, Kirsten Moana. *Apocalyptic Dread: American Film at the Turn of the Millennium*. Albany: State University of New York Press, 2007.

Troy, Gil. *The Age of Clinton: America in the 1990s*. New York: St. Martin's Press, 2015.

Wee, Valerie. *The Scream Trilogy, Hypermodernism and the Late Nineties Teen Slasher Film*. Journal of Film of Video, 57:3, Fall 2005.

Zeisler, Andi. *We Were Feminists Once: From Riot Grrrl to Covergirl, the Buying and Selling of a Political Movement*. New York: Public Affairs, 2016.

Index

AIDS 13
Airplane (1980) 151
American Dream 6, 17, 18, 23, 170
American Pie (1999) 79
Amos, Tori 17
The Amy Fisher Story (1993) 131
Andy Hardy (film series) 27
Apocalypse Now (1979) 27
Apple, Fiona 17

The Backstreet Boys 17
Balaban, Bob 39
Barrymore, Drew 65, 131
Beavis and Butthead Do America (1996) 66
Berkley, Elizabeth 52
Best in Show (2000) 39
Bikini Kill 16
Bjork 17
The Blair Witch Project (1999) 3, 153
The Body Snatchers (book) 109
Branch Davidians 22
Brando, Marlon 27
The Breakfast Club (1985) 11, 109
The Breeders 17
Bring It On (2000) 79
Broaddrick, Juanita 20
Brown Simpson, Nicole 22
Buffy the Vampire Slayer (1992) 4, 32–38
Buffy the Vampire Slayer (television series) 9, 32, 55
Bush, George H.W. 13, 19

Cabin Fever (2002) 150, 163
Campbell, Neve 65
Campfire Tales (1997) 146
Candyman (1992) 3, 93, 153
Carrie (1976) 27, 127
Carrie (book) 127
Charmed 55
Cherry Falls (2000) 4, 140–145
Children of the Corn: Genesis (2011) 164
Children of the Corn III: Urban Harvest (1995) 64
Clerks (1994) 63
Clinton, Bill 19–21, 24, 31, 131, 169

Clinton, Hillary Rodham 20, 21, 24
Close Encounters of the Third Kind (1977) 39
Clueless (1995) 32, 169
CNN 22
Cobain, Kurt 17, 18, 24
Cold War 6, 13
Cole, Paula 95
Columbine shootings 11, 23–24, 78, 114, 135, 150
Cox, Courteney 65, 170
The Craft (1996) 55–62, 170
Craven, Wes 5, 12, 63, 65–66, 164
The Crow (1994) 64
The Crucible (play) 117
Cruel Intentions (1999) 79
The Crush (1993) 43–48
The Crying Game (1992) 64

Dangerous Minds (1995) 116
Dawson's Creek 9, 95, 171
Dead Poets Society (1989) 116
Destiny's Child 17
Dimension Extreme 163
Dimension Films 11, 64, 107, 108, 114, 121, 122, 136, 151, 163
Disturbing Behavior (1998) 9, 103–108, 111
Dog Day Afternoon (1975) 27
Don't Be a Menace to South Central While Drinking Your Juice in the Hood (1996) 152
double-parenting 45
Down to You (2000) 131
Dressed to Kill (1980) 143

EC Comixs 39
Eden Lake (2008) 163
Edward Scissorhands (1990) 40
Elastica 17
Elliott, Missy 17
Englund, Robert 96
Evil Dead II (1987) 137
The Exorcist (1973) 119

The Faculty (1998) 9, 78, 108–114
Fatal Attraction (1987) 15, 49–50
Fear (1996) 49–54

184 Index

Final Destination (2000) 145–151, 157
Final Girl 4, 5, 8, 9, 28, 65, 68, 75, 101, 124, 125, 167
A Fish Called Wanda (1988) 121
Flowers, Gennifer 21
Frankenstein (book) 125–126
Friday the 13th (1980) 4, 29, 71
Friday the 13th Part 2 (1981) 5, 124
Fright Night (1985) 30

Garbage 17
Generation X 6, 18
Gidget (1959) 27
Goldman, Ron 22
Good Will Hunting (1997) 64
Grand Guignol 150
The Great Dictator (1940) 151
The Grudge (2004) 158
Grunge 13
Guest, Christopher 39

Halloween (1978) 4, 68, 71, 121
Halloween H20 (1998) 9, 78, 114, 121–127
Halloween: The Curse of Michael Myers (1995) 64, 122
Halloween 3: Season of the Witch (1982) 121
Halloween 4: The Return of Michael Myers (1988) 122
Hanna, Kathleen 16
Harry Potter (book series) 55
The Haunting (1963) 31
Haxan (1922) 55
Heavens to Betsey 16
Hellraiser: Revelations (2011) 164
Hellraiser III: Hell on Earth (1992) 64
Hill, Anita 6, 10, 13, 14, 15, 24, 31, 59
Hole 17
Hostel (2005) 150
Hughes, John 27, 28

I Know What You Did Last Summer (1997) 78, 82–87, 136, 151, 152, 169
I Married a Witch (1942) 55
I Still Know What You Did Last Summer (1998) 87–91
Idle Hands (1999) 9, 134–139
I'll Always Know What You Did Last Summer (2006) 160–163
I'm Gonna Git You Sucka (1988) 152
In Living Color 151, 152
Industrial Revolution 25
Inglourious Basterds (2009) 163
Inside (2007) 163
internet 10, 20, 150
intertextuality 6, 10
Invasion of the Body Snatchers (1956) 109

Jacobs, Marc 31
Jason Goes to Hell: The Final Friday (1993) 39
Jawbreaker (1999) 79
Jones, Paula 20

Kids (1995) 32
King, Rodney 6, 18
Konrad, Cathy 65
Koresh, David 22
KRS-One 18
Kruger, Ehren 78, 164

Lambert, Mary 157
The Last House on the Left (1972) 65
Lewinsky, Monica 20, 131, 171
Life Is Beautiful (1997) 64
Lilith Fair 17
Lolita (1962) 131
Los Angeles riots 6, 13, 19
The Lost Boys (1987) 30, 36
Love Story (1970) 48
Low Down Dirty Shame (1994) 152

Malleus Maleficarum 56
Manson, Marilyn 23
The Matrix (1999) 153
McVeigh, Timothy 22
The Melvins 17
MGM 27, 103, 107
A Mighty Wind (2003) 39
Milano, Alyssa 52
Miramax 63, 163
Morissette, Alanis 17
Multiplexes 28
My Boyfriend's Back (1993) 38–42

Never Been Kissed (1999) 143
New Line Cinema 146
A Nightmare on Elm Street (1984) 4, 65, 71, 95
A Nightmare on Elm Street: Dream Warriors (1987) 124
A Nightmare on Elm Street 4: The Dream Master (1988) 5
Nirvana 6, 17, 31
No Doubt 17
*NSYNC 17
Nutter, David 103, 107
NWA 18

Party of Five 9, 65
Pearl Jam 17
The People Under the Stairs (1991) 65, 153
Pet Sematary (1989) 157
Pet Sematary 2 (1992) 157
Phair, Liz 17
The Piano (1993) 64
The Pixies 17
Poison Ivy (1992) 127, 131
Psycho (1960) 31, 125, 143
Pulp Fiction (1994) 63

Rack, B.J. 65
The Rage: Carrie 2 (1999) 127–130
Ramsay, JonBenet 171
Rap music 18
The Reader (2008) 163

Index

Rebel Without a Cause (1955) 27
Regan, Ronald 6, 13, 169
Reservoir Dogs (1992) 6, 63
The Ring (2002) 31, 78, 158, 161
Ringwald, Molly 28
Riot Grrrl 6, 13, 16, 17, 31, 32, 36, 55
Rooney, Mickey 27
Rosemary's Baby (1968) 55
Rubel Zuzui, Fran 32

Sabrina, the Teenage Witch 55
Salem Witch Trials 117–118
Salt-N-Pepa 17
Sassy Magazine 33
Saturday Night Live 151
Save the Last Dance (2001) 48, 131
Saved by the Bell 52
Saw (2004) 157
Say Anything (1989) 48
Scary Movie (2000) 151–155
Scream (1996) 6, 11, 63–72, 92, 93, 114, 121, 124, 125, 136, 152, 169, 170
Scream 2 (1997) 72–78, 81, 114, 125, 170
Scream 3 (2000) 78–82, 151, 163, 164
Scream 4 (2011) 164–168
The Serpent and the Rainbow (1988) 65
Shakespeare in Love (1998) 64, 154
Shapiro, Alan 43
She's All That (1999) 79
Showgirls (1995) 52
Silence of the Lambs (1991) 3
Simpson, O.J. 11, 22
The Simpsons 6, 169
Sinatra, Frank 25
slasher films 3, 7, 28, 63, 78, 84
Sling Blade (1996) 64
The Smashing Pumpkins 17
Snow White and the Seven Dwarfs (1937) 55
Sonic Youth 17
Soviet Union 13
The Spice Girls 17, 33
Starbucks 32
Stiles, Julia 131
Stone Temple Pilots 17
Suspiria (1977) 55
Swamp Thing (1982) 65

Tales from the Hood (1995) 153
Taxi Driver (1976) 27
Teaching Mrs. Tingle (1999) 114–120
Team Dresch 16

teenagers 25
10 Things I Hate About You (1999) 79, 131
There's Nothing Out There (1991) 6
The Thing (1982) 109
Third Wave feminism 15, 31, 36, 55, 105
Thomas, Clarence 14, 15, 24, 59
Timberlake, Justin 25
TLC 17
Tommy Hilfiger 114
Toronto International Film Festival 8
toxic masculinity 9, 158
Trading Places (1983) 121
True Lies (1995) 121

Urban Legend (1998) 92–98, 151
Urban Legends: Bloody Mary (2005) 156–160
Urban Legends: Final Cut (2000) 98–102

A Vampire in Brooklyn (1995) 74, 153
Varsity Blues (1999) 79

Waco siege 22
Walker, Rebecca 6
Wayans, Kennen Ivory 151
Wayans, Marlon 151
Wayans, Shawn 151
WB (network) 8, 32
Weinstein, Bob 63, 65, 66, 107, 108, 163
Weinstein, Harvey 63, 66, 107, 108, 163
The Weinstein Company 163
Whedon, Joss 34, 35
Who's the Boss? 52
Wicked (1998) 131–134
The Wild One (1953) 27
witches 55–62
The Witches (1990) 55
The Witches of Eastwick (1987) 55
Wiley, Kathleen 21
Williamson, Kevin 63, 64, 78, 108–109, 122, 164, 169, 171
Winfrey, Oprah 23
The Wizard of Oz (1939) 55, 119
Wong, James 147
Wood, Cary 64

The X Files 146, 147

Young Frankenstein (1974) 151

Zappia, Robert 122
zines 16

www.ingramcontent.com/pod-product-compliance
Ingram Content Group UK Ltd.
Pitfield, Milton Keynes, MK11 3LW, UK
UKHW042013140426
5217IPUK00015B/1143